Improving Inter-professional Collaborations

Inter-professional collaborations are invaluable relationships that can prevent the social exclusion of children and young people and are now a common feature of welfare policies worldwide.

Drawing on a four-year study of the skills and understanding required of practitioners in order to establish the most effective interagency collaborations, this comprehensive text:

- gives examples from practitioners developing inter-professional practices to allow readers to reflect on their relevance for their own work;
- emphasises what needs to be learnt for responsive inter-professional work and how that learning can be promoted;
- examines how professional and organisational learning are intertwined;
- suggests how organisations can provide conditions to support the enhanced forms of professional practices revealed in the study;
- reveals the professional motives driving the practices as well as how they are founded and sustained.

Full of ideas to help shape collaborative inter-professional practice, this book shows that specialist expertise is distributed across local networks. The reader is encouraged to develop the capacity to recognise the expertise of others and to negotiate their work with others.

This book is essential reading for practitioners in education and educational psychology or social work, and offers crucial insights for local strategists and those involved in professional development work.

The book also has a great deal to offer researchers working in the area of cultural historical activity theory (CHAT). The four-year study was framed by CHAT and offers a well-worked example of how CHAT can be used to reveal sense-making in new practices and the organisational implications of enhanced professional decision-making.

As well as being important contributors to the developing CHAT field, the five authors have worked in the area of social exclusion and professional learning for several years and have brought inter-disciplinary strengths to this account of inter-professional work.

Anne Edwards is Professor of Educational Studies and Director of Research at Oxford University.

Harry Daniels is Professor of Education at the University of Bath.

Tony Gallagher is Professor of Education at Queen's University, Belfast.

Jane Leadbetter and **Paul Warmington** are Senior Lecturers in the School of Education at the University of Birmingham.

Improving Learning TLRP

Series Editor: Andrew Pollard, Director of the ESRC Teaching and Learning Programme

Improving Classroom Learning with ICT
Rosamund Sutherland, Susan Robertson and Peter John

Improving Learning in College: rethinking literacies across the curriculum (forthcoming)
*Roz Ivanic, Richard Edwards, David Barton, Zoe Fowler,
Gregg Mannion, Kate Miller and Marilyn Martin-Jones*

Improving Learning in Later Life (forthcoming)
Alexandra Withnall

Improving Mathematics at Work: the need for techno-mathematical literacies (forthcoming)
Celia Hoyles, Richard Noss, Phillip Kent and Arthur Bakker

Improving Research through User Engagement (forthcoming)
Mark Rickinson, Anne Edwards and Judy Sebba

Improving the Context for Inclusion: how teachers & educational psychologists can use action research to work together to develop inclusion (forthcoming)
Sue Davies, Andrew Howes, Sam Fox, Sian Swann, Heddwen Davies

Improving What is Learned at University: an exploration of the social and organisational diversity of university education (forthcoming)
John Brennan

Improving Inter-professional Collaborations

Multi-agency working for children's wellbeing

Anne Edwards, Harry Daniels,
Tony Gallagher, Jane Leadbetter
and Paul Warmington

Routledge
Taylor & Francis Group

LONDON AND NEW YORK

First published 2009
by Routledge
2 Park Square, Milton Park, Abingdon, Oxon OX14 4RN

Simultaneously published in the USA and Canada
by Routledge
270 Madison Avenue, New York, NY 10016

Routledge is an imprint of the Taylor & Francis Group, an informa business

© 2009 Anne Edwards, Harry Daniels, Tony Gallagher, Jane Leadbetter and Paul Warmington

Typeset in Charter ITC and Stone Sans by
Keystroke, 28 High Street, Tettenhall, Wolverhampton
Printed and bound in Great Britain by
TJ International, Padstow, Cornwall

British Library Cataloguing in Publication Data
A catalogue record for this book is available from the British Library

Library of Congress Cataloging in Publication Data
Improving inter-professional collaborations : learning to do multi-agency work
Anne Edwards . . . [et al.].
       p. cm. — (Improving learning)
     Includes bibliographical references and index.
    1. Action research in education—Great Britain—Case studies.
    2. Group work in education—Great Britain—Case studies.
    3. Marginality, Social—Great Britain—Case studies.
    4. Education—Parent participation—Great Britain—Case studies.
    I. Edwards, Anne, 1946–
    LB1028.24.I36 2008
    362.7–dc22   2008029199

ISBN 10: 0–415–46869–8 (hbk)
ISBN 10: 0–415–46870–1 (pbk)
ISBN 10: 0–203–88405–1 (ebk)

ISBN 13: 978–0–415–46869–5 (hbk)
ISBN 13: 978–0–415–46870–1 (pbk)
ISBN 13: 978–0–203–88405–8 (ebk)

Contents

Illustrations

Figures

Boxes

Tables

Series editor's preface

The *Improving Learning* series showcases findings from projects within ESRC's Teaching and Learning Research Programme (TLRP) – the UK's largest ever co-ordinated educational research initiative.

Books in the *Improving Learning* series are explicitly designed to support 'evidence-informed' decisions in educational practice and policy-making. In particular, they combine rigorous social and educational science with high awareness of the significance of the issues being researched.

Working closely with practitioners, organisations and agencies covering all educational sectors, the Programme has supported many of the UK's best researchers to work on the direct improvement of policy and practice to support learning. Over sixty projects have been supported, covering many issues across the lifecourse. We are proud to present the results of this work through books in the *Improving Learning* series.

Each book provides a concise, accessible and definitive *overview* of innovative findings from a TLRP investment. If more advanced information is required, the books may be used as a gateway to academic journals, monographs, websites, etc. On the other hand, shorter summaries and *Research Briefings* on key findings are also available via the Programme's website at www.tlrp.org.

We hope that you will find the analysis and findings presented in this book are helpful to you in your work on improving outcomes for learners.

Andrew Pollard
Director, TLRP
Institute of Education, University of London

Introduction

In this book we discuss what we learnt about professional learning in inter-professional collaborations, which aimed at preventing the social exclusion of children and young people during a four-year study. The research project was funded by the Economic and Social Research Council (ESRC) Teaching and Learning Research Programme (TLRP).

Our focus was twofold:

1 What and how did professionals learn as they developed new ways of working to provide joined-up responses to support children and families.
2 What were the organisational conditions for their learning.

The study started in January 2004 and captured a period of change in English and Northern Irish local authorities, which included developing interagency responses to the problems of social exclusion. In particular, the service providers with whom we worked were aiming at disrupting the trajectories of exclusion of children and young people and at preventing what might seem the inevitable process of their becoming excluded from making a contribution to society or benefiting from what society had to offer. These providers included: education, health and social care and, in some cases, the voluntary and community sector.

The book is in three parts. In Part I (Chapters 1 and 2) we outline the background to the current focus on the prevention of social exclusion with children and young people; introduce briefly the Cultural Historical Activity Theory (CHAT) analytic framework we used; and consider the implications of increased inter-professional collaboration for the professions.

In Part II (Chapters 3 to 6), we set out what we learnt from our research in five English and two Northern Irish longitudinal case studies. We identify what practitioners and their organisations were learning during this period of change, how that learning was supported and the challenges they faced. Our conclusion is that although there is no uniform model of inter-professional working that can be rolled out, and nor should there be, there are some useful principles that can lead to inter-professional work being an enriched form of professional practice. Interestingly, and contrary to our expectations, we found little evidence that practitioners were bringing parents or carers into partnership with them. We therefore suggest this is an area that remains to be developed once practitioners have become more secure in the inter-professional practices they are developing.

In Part 3, we consider the implications of the study for current moves towards inter-professional work, wherever it is located, and for how it might be examined. In Chapter 7 we examine the implications of what we saw for professional learning; in Chapter 8 we draw on Basil Bernstein's ideas to consider how organisations might enable it; and in the final chapter we outline what we think are the implications of this study for the development of CHAT.

The Learning in and for Interagency Working (LIW) study was framed by CHAT because it allowed us to look at three intertwined layers of change: individual professional sense-making and learning; collaborative meaning-making and action; and collective or systemic responses and development. It was also important to place these processes within wider systemic changes in national welfare systems.

We do not offer a blueprint for delivering a programme of professional learning. Rather, our study suggests that change processes need to recognise the roots of current practices; work on identifying desired future practices and the values that underpin them; and analyse what needs to be done to reshape current practices so that new forms of work can be developed. We therefore hope that the practices and ideas generated by the professionals in this study provide useful starting points for current programmes of professional development.

We also think that the tools of CHAT are useful for this kind of work as they remind us of the multi-layered nature of our institutions and the need to look at change simultaneously for individual, inter-actional and collective levels of action. We did not find any examples of tightly synchronised multi-layered responses to changes in policies for vulnerable children in the sites in which we worked. This was not surprising, as changes at one level are bound to nudge forward changes at another. For this reason we became increasingly interested in what occurred not only at the boundaries between professions but also at the boundaries between different layers in the organisational hierarchies in the local authorities where we worked.

Acknowledgements

We learnt a lot while undertaking this study and are therefore extremely grateful to the local authorities and the practitioners in them who generously collaborated with us. We have provided feedback our findings to them and, for reasons of confidentiality, do not want to name them here, but they know how much we owe to them. We particularly thank the three 'local authority researchers' who were seconded on a part-time basis to the English element of the study over the last two years of the project. They also know who they are and we hope they know how much we think they contributed to the study. We would also like to thank everyone who attended our regional workshops early and late in the study as these were so important for us in testing the wider relevance of our ideas and findings. Particular thanks go to Alan Brown, Margaret Threadgold and Klaus Wedell for their wise and sustained advice on the Project Reference Group and to Dame Gillian Pugh for so skilfully guiding the project dissemination conference and for the helpful advice that followed it.

The research team was also a multi-centred system of distributed expertise. In Bath, Harry Daniels worked with Anna Popova and Mariann Martsin; in Birmingham, Jane Leadbetter, Deirdre Martin and Paul Warmington were involved throughout the study, Sarah Parsons for the first year and Penny Smith for the last year; in Oxford, Anne Edwards worked with Apostol Apostolov and Ioanna Kinti. David Middleton and Steve Brown contributed from the University of Loughborough, and in Steve's case more latterly from the University of Leicester. Joan Lloyd held everything together in Birmingham over the first year, and Louise Chambers and then Kate Youngs picked up the reins in Bath for the final three years. In Northern Ireland the team for the two-year study was Tony Gallagher, Rosemary Kilpatrick and Karen Carlisle.

In addition, we benefited hugely early on in the study from regular meetings with Yrjö Engeström and his colleagues at the Center for Activity Theory and Developmental Work Research at the University of Helsinki and would particularly like to thank Yryö Engeström and Hanna Toiviainen for their contributions to the study. Colleagues at the Intermedia Centre at the University of Oslo joined in discussions with us as we developed ideas. We would therefore also like to thank Sten Ludvigsen and Trond Eliv Hauge for making those conversations possible. Also in Oslo, we have enjoyed conversations with the Prolearn and LIKE project teams led by Karen Jensen and Monika Nerland, which have informed the development of our ideas about being a professional

This book is a collaboration, drawing heavily on the analyses undertaken by the whole team over the four years of the study. Inevitably there were lead authors: Harry Daniels took the lead on Chapter 8 and part of Chapter 3 and Anne Edwards on the remaining chapters with Chapter 9 as a joint effort. Tony Gallagher provided the Northern Ireland details and Jane Leadbetter and Paul Warmington contributed with sections and critical commentary. Papers by Jane, Paul and the rest of the team have also helped shape this text. These are all available on www.bath.ac.uk/research/liw/.

We end with particular thanks to the professionals in England and in Northern Ireland who put up with us and allowed us to share in their learning. They probably have a very strong idea of how much we have learnt from working with them, we just hope that it was reciprocal.

Part I

What is the issue?

Chapter 1

Social inclusion and inter-professional collaboration

Introduction

The research project on which this book is based was funded by the Teaching and Learning Research Programme (TLRP) and ran from January 2004 to December 2007 at a time of major shifts in the organisation of services for children and young people. Over the four years of the study we worked with practitioners such as educational psychologists, children and families workers, teachers, education welfare officers, health professionals, speech and language therapists and colleagues from the voluntary sector who were all learning to work together in ways they had not done before in order to support the social inclusion of children and young people. They were learning to do this work while relationships between their organisations reconfigured around them. They remained focused on what they saw as the needs of children and adjusted their practices. In many ways, their practices raced ahead of both local and national strategies as they worked creatively for children in shifting systems. LIW was set up to capture the learning that occurred in these developing practices and the conditions that made learning possible. Two years into the study a research team based in Northern Ireland received TLRP funding to extend the LIW work in a different context. The Northern Irish LIW study did not entirely replicate the main study, but was an important sounding board for the ideas developed in the English analyses. In this chapter we outline the development of UK policy on the prevention of social exclusion through inter-agency collaborations and introduce the LIW study.

What is social inclusion?

The idea of social inclusion of children is not an easy idea to pin down. It raises all sorts of questions about how social practices can become more inclusive and the contribution of disadvantaged children and young people to them. Social inclusion is, nonetheless, seen as desirable because of concerns with equity and with the disruption that socially excluded youngsters can cause. Social exclusion is perhaps easier to describe. It was discussed with intensity in Europe during the 1990s because of serious concerns about the fragility of society. In 1993, for example, an early definition of the social exclusion of children and adults was provided in a European Commission Green Paper on *European Social Policy Options for the Union*.

> Social exclusion does not only mean insufficient income. It even goes beyond participation in working life; it is manifest in fields such as housing, education, health and access to services. It affects not only individuals who have suffered serious set backs, but social groups, particularly in urban and rural areas, who are subject to discrimination, segregation or the weakening of traditional forms of social relations. More generally by highlighting the flaws in the social fabric, it suggests something more than social inequality and, concomitantly, carries with it the risk of a dual or fragmented society.
>
> (Commission of the European Communities 1993: 20–1)

Here we can see that social exclusion is being presented as a complex phenomenon that threatens the wellbeing of both individuals and their communities.

Finding ways of including disadvantaged children in the opportunities available for them became even more of a priority as a result of other strands being woven into the argument for it. One of these strands is economic. The 1990s saw a growing fear that there were soon to be too few skilled workers to support the rapidly increasing number of elderly. During that period the idea of a child 'at risk' of not being able to contribute to society began to replace the notion of disadvantage. From the Organisation for Economic Cooperation and Development (OECD) perspective, children and young people who were 'at risk' were likely to fail in the school system and unlikely to enter work (OECD 1998). As Levitas (1998) has observed, inclusion had become an individual obligation that needed to be actively performed.

Social inclusion was therefore becoming recast, with the idea of entitlement to integration into society as both an individual right and a societal necessity. As Room explained at the time:

> Social exclusion is the process of becoming detached from the organisations and communities of which the society is composed and from the rights and responsibilities that they embody.
>
> (Room 1995: 243)

The shift, from seeing problems in terms of being disadvantaged to being 'at risk' of being excluded from what society both offers and requires, was regarded as helpful by policy-makers. It was future-oriented and allowed the State to think about how it might prevent the exclusion of children from what binds society together and their responsibilities to society. The 'prevention of social exclusion' therefore emerged as a new core concept in welfare services in England in the late 1990s (Bynner 2001; France and Utting 2005).

The 'prevention of social exclusion' is as slippery a term as 'social inclusion'. It is usually linked with the idea of early intervention at the initial signs of vulnerability. Most work on early intervention has focused on the early years of life in initiatives such as Head Start in the US and Sure Start in England (Glass 1999, 2005). This rather limited understanding of early intervention was particularly expanded in the report of Policy Action Team 12 in the UK, which argued that children and young people can become vulnerable at different stages of their lives through changes in their life circumstances and that early inter-vention needs to include acting at the early signs of vulnerability, regardless of age, to prevent ultimate social exclusion (Home Office, 2000).

Of course vulnerability is often complex and may not be evident unless one looks across all aspects of a child's life: parenting, schooling, housing and so on. There are two important ideas for professional practice embedded in these developing understandings. First, social exclusion should be seen as a dynamic process and not a static condi-tion (Walker 1995). The dynamic is the outcome of interactions of effects across different domains of a child's life and therefore can be disrupted if the responses to it are also multi-dimensional. That means that practitioners, working together, can make a difference. Second, because vulnerability may not be evident until a picture of accu-mulated difficultly is picked up by looking across a child's life, all services that work with children need to be brought into the process of prevention. Practitioners working in universal services, that is, services open to all children and young people, have a role to play in spotting vulnerability, if not in responding to it with specific support. As we shall see, these expectations have called for new forms of inter-professional work: new ways of looking at children with other professionals and new ways of responding to the picture of the child that emerges.

Box 1.1 Social inclusion

Social inclusion is therefore a much broader idea than, for example, being included in the school curriculum by receiving extra support. It ranges across the whole of a child's life and is evident in their ability to experience what society has made possible. Being socially included involves having accessible resources as well as direct help, and most certainly includes the right to make some contribution to developing the social conditions one experiences. It is the beginnings of responsible citizenship and resonates strongly with Northern European ideas of *Bildung* and the general wellbeing of the developing child in relation to the moral order of general society. Socially included children or young people are able to navigate the opportunities available and the difficulties they meet in their lives so that they avoid becoming disconnected from those opportunities. For most children the navigation involves making choices between opportunities. For some, at times, the difficulties threaten to throw them off track. It is at this point that they become vulnerable and require extra responsive help.

Policy responses

It was quickly apparent that the welfare services that work with children should find ways of enabling collaboration between practitioners (Home Office 2000; OECD 1998) to enable responsive interventions to give support to children who appear vulnerable. This belief lay behind a raft of measures in England that aimed at producing joined up responses to the multi-dimensional problem of social exclusion in England. These included establishing the government's Social Exclusion Unit, the Green Paper *Every Child Matters* (DfES 2003), and the subsequent *Children Act* (DfES 2004), which together set out an agenda for more responsive inter-professional work that recognised the complexity of the problem. Actual government initiatives have included Sure Start, which worked with children and their families from birth (Glass 1999; Melhuish *et al.* 2005); the Children's Fund, which set up local partnerships to encourage interagency collaborations across services working with children aged five to thirteen (Edwards *et al.* 2006); On-Track, which focused on children and crime prevention in targeted areas (France *et al.* 2004); Local Network Funding (DfES 2005); and extended schools (Cummings *et al.* 2004), which offered support for families, activities for children, community access and quick access to other services.

The need for practitioners to be able to understand the totality of a child's life circumstances has led to major reconfigurations of children's services in local authorities in England. We have seen, for example, the merging of education and social care services under single directorates in English local authorities and a reorganisation in central government to produce, in 2007, the Department for Children, Schools and Families (DCSF). This merging has the potential to produce the infrastructural conditions for inter-professional work, but it represents a massive shift. The Policy Action Team 12, when looking at services for young people, reported that collaboration between services was not being achieved because local authority budgets for intervening in a crisis were different from those that funded preventative activities; priorities for services set out in policy guidance did not encourage collaboration; and professional cultures worked against the kinds of collaborations that were needed (Home Office 2000). The LIW study found many of these difficulties still in place when it completed its report in 2008.

Another element of the policy response to the problem of social exclusion reflected the link between exclusion and lack of engagement with the democratic processes of society, which marked European discussions during the 1990s. Alongside increased attention to collaboration between professionals was an expectation that citizens identified as vulnerable would participate in the development of the services that were to be provided for them. Sinclair and Franklin (2000: 2) summarised the reasons for involving children as: upholding children's rights; fulfilling legal responsibilities; improving services; improving decision-making; enhancing democratic processes; promoting children's protection; enhancing children's skills; empowering; and enhancing self-esteem. The Children's Fund, for example, reflected the view in government that children should play a greater role in developing policy and practice. In 2000 its strategy document stated:

> we want to hear the voices of young people influencing and shaping local services; contributing to their local communities; feeling heard; feeling valued; being treated as responsible citizens.
>
> (Children and Young People's Unit 2000: 27)

This strategy required service providers to become more responsive to the needs and strengths of the groups with whom they were working. However, it was not always easy for them to adjust from being the expert who inhabited a culture of specific expertise to learn to recognise the expertise that parents and carers brought to discussions of their children and neighbourhoods (Anning *et al.* 2006; Edwards *et al.* 2006).

In this book we are focusing on the professionals and the cultures that shape them, and that they also shape, as they undertake new work. The policy and infrastructural changes during 2004–07 formed crucial background elements, and the ways in which they occurred impacted on the possibilities for action for the professionals. A theme that runs through this book is the interaction between local authority systems, the more local work systems of the professionals with whom we worked, and the professional learning that arose in new inter-professional practices.

Professionals in changing systems

The 2007 discussion paper produced by the UK Treasury, as a result of its detailed policy review of services for children, outlined the need for a broad interpretation of social inclusion and a systemic response:

> the system needs to be capable of providing a continuum of support across services throughout childhood and to be able to intervene when poor outcomes do arise . . . new interventions would still be needed to deal with those who will begin to signal a higher likelihood of poor outcomes at a later age but who had not done so before.
>
> (Treasury-DfES 2007: 19)

The paper continued:

> The need to identify children experiencing poor outcomes, and to monitor children to identify who might be showing signs of developing poor outcomes, implies a key role for universal services.

These services, such as health visitors, GPs, children's centres and especially schools – which have constant contact with children throughout their childhood – could play the primary role in identifying which children might be vulnerable.

(ibid: 19)

Box 1.2 The need for a whole system approach

The way forward for professionals, it argued, is to recognise that targeted and specialist services are vital for prevention and early intervention, but prevention also depends on the work of these universal services. Prevention needs 'a whole system approach' and the 'full engagement of universal services, especially schools'.

A whole system approach marks a considerable change for services that are used to working to their own professional standards on their own professional goals. In the LIW study we focused on the changes in practice identified by the practitioners as they began to work across organisational boundaries with other professionals. Through examining their developing practices and their frustrations with them, we identified the organisational shifts that were necessary. These frustrations were usually related to the old rules that still governed new practices and the barriers that existed at the organisational boundaries that were tested by new practices. For example, systems of referral that meant that organisations passed on 'bits of the child', as one practitioner put it, from one to the other, were opened up for scrutiny and criticism of how slow the respective organisations were in enabling parallel inter-professional collaboration that was more responsive to the needs of children.

Our main focus, however, was the learning that occurred in doing interagency work. Here again practitioner frustrations were important because, as they were discussed, the ways in which they were understood were revealed to the research team. We will look in detail at what practitioners were learning in Chapter 4. At this point we will simply point to two major changes demanded of professionals. Discussion of these, and others, is developed in later chapters. First, practitioners learnt that they needed to look beyond the boundaries of their organisations at what else was going on in children's lives and, at the very least, to develop some understanding of how other professionals interpreted specific children, their needs and strengths. Second, this outward-looking stance was accompanied by a revived focus on individual children as people with complex lives who were interconnected with their families and communities. The complexity of children's worlds was no longer hidden from practitioners by their looking at them using the narrow lenses of a tightly focused profession. Instead, areas of children's lives that were beyond the influence of practitioners as individual specialists were revealed.

Initially these revelations were met by worries about professionals being expected to become the all-purpose generalist practitioner, the complete problem-solver. Edwards outlined these practitioner concerns in a paper drawing on her study of the Children's Fund and, arguing against generalist practice, produced a list of elements of the new multi-agency working – see Box 1.3.

Box 1.3 Features of inter-professional practice

- A focus on children and young people as whole people, that is, not as specific 'needs'.
- Following the child's trajectory.
- An ability to talk across professional boundaries.
- An understanding of what other practitioners are able to offer the responsive package of protection that is built around the child or young person.
- Acknowledgement of the capacity of service users and their families to help tailor the services they are receiving.
- An understanding that changing the trajectories of exclusion of children and young people involves not only building confidence and skills, but also a reconfiguring of the opportunities available to them – that is, systems-wide change.

(Edwards 2004: 5)

Lying behind these features is a belief in the importance of sustaining the specialist expertise of individual practitioners and the suggestion that instead of thinking of generalist practice, we should see practitioners as parts of local systems of distributed expertise. We will discuss expertise in more detail in later chapters; the key point here is that in inter-professional work, specialist expertise becomes more rather than less important, as does the need to be quite clear about the limits of one's expertise and to know when to work with others. The Treasury discussion paper (Treasury-DfES 2007) makes this very clear through its distinction between the role of universal services in identifying problems and the role of more specialist services in working together on them.

However, Edwards' list did not acknowledge the different trigger points for professional action across professions and the extent to which these are shaped by how each organisation categorises children. For example, trigger points in schools are usually related to behavioural problems, while those in children's services are shaped by understandings of levels of need (Hardiker 1999) with, as Jack observes, professional identity often associated with the capacity to work with children in the greatest need (Jack 2006). The practitioners we worked with struggled with these differences and with the assessment systems that were being introduced by their local authorities as tools or resources for making work manageable. These struggles revealed their thinking and the need for organisational adjustments.

Another important aspect of the adjustments we observed in local systems were the different time scales involved in achieving change through a systemic approach, and the capacity of the organisations in which practices were changing to learn from and respond to these changes. This is not an uncommon problem when new practices are being developed (Schulz 2001). In the LIW study, we observed that local strategists' time-scales differed from the practitioners, who were often far more aware of the organisational implications of inter-professional work, while the tools created to support practices were frequently lagging behind the practices in their development. This highlighted for us the need for systemic approaches to change to include time for systemic learning. Time is needed for strategy to learn seriously from practice, and for the development of strategies that are informed by the learning that is occurring in practice as practitioners develop new ways of working. We pursue this theme later in the book.

Child-centred practices

As we have already indicated, practitioners involved in preventing children's social exclusion share a common interest in children's wellbeing based in sets of professional values that overlap at the very least. This shared focus, we suggest, is in line with the government's reform agenda for public services by 'putting the customer first' (Office of Public Services Reform 2002: 7). It encourages an approach to preventative work that involves practitioners in following each child, at the expense of a concern with the category systems of their home organisations and how they might be sustained. In other words, we are proposing that inter-professional work is more likely to be child-led than service-led.

Reflecting the child-led focus of inter-professional work, policy developments for the prevention of social exclusion have drawn heavily on research on the resilience of vulnerable children, which originated in developmental psychology in the US and elsewhere. The research and its implementation tended to centre on developing individual strengths to prevent a vulnerability to adversity (Garmezy 1991; Masten and Garmezy 1985). The argument is that resilience is a capacity for adaptation to appropriate developmental pathways despite disruptions such as family crises, and that the best predictors of resilience are relationships with 'caring prosocial adults' and 'good intellectual functioning' (Masten and Coatsworth 1998). The origins of resilience in children 'at risk' are therefore similar to the development of competence in children in more stable and nurturing situations. The more psychological versions of resilience are also contested (Evans *et al.* 2006; Little *et al.* 2004), as they can under-emphasise the need for the worlds inhabited by children to adapt to their needs and underplays the capacity of children to shape their own situations (Edwards and Apostolov 2007).

Attention to environment and the protective factors to be found in it is therefore also a strand in work on resilience. Luthar (1993), for example, has suggested that resilience lies more in the contexts and relationships in which development occurs than in individuals' personal attributes. Resilience is now recognized as a dynamic process of interaction between sociocultural contexts and developing individuals (Howard *et al.* 1999). The development of contexts to build resilience has included work on and with families, where it meshes particularly with strength-based approaches to family therapy (Walsh 2002), and aims at enabling families to 'bounce-back from adversity' (Hawley and DeHaan 1996). It has also included attention to integrated service delivery that operates with families and communities as well as with vulnerable individuals (Luthar and Cicchetti 2000; Warren *et al.* 2006).

Box 1.4 Disrupting children's trajectories of exclusion

A focus on individual children and their support networks brings coherence to inter-professional work and for that reason, throughout the book, we will talk about the work that is done on supporting, or if necessary disrupting, children's trajectories to ensure that they are being directed from social exclusion to inclusion in and engagement with what society can offer. The idea of a trajectory has been useful in helping us see inter-professional work as collaborations over shared professional problems, however differently they might be interpreted by the collaborating practitioners. It has also allowed us to acknowledge the dynamic shaping of trajectories of vulnerability and how they may change over time (Walker 1995). Following children's trajectories has required practitioners to move from working only with the stable categorisations of their own organisations to engage with those in play when other professionals identify children's strengths and needs. It has revealed alternative interpretations and the validity of the responses made by other professionals.

Sampling sites for the LIW study

The LIW study was based in five local authorities in England and in two case study sites in Northern Ireland. The seven sites are described in Chapter 3. Here we explain how we selected them in relation to the kinds of inter-professional work that was beginning to emerge in them.

We needed to identify places where new understandings were being developed in new practices. To do that we drew on the work of Victor and Boynton (1998) who identified five types of work: craft, mass production, process enhancement, mass customisation, and co-configuration (Figure 1.1). The sites we selected were, according to evidence, gathered in interviews with senior local authority staff, moving from mass customisation, that is, from careful targeting of specialist provision, to co-configuration, which is a way of labelling responsive interactions in inter-professional work. The idea of co-configuration was an important element in the LIW study and is therefore worth elaborating here.

According to Victor and Boynton, each type of work generates and requires a certain type of knowledge that is produced in different kinds

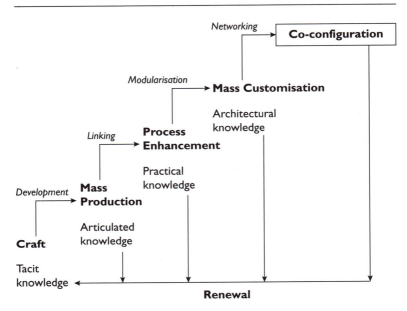

Figure 1.1 Historical forms of work (adapted from Victor and Boynton, 1998)

of relationships. They suggest that change occurs through learning and the leveraging of the knowledge produced into new, and arguably more effective, types of work.

Looking at each stage in Figure 1.1 in turn, they explain that what craftworkers know about their work rests in their personal intuition and experience and in the use of their tools. When these practitioners invent solutions, they create tacit knowledge that is tightly coupled with experience, technique and tools. This kind of work is often regarded as intuitive and is easily recognisable in, for example, informal youth work settings. The articulation of tacit knowledge may lead to the next stage where it can become regarded as 'good practice' with the expectation that it is mass produced to become the norm for all.

Learning is an important driver for movement through each stage. Mass production workers follow instructions yet also learn about work through observation and reflection. They learn where the instructions are effective and where they are not. This learning leads to a new type of knowledge, which Victor and Boynton call practical knowledge. Practical knowledge is in turn enhanced through linking processes. For example, these processes may involve setting up a team system where practitioners focus on improving work processes, which promotes the sharing of ideas within the team and which fosters collaboration across teams. As we can see, progression through the stages involves increasing transparency and clear articulation of the knowledge being brought into play.

The move to mass customisation brings greater precision. To take an example from children's services, it would involve the careful shaping of a specific service, through creating modules or tailored forms of provision that can be specifically targeted at particular groups. One difference between this work and what happens in work we would label co-configuration is that with mass customisation there is little opportunity for ongoing reshaping of services; whereas the emphasis of co-configuration work is on the continual development of the service with others. Another difference is that the networks of co-configuration involve the users of the service alongside practitioners in the development work and everyone is involved in learning. As Victor and Boynton explain, albeit in the language of industry:

> The work of co-configuration involves building and sustaining a fully integrated system that can sense, respond, and adapt to the individual experience of the customer. When a firm does co-configuration work, it creates a product that can learn and adapt, but it also builds an ongoing relationship between each customer-product pair and the company. Doing mass customization requires designing a product at least once for each customer. This design process requires the company to sense and respond to the individual customer's needs. But co-configuration work takes this relationship up one level – it brings the value of an intelligent and 'adapting' product. The company then continues to work with this customer-product pair to make the product more responsive to each user. In this way, the customization work becomes continuous. . . . Unlike previous work, co-configuration work never results in a 'finished' product. Instead, a living, growing network develops between customer, product, and company.
>
> (Victor and Boynton 1998: 195)

Although this model of changing practices originated in the Harvard Business School and does not discuss the provision of welfare services, it resonated strongly with the senior staff responsible for reconfiguring children's services in local authorities in England when the team discussed it with them at the start of LIW.

Box 1.5 Co-configuration

Co-configuration is a way of labelling practices that are currently emerging in inter-professional work where practitioners work together to help shape a child's trajectory. It also allows us to recognise the point made by Furlong and Cartmel (1997) that young people currently find themselves negotiating risks that were largely unknown to their parents and that those negotiations take place at an individual level even though they are shaped by wider structural changes. Finally, for us, as CHAT researchers, an added attraction of the Victor and Boynton model is its focus on how changes in conceptual tools, that is the knowledge in use, are intertwined with changes in individual practices and in the services and systems in which they are produced.

The implications of co-configuration work for practice in children's services are considerable. Co-configuration in responsive and collaborating services requires flexible working in which no single actor has the sole, fixed responsibility and control. It requires participants to be able to recognise and engage relationally with the expertise distributed across rapidly changing work places (Edwards 2005) and to work in new ways with those who hitherto had been seen mainly as clients. It has the potential to involve children and families in repositioning themselves in and thereby reshaping the social conditions of their development as they work on them and change them (Edwards and Apostolov 2007). It therefore echoes emphases on individual responsibility and participation in society as a route to the prevention of social exclusion. As we embarked on the study in the selected sites, we knew that we would be examining these processes as they arose and therefore needed to work in a sustained way over substantial periods of time to trace their development.

An outline of the LIW project

While looking at the emergent inter-professional practices involved in working with vulnerable young people we had three aims:

- the identification of new professional practices;
- the creation with practitioners of new knowledge rooted in reflective, systemic analysis of these practices, which could be used to develop inter-professional work;

- placing the emergent inter-professional practice within an understanding of the historically changing character of service provision and user-engagement.

In pursuing these aims we used the theoretical tools of Cultural Historical Activity Theory (CHAT), which has its roots in the work of Vygotsky (1978, 1987, 1997a, 1997b, 1999) and is explained in Daniels (2001). CHAT frameworks locate individual learning and development in the environmental conditions for thinking and acting (Cole 1996) and are discussed more fully in Appendix A.

Box 1.6 Vygotsky and dual stimulation

Vygotsky's contribution to revealing for us how people were making sense of new practices was profound. His big contribution to psychology was to make accessible for analysis what he termed 'consciousness' and what we would now see as how people think and make sense of the world. The argument was that people reveal their understandings in the way that they interpret a problem and use the tools that are available to them to work on it. That is, understanding is revealed in the act. These tools may be material artefacts such as calculators, but they also include the conceptual tools revealed in how language is used while working on a task. Vygotsky argued that people could be helped to reveal thinking through a method that he called dual stimulation. He explained it as follows:

> By using this approach, we do not limit ourselves to the usual method of offering the subject simple stimuli to which we expect a direct response. Rather, we simultaneously offer a second series of stimuli that have a special function. In this way, we are able to study the process of accomplishing a task by the aid of specific auxiliary means; thus we are also able to discover the inner structure and development of higher psychological processes.
>
> (Vygotsky 1978: 74)

A simple example of dual stimulation is to give a child a task and a tool, which may be an intellectual tool, and to see how they use the tool to work on the task. How they are making sense of the task and the tool will be revealed in their actions, which will, of course include the language they use.

As we shall see, dual stimulation was central to our methodology, so we now outline briefly what we did over the four years of the study. In Stages 1 and 2 of the project we produced a literature review (Warmington *et al.* 2005); conducted a series of regional workshops with seventeen English local authorities; and began to frame our understanding of what and how practitioners were learning as they developed inter-professional work. In Stage 3 we moved to a detailed examination of these work practices in small-scale intensive studies in two local authorities over a period of six months. In the first authority we worked with a Youth Offending Team (YOT) and in the second with a newly created Multi-Agency Team, a 'virtual' team comprising professionals from a range of services and agencies. In the 18-month Stage 4 we repeated the intervention research on a larger scale in three local authorities over a period of twelve months in three multi-agency settings: an extended school, a Children in Public Care (CiPC) team, and a Multi-Professional Team. The interventions allowed us to reveal the ideas in use, the frustrations met and solutions found by the practitioners. In the final stage we tested our findings from Stages 3 and 4 with other welfare professionals and in the Northern Irish study to assess how relevant the ideas were for their developing inter-professional activities.

Our work in the English case study sites was oriented around a series of two-hour structured sessions in each site. The methodology we used in these sessions was Developmental Work Research (DWR) (Engeström 2007a). DWR is based on the Vygotskian idea of dual stimulation, which is used to help practitioners reveal the thinking that is embedded in their accounts of their practices and the systemic tensions and contradictions they encountered when developing new ways of working. The 'second series stimuli' offered in DWR are the conceptual tools of activity theory (see Appendix A). These are provided by the research team to enable participants to analyse and make sense of their everyday practices.

In the DWR sessions, evidence of the practices, gathered in interviews, previous sessions or compiled with practitioners as case study examples, was presented by the facilitators. Participants were then helped to examine those practices using activity theory. In doing so they revealed the conceptual tools they were using as they engaged in or hoped to develop their work. This methodology enabled the LIW team to see what practitioners were learning in order to undertake inter-professional collaborations and what adjustments they were making to existing practices and their own positions as professionals within those practices. The analysis of talk in the sessions is outlined in Chapters 8 and 9 and is discussed in Middleton *et al.* (in press).

When DWR is used in the intensive form developed by Engeström and his colleagues in Helsinki (Engeström 2007a; Engeström *et al.* 2003a), the explicit aim of the processes is to promote learning at the level of the activity system – for example a work team – in which the intervention is occurring. The researchers are invited into organisations to help them achieve systemic change.

Our use of DWR differed as we used it as a tool in a research study where we selected sites in order to achieve the sample we needed and then negotiated entry into them. In every local authority the senior people with whom we negotiated entry were keen to embrace the expansive learning potential of DWR. However, we worked most closely with practitioners and not with the strategists who gave us access. Consequently, although this varied across sites, we needed to limit our expectations of significant systemic change as a result of our intervention and instead to focus more on the purposes of the research study, which were to reveal what and how practitioners were learning as they embarked on a joined-up approach to preventing social exclusion.

The case studies that were based in Northern Ireland operated in a slightly different way. The Northern Ireland project was an extension of the English study and started two years after the English one. It was based on the premise that the situation there differed in potentially significant ways and hence would add important variation to the range of circumstances we were exploring. As a part of the UK, Northern Ireland largely follows the policy path adopted in England, but normally after a short time-lag. This pattern became even more evident during the long period of Direct Rule when no locally elected Assembly was in operation. Two particular features of Northern Ireland were deemed to be of particular interest. First, as a consequence of denominational influence in education, there is a more complex pattern of school ownership in Northern Ireland, as compared with England, and the role of local authorities is less important. These denominational divisions could complicate collaborative engagement between schools. Second, during the period of Direct Rule significant resources were put into a community development strategy in order to construct strong networks within communities that had suffered violence and disruption. The logic of the strategy was that the networks would enhance community confidence and provide foundations for bridging efforts between divided communities. The main consequence is that the role of voluntary and community organisations has become very significant in the delivery of a range of public policy areas.

As an initial step, the Northern Irish team held twenty one-to-one interviews and two focus groups with professionals. The purpose was to establish an overall picture of collaborative working in Northern Ireland and to assess the extent to which professionals engaged in this work were concerned to improve or develop existing practice. In addition, the first stage would be used to identify potential research sites for more detailed scrutiny. Two sites were subsequently identified, although in one of these we worked in two distinct areas, giving us a total of three research sites for application of the modified DWR methodology. The Northern Irish sites were very important in ensuring that the ideas developed in the England study were not only of local relevance.

Conclusion

In this chapter we have set out the policy context for changes in the ways that UK welfare professionals are being expected to work. We have then outlined the research study on which this book is based and in particular have highlighted (i) the importance of the idea of co-configuration to our thinking about inter-professional work and (ii) how DWR methods were used to reveal the ideas being developed by practitioners as they started to work across professional boundaries to disrupt children's trajectories of social exclusion.

Chapter 2

Professional learning for inter-professional collaboration

Introduction

Professional action is usually marked by the need to make informed decisions based on analyses of tasks or problems. Professionals are therefore not usually engaged in rigid and predictable work practices where routine dominates. To reflect that view of professional action we see professional learning as a process of increasingly informed sense-making and action. In this chapter we explain what we mean by learning and introduce ideas that are developed throughout the book. These include collaboration, boundary work, distributed expertise and responsible agency. We conclude by pointing to the need to pay attention to the organisational conditions necessary for professional learning.

Learning and professional identity

We are not suggesting by our use of 'informed' that learning is simply a matter of acquiring knowledge and applying it. The 1990s debate (Anderson *et al.* 1996, 1997; Greeno 1997) over whether learning was the acquisition and application of knowledge or simply a matter of participation in social practices was usefully brought to a close with Sfard's 1998 paper on why we need to think of learning as processes of both acquisition and participation. That is, we internalise the ideas that are important in our culture, we organise them into schema that have a logic for us and reveal them in our problem-solving.

However, our responses to the problems we are working on are also shaped by the situations in which they are presented, how we are positioned in them and what resources they offer. For example, if a teacher is presented with the problem of a child who is not behaving in class, she will interpret the child's behaviour by drawing on her experience and training, and will respond in ways that are shaped by the established social practices of the school, following agreed procedures. In other words, she will act as a participant in the established school practices while also using her professional knowledge to assess the child's needs. As we shall see, one of the challenges for the professionals we worked with was that the social practices of their workplaces did not always allow them to work with the ideas about the prevention of social exclusion that they were developing with other practitioners.

The links between professional learning and organisational practices are important, so let's explore them a little further. There is a vast literature on learning in the workplace. Some, such as the work of Jean Lave, offer classic examples of learning apprenticeships based on participation in established social practices. Her famous study of West African tailors (Lave 1997) shows how apprentice tailors are inducted into long-established work practices through observation and by being given small manageable tasks that over time absorb them into the more complex practices of the workplace.

In another classic study of working practices in a dairy warehouse, Scribner placed more emphasis on cognitive processes and illustrated what she described as 'mind in action' (Scribner 1997). Scribner observed how workers accomplished tasks within activities and how their thinking and acting were shaped by these activities. Interestingly, the dairymen in Scribner's study worked creatively, building on their expertise in using existing resources to solve problems by inventing strategies and bending rules. Focusing on how work conditions give rise to ways of thinking and acting, Scribner concluded 'skilled practical thinking at work is goal-directed and varies adaptively with the changing properties of problems and changing conditions in the task environment' (ibid: 367).

The main message from this and similar studies is as follows. Professional knowledge may be embedded in: routines; relationships; material artefacts, such as order forms in the dairy or assessment systems for care workers; and how language is used to discuss work. However, we also need to recognise that people work purposefully with these resources to achieve the goals of practice.

We agree, following Lave, that professional learning involves being able to recognise, access, use and contribute to the knowledge that is embedded in the social practices of the workplace and the resources used there. However, we follow the more cognitive line presented in

Scribner's study of dairy workers and suggest that a focus solely on social practices does not take into account the extensive and often generalisable knowledge that underpins expert adaptive professional practice. One cannot, for example, become a history teacher simply by watching other history teachers; there is a knowledge base that includes knowledge of history, knowledge of the curriculum and knowledge of how children learn.

Box 2.1 Purposeful agency in professional practices

To see learning in the workplace as merely induction into existing practices is particularly problematic when considering the kind of work we were studying, where practitioners were developing new ways of working together and in doing so were rethinking their practices. It seems to us that studies of professional action and learning in the workplace should recognise that professional practice is propelled forward by knowledgeable action on the problems of practice; and that means that there is some degree of purposeful agency in these practices.

Other studies have also recognised the importance of what individuals bring to the workplace, alongside how workplaces assist or restrict possibilities for learning (see, for example, Billett 2002; Fuller and Unwin 1998, 2003). Eraut's TLRP study of the professional development of accountants, nurses and engineers during their first three years in the workplace (Eraut 2007) exemplifies this approach. His grounded analyses of the processes of developing expertise has separated features of individuals from aspects of the context and then looked at how each affected learning at work. He suggested that individual experiences such as feeling supported, achieving a balance between the perceived value of the work and the degree of challenge, and being able to take decisions based on judgements positioned people as effective learners. He also identified what he termed 'contextual factors', such as how work is structured, how easy it is to form helpful relationships, and reasonable expectations of their performance, which could be manipulated to create a 'learning organisation', by which he means a workplace that is conducive to learning.

Eraut's emphasis on the emotional aspects of learning at work, the interactions, individual intentionality, and the value of the task, together with attention to how work is structured, are all important contributions to understanding learning in the workplace. They recognise that workplace learning is more than induction into existing practices, that worker engagement is crucial and that the practices of the workplace can be mindfully structured to support professionals as engaged decision-makers. Eraut's work can be categorised as an interactionist account of professional learning. It separates individual from context and then explores how individuals interact with each other and with contexts to develop their understandings of their workplace and their actions within them.

The sociocultural line that we have been taking does not start with a separation of individual from context. Instead it focuses on how learning professionals, in the actions they take, engage with the knowledge that is mediated by the situation in which action is occurring. For example, the expected way for a teacher to work with a child with disturbing behaviour in school will be different from those expected of a youth worker on a Friday night. People learning to be teachers or youth workers will work with the child using the ideas embedded in the expectations and procedures, which will in turn reflect the practices of the different workplaces. These ideas will shape how they interpret the child and how they work with her. Professional learning, following this framework, can be characterised as developing an increasingly complex interpretation of the child and her strengths and needs, and by knowing how to use available professional resources to take appropriate action based on that interpretation.

This understanding of professional learning means that we acknowledge that it can involve professionals in developing mental schema of relevant professional knowledge that they can call upon when necessary. However, it also suggests that we can simultaneously view it as a capacity to decode a setting and the actions within it, to look for patterns in tasks or problems, and to recognise resources that might support responsible action (Edwards *et al.* 2002). Professional learning from the sociocultural perspective we have just outlined is therefore not simply a matter of acquiring concepts that are systematically stored and then used when needed, though it does involve internalisation. Neither is learning simply a matter of being swept up by the social practices of what Lave and Wenger (1991) have called a 'community of practice'.

Professionals are by definition knowledgeable and agentic decision-makers, yet at the same time operate within established sets of social practices that shape the possibilities for action available to them. Their professional identities are therefore bound up with the expectations held of them. For example, a child would expect a teacher to work with her in a different way from a youth worker. She may also expect high school teachers to operate differently from primary school teachers. Within schools, different roles and responsibilities mean, for example, that form tutors are usually expected to pass the most troubling children to more senior staff, and of those senior staff only some will have easy access to the other professionals who may help the child.

Holland *et al.* (Holland *et al.* 1998) have looked at a variety of organisations and settings and have described each as a 'figured world' with inscribed social practices that shape the ways in which people can function within them. The idea of navigating the opportunities available to us as actors in the figured world of recognisable practices is a useful way of thinking about professional action. In the case of a school, these practices will be historically formed, central to the maintenance of order and therefore relatively easy to understand but difficult to negotiate and change. Holland and her colleagues, however, are not suggesting that lives are necessarily pre-determined by the practices in which people operate. Holland and Lachicotte (2007), for example, point out that we are able to regulate our behaviours by creating new cultural resources, which in turn shape our behaviours. The non-drinking alcoholics discussed in Holland *et al.* (1998) are one example of how people can act on their worlds to create new practices to support desired changes in behaviours.

Billett (2006), looking more closely at individual action, similarly sees participation in work practices as a form of negotiation and decision-making taken forward by a sense of personal agency. Like Holland *et al.*, Billett argues we should recognise the capacity of individuals to shape and reshape cultural practices and thereby their own learning. Both Holland *et al.* and Billett are drawing on Vygotsky's idea of externalisation, which we discuss in the next section. In brief, externalisation is shorthand for recognising that we shape our worlds as well as being shaped by them.

Billett's linking of learning with the negotiating and reshaping of cultural practices takes us to professional identity. We agree with Roth *et al.* (2004) that identity is not a stable characteristic, but is negotiated and accomplished within activities.

Box 2.2 Identity

Identity is therefore a way of describing how people are located within and participate in the practices which that comprise an activity such as the prevention of social exclusion. When the activity itself is new and is being negotiated, it follows that professional identities are also under negotiation.

Learning can occur in negotiations in work systems that are open and changing. But it can also occur when people work outside their home systems with other practitioners. In those circumstances there may be challenges for professionals who are developing practices in collaboration with other practitioners when new practices are running ahead of the practices that are valued in their home workplaces. The negotiation of changing identities is perhaps particularly challenging for practitioners who are relatively low status and who work in systems of high accountability. We are very aware of the vulnerability of some professionals when they are working collaboratively outside the known and well-supported social practices of their home organisations. Yet it is difficult for them to avoid learning in those situations.

As Sfard and Prusak (2005) have explained, one cannot separate learning from identity formation because when one learns something, new one is positioned differently in relation it. For example, as a result of working alongside a children and families worker, a teacher may more frequently see troublesome children as troubled and so work differently with them. This change in position may not fit with the social practices or figured world of the school, which may be built on the expectation that teachers should work primarily on the main-tenance of order. These kinds of tensions between the individual learning that occurs outside organisations and the figured worlds of organisations have been central to our study of professional learning in and for interagency working. Cultural Historical Activity Theory (CHAT) has provided us with the tools to understand these tensions by asking us to look at situated activities over time as well as at the individual sense-making of practitioners.

A CHAT view of professional learning

Box 2.3 Professional learning in the LIW study

In the Learning for and in Interagency Working (LIW) study we set out to identify what professionals were thinking and doing when they worked in the fluid and responsive ways we have described as 'co-configuration' in Chapter 1. We wanted to find out what practitioners needed to know, what adjustments were made to their senses of who they were as professionals, and how the social practices of their workplaces interacted with their learning. We therefore saw professional learning as including both intellectual and emotional change and as intertwined with the histories, practices and intentions of practitioners' organisations.

CHAT gave us the lens we needed to look at this because, in line with a sociocultural account of learning, it does not separate what is learnt from how individuals act in and on their worlds. It then goes further to demand a focus on the activities in which people are participating and how they shape and are shaped by what participants think and do. It is worth going back briefly to the origins of CHAT. Vygotsky, the founding father of CHAT, writing in Moscow in the late 1920s and early 1930s, worked on a fresh understanding of human development that reflected the Marxism of that time and place. Central to this understanding was the idea that learning involves both internalisation and externalisation. By this he meant that we not only take in ideas that are important in our culture as we work with others, but these ideas are also part of how we act on our worlds and shape them and so change them. This dialectic, or ongoing interaction, can be summarised by the idea that we are both shaped by and shape the worlds we inhabit. We may enter worlds that have been shaped by those who went before us, but these worlds may also be changed by our actions in them.

This idea is particularly helpful when we are looking at the development of new practices because it recognises the dynamic nature of the relationships between knowledge, actions and social practices. It helps us to examine what happens when, for example, a new idea such as the prevention of social exclusion is introduced into professional activities. It does this by asking us to look simultaneously at change at the levels of individual actions and interactions, at the nature and purpose of the activity, and at the system or systems in which the activity is located.

Let's look in a little more depth at what we mean by activity, as it is the central idea in CHAT. For the purposes of this discussion we will take the prevention of social exclusion as the main activity of the professionals we worked with. The activity may differ from place to place, depending on local histories, practices and intentions. However, in the context of the risk and resilience framework that is underpinning policies for prevention (see Chapter 1) we would expect that activities would ultimately focus on children's trajectories of vulnerability, with the intention of working on them to disrupt and alter them. The focus of an activity tells you a great deal about the nature of an activity in different settings. We shall use CHAT terminology to explain.

Leont'ev, a close colleague of Vygotsky, shifted attention from Vygotsky's concern with how we use ideas or concepts in our actions on the world and instead looked at how we interpret the world as we act on it by engaging in activities. Leont'ev therefore developed the idea that how we act in the world needs to be understood by examining the activity as well the actions that contribute to it. The key to understanding the activity is to understand its focus from the perspective of those who are taking part in it. Leont'ev termed the focus of the activity the 'object' of activity and explained its importance as follows.

> The main thing which distinguishes one activity from another, however, is the difference in their objects. It is exactly the object of an activity that gives it its determined direction. According to the terminology I have proposed, the object of an activity is its true motive.
>
> (Leont'ev 1978: 62)

Box 2.4 Object motives in inter-professional work

In summary, our interpretations of tasks or problems are shaped by the activities in which they occur. In turn the interpreted tasks elicit our responses to them. These interactions present particular challenges for inter-professional work. If we think of a child's trajectory as the object of activity that is being worked on by perhaps a teacher, a housing charity worker and a children and families worker, we would expect that each practitioner would view the trajectory slightly differently, even though they were all ultimately concerned about the child's wellbeing. Their interpretation of the child's trajectory will elicit the actions they take to work on the trajectory. If we return to the idea of externalisation that Vygotsky emphasised, we can see that practitioners will first interpret and then act on the trajectory using the ideas and practices of their professions.

The challenge for inter-professional work is to co-ordinate interpretations and responses across professions so that practitioners work in timely and responsive ways with vulnerable children and with each other. The activity, prevention of social exclusion through interprofessional work, is particularly interesting, because the activity, as currently configured by the policies discussed in Chapter 1, is a relatively new one. We have been able to capture professional sensemaking and actions in an activity that is itself changing as practitioners increasingly recognise its complexity and the implications for themselves and their organisations.

We have so far been talking about activities rather than activity systems. This is in part because our case studies of professional learning were all engaged in a similar activity, the prevention of social exclusion, but the conditions for and approaches to that engagement, as we shall see in Chapter 3, varied across sites. An activity system is often an object-oriented work system with historically embedded rules or expectations with an evident division of labour in how people work on an object. An activity theory analysis therefore allows us to compare, for example, differences in how the work is shared out in different settings, or whether the rules in place are helping or hindering the work that people want to do (Engeström 1999a).

Engeström's development of activity theory with its emphasis on activity systems is outlined in Appendix A. His analyses of activity systems centre on systemic learning, that is, on how work systems change as a result of working on and transforming the object of activity (Engeström 1999a, 1999b). At this point we shall simply draw attention to the importance of contradictions to these changes. The different types of contradiction are discussed in Chapter 6. Contradictions to be met in inter-professional work may include several ways of interpreting the object of activity within one work group; sharing out the work in ways that makes responsive work on a child's trajectory difficult; or differences in the way that collaborating work systems are able to work together. These contradictions are seen as the drivers of change within work systems. For that reason they should be explored and worked on.

Although our primary focus in the LIW study was professional learning, we tried to capture both individual and collective learning, and to recognise that they are strongly intertwined. Individual professional learning cannot easily occur within systems that are themselves resistant to recognising contradictions and to learning from them.

Approaches to inter-professional work

Our discussion so far has centred on the development of professional knowledge, with the implicit assumption that professional learning involves the development of specialist expertise. We intend to continue this line of argument, as we are not suggesting that inter-professional work should lead to the development of multi-professional workers who operate only with sets of generic skills, which mean they try to be all things to all people. There are certainly some generic skills that enable people to collaborate across professional boundaries, and we shall discuss them in Chapter 4, but for us the specialist professional expertise that practitioners bring to complex problems is paramount.

There are currently three broad models for inter-professional work when working across professional boundaries and with children and families: multi-professional teams; the co-location of services; and local networks made up of practitioners with different kinds of expertise. We shall look briefly at each of them and explore the variations within them as we describe our study in later chapters.

Multi-professional teams

These emerged during the period of the study as one response to the policy agenda outlined in Chapter 1. They were the outcome of radical restructuring of service provision within local authorities and typically comprised: educational psychologists, children and families workers, education welfare officers and specialist teachers. The teams had responsibility for the delivery of services within localities and were often connected to specific schools. In some ways they resembled existing multi-professional teams such as Youth Offending Teams (YOT) but had a slightly more open brief. We observed that the time needed to enable these teams to learn to work as object-oriented work systems, with shared understandings of goals, should not be under-estimated.

In addition to these new teams, we also came across more loosely coupled work teams, exemplified by the Children in Public Care (CiPC) team described in Chapter 3. These might comprise educational psychologists, children and families workers, education welfare officers and also teachers. They met regularly as teams, but members also worked separately on other aspects of their workload. In the LIW case study example, when they met their focus was clearly defined, and they spent little time working on developing themselves as a team. The team was a resource that enabled them to work on supporting the developmental trajectories of specific children.

Co-location of services

This version of service organisation was much discussed by local authorities during the period of the study. However, although we visited new buildings where co-located teams for children of all ages were being established, co-location was limited mainly to early years provision in Sure Start programmes (Glass 1999; Melhuish *et al*. 2005) and early excellence centres (Pascal *et al*. 2001). The development of extended schools in England (Cummings *et al*. 2004; Dyson *et al*. 2002) may lead to an increased use of school sites as bases for other services, but we found very little evidence of that occurring during the period of the study.

Co-location of services within the same setting in a locality has the potential to encourage inter-professional collaboration and to enable more timely responsive work with children and families. However, it is unsafe to assume that co-location necessarily means collaboration. As Roaf (2002: 146) observes, joined up working of this kind at locality levels 'depends on effective co-ordination and network-brokering elsewhere in the system, particularly within agencies'.

Local networks

Informal local networks of inter-professional support for children and families are not new. They may be the result of previous collaborations in short-term funded initiatives, or they may have emerged over time as practitioners have learnt who to turn to when they need specific expertise to help with a client. Networks, however, can mean very different configurations, ranging from informal local links that can be called upon when a need for help arises to more formally configured linkages, where practitioners are expected to work together to help children and families. They can also be premised on quite different ideas about how to work together. These can range from sequential forms of collaboration, where a child is passed from one expert to another, to parallel collaborations where support is wrapped around a child or family with professionals timing their own interventions in relation to the needs of the client and the work of other professionals involved in the case. The latter form of collaboration, sometimes characterised by Engeström *et al.* (1999) as 'knotworking' or tying threads of support around a client, is difficult to achieve in current multi-professional networks, though the orchestration of these threads by keyworkers may help to promote this kind of timely and responsive work.

When we planned the project, we had expected to find more examples of local networks of inter-professional collaboration than we did. Those local authorities that were moving from mass-customisation to co-configuration of service provision (see Chapter 1) tended to opt for developing multi-professional teams. In Chapter 3 we discuss the development of a local network of services around an extended school and outline the challenges that it presented for practitioners in and out of the school. The difficulties that Roaf observed with co-located services would certainly suggest that local responsive networks are unlikely to emerge until employing agencies have made fluid and responsive collaborations a priority. Engeström (2005) has discussed the problem of organisational capacity for collaboration from a CHAT perspective, arguing that organisations where workers need to collaborate across institutional boundaries need to develop what he terms 'collaborative intentionality capital' or a developed propensity for collaboration as an organisational resource. Our work with both teams and networks would support this argument.

New kinds of work in different forms of collaboration

We have been using the term 'collaboration' without so far questioning its meaning and the demands it can make on professionals and organisations. The National Evaluation of the Children's Fund used the following definitions.

Box 2.5 NECF definitions of collaboration

- *Integrated services*   Services that have joined together as working teams to give support jointly to children, young people and their families. These may be evident at management level, for example, in children's trusts or in teams at the point of service delivery.

- *Collaboration*   Working together on joint projects, recognising a common aim and the different contributions that can be made towards achieving it.

- *Co-ordination*   Working together under the direction of a co-ordinator who orchestrates the contribution of each party to the child or young person's pathway.

- *Co-operation*   Working with others to achieve outcomes without noticeable changes in current practices.

(NECF 2004: 6)

The different approaches to inter-professional work that we outlined in the previous section each reflects one or more of these forms of interaction. Each type of interaction requires professionals to work with sensitivity to the purposes and practices of other practitioners, but they differ in the extent to which practitioners may be expected to develop new ways of interpreting, discussing and responding to cases with other practitioners.

One way of looking at the potential impact of inter-professional collaboration on practitioners has been outlined by Engeström *et al.* (1997) in their study of law courts. They use slightly different terminology from NECF to distinguish between what they call 'co-ordination, co-operation and communication' and use these terms to tease out different degrees of collaboration.

Co-ordination for Engeström *et al.* is the least demanding form of working together and is outlined in Figure 2.1. Here there is an agreed script or set of rules of working that co-ordinates the behaviour of each practitioner. Practitioners do not question or contribute to the script or develop new rules as a result of their work on their assigned tasks. This kind of work is akin to sequential referrals where a child is passed from service to service without the services needing to make adjustments to their own work to accommodate the interpretations and responses of other professionals and reflects what NECF termed 'co-operation'.

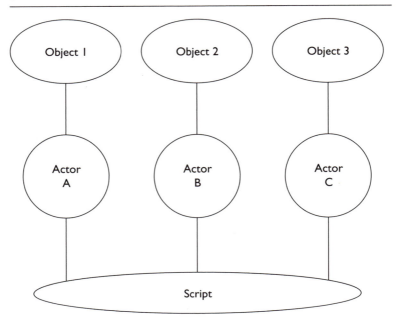

Figure 2.1 The general structure of co-ordination

In Engeström's typology, co-operation (Figure 2.2) resonates with both co-operation and co-ordination in the NECF framework. Engeström *et al.* explain:

> By *co-operation* we mean modes of interaction in which the actors, instead of each focusing on performing their assigned roles . . . focus on a shared problem, trying to find mutually acceptable ways to conceptualise and solve it. The participants go beyond the confines of the given script, yet do it without explicitly questioning or reconceptualising the script.
>
> (1997: 372)

In Figure 2.2, Engeström *et al.* have represented a form of inter-professional collaboration where individual expertise is kept intact, although understandings of the object of activity are enhanced through joint work. What distinguishes it from communication (Figure 2.3) is that participants represented in Figure 2.2 do not question the rules that govern their practices in order to erode differences between professionals and their practices.

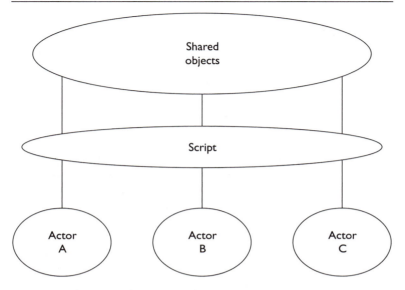

Figure 2.2 The general structure of co-operation

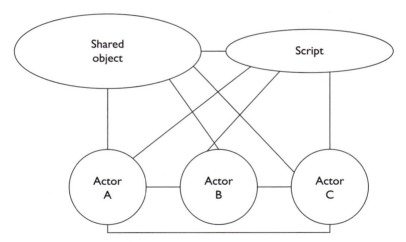

Figure 2.3 The general structure of communication

In Figure 2.3, practitioners work on their own organisations to question the rules that govern the ways they work together on shared objects. By describing this version of working together as communication, rather than collaboration, Engeström *et al.* are going further than the NECF description of collaboration to suggest (a) that collaboration involves disruptions to the rules, division of labour and social practices in an organisation and (b) that the new forms of collaboration that arise are accompanied by new linguistic and material tools to allow the new work to be done.

These are both very important points and will be developed in the chapters that follow. For example, we shall be arguing that new professional identities arise when the division of labour in an organisation is disrupted and people are repositioned within reconfigured practices, and that tools are developed and used in ways that reveal the repositioning and the learning that has taken place.

The models produced by Engeström *et al.* in the 1997 study also raise questions about hybridity, that is, the extent to which expertise remains discrete as a result of inter-professional collaborations. Our CHAT analyses suggest that much will depend on the histories of organisations and their wider social networks. In places where expertise is rarely made explicit, it may be expected that the idea of the hybrid generic multi-agency worker is seen as a solution to a problem posed by the policies we outlined in Chapter 1. We would suggest that this is not the best way forward. Instead, where expertise is not easily explained, work should be done to help practitioners identify and make explicit their particular contributions to the inter-professional endeavour.

The prevention of social exclusion is, as outlined in Chapter 1, a complex task calling for multiple forms of expertise. Consequently the changes in practice that need to occur include learning how to work with other professionals to expand understandings of the problems of practice, and learning to know how to work with them to respond to those expanded understandings. In the next section we shall outline the ideas that we have used and developed to get some purchase on the expansions of understandings and practice we observed over the four years of the study.

Key concepts for understanding professional learning in the LIW study

The big challenge for the professionals who were moving towards fluid forms of inter-professional work can be summarised as working outside what Sennett (1999: 21) has described as the safety of their 'institutional supports'. We suggest that this kind of work calls for an enhanced form of professional practice where professionals contribute to local systems of distributed expertise, whether they are members of teams, co-located services or co-ordinated networks.

Importantly, when existing organisations have been disrupted to form multi-professional teams, as we shall see in Chapter 3, energy goes into making the team work well. However, when there has been less disruption and people retain their affiliation to their home organisations while working with other practitioners, they may find themselves either placed at the boundaries of their organisations and their practices, or positioned as boundary crossers who work both inside and outside their institutional shelters. As we explored these phenomena, we developed concepts that helped us to explain what was occurring and to examine the implications for practice. The concepts fall under the following headings: boundary work, distributed expertise, and agency and responsibility. We shall now look at each in turn.

Boundary work

As we undertook our analysis, the importance of the boundaries between different work systems became increasingly clear. The actual boundaries are outlined in Chapter 3 and how they operated as sites for learning is discussed in Chapter 5. Here our focus is on why boundaries were so important. Above all, they were places where professional identities were called into question. For example, practitioners who were not members of discrete teams, yet were collaborating with other professionals, found themselves positioned as boundary workers looking out from their home organisations towards the other professionals and looking inward to the expectations of their primary workplaces.

The wealth of work on boundaries (e.g., Churchman 1979; Midgley *et al*. 1998) reminds us that boundaries are socially constructed to define what and who is included within systems. They are therefore inextricably linked to professional identity. We know from Kerosuo's work on boundaries between health professionals (Kerosuo 2003) that organisational boundaries are likely to be complex, unstable and negotiable, and are often sites of struggle and of adjustments in identity. Holland and Lave's studies of identity shifts as people move across settings or when settings change, similarly suggest that new identities are formed in the practices that arise at boundaries between sets of social practices (Holland and Lave 2001).

In our study we observed the tensions that professionals experienced while working at the boundaries of familiar practices. We termed their predicament 'balancing on the boundaries' to capture how they were holding on to the security of established patterns of workplace practices while being pulled forward to new forms of collaboration by their beliefs that these would benefit children. Their identity struggles were clear and often painful.

As we thought about the importance of boundary work, and particularly the impact of the Developmental Work Research (DWR) sessions we ran with mixed groups of professionals (see Chapter 1 and Appendix A), the idea of a 'boundary zone' (Konkola 2001) became increasingly useful. Boundary zones as described, perhaps somewhat idealistically, by Konkola are neutral spaces on the boundaries of more than one organisation where the values and professional priorities of each practitioner are respected, where information can be shared, and where trust can be built. They are not activity systems working on a common and contested object; rather they are places where local expertise can be made explicit so that it might be drawn on later.

We first became aware of their importance for professional learning in the National Evaluation of the Children's Fund (NECF) (Edwards in press a). We saw there that long-term sustained and supported meetings of practitioners from different professions, set up to build trust and to talk about cases in relatively informal ways, helped to build local networks of responsive support for vulnerable children. As one practitioner in that study explained:

> it's about understanding at a deeper level. It's about connections. Maybe you are not sure about the child we are thinking about; but as we talk it through there may be a connection and if not for that child, maybe for another.

These spaces operated as springboards for new linkages between practitioners. We described the linking as etching new trails across local landscapes to work together to reconfigure the trajectories of children (Edwards et al. 2006). The links that arose from these boundary spaces increased practitioners' access to both human and material resources.

Our DWR sessions with case study participants also operated as boundary zones. However, these sessions achieved more than the less structured Children's Fund practitioner meetings managed to do. Because the DWR sessions were structured to elicit how people were making sense of new practices, they helped to build understandings of practices and their purposes, which could be shared quite explicitly across professional boundaries. For example, it became clear to all participants in the sessions that inter-professional work required that they reflected quite profoundly on their own personal and professional values.

It seems that spaces where practitioners could share meanings, begin to understand the specialist strengths of others, and explore new identity positions alongside other professionals were useful. Sometimes these spaces were used quite overtly by participants to bring other professionals onside while relationships between services were being reconfigured. In Chapter 5 we shall examine how they were used as pedagogic spaces by some participants in order to take forward the thinking of other practitioners.

Distributed expertise

Another key concept used in the study was expertise, or more specifically as we indicated in Chapter 1, distributed expertise. CHAT analysts, looking at expertise in the workplace present it as a collective attribute spread across systems that is drawn upon to accomplish tasks; expertise therefore lies in both the system and the individuals' ability to recognise and negotiate its use. Expertise, from a CHAT perspective, has been described as the 'collaborative and discursive construction of tasks, solutions, visions, breakdowns and innovations' within and across systems rather than individual mastery of specific areas of relatively stable activity (Engeström and Middleton 1996: 4).

For example, in NECF, we observed emergent awareness of the expertise distributed across a local system when a teacher was faced with the distress of a newly arrived Angolan child from an asylum-seeking family. Through the meetings we just outlined the teacher became aware of an art therapy group the child could join, and was able to take the child's mother to an agency who could give her the specialist trauma counselling she needed. These links were examples of the trails that were being etched across localities that could be followed later by other practitioners (Edwards *et al.* 2006).

Viewing expertise as the negotiated accomplishment of tasks, and viewing expert preventative practices as the negotiated accomplishment of preventing social exclusion, requires us to see expert inter-professional work as resourceful practice that operates across systems. Professionals need to become adept at recognising and working with (i) the professional resources that other practitioners bring to bear on interpreting a problem of practice, and (ii) the resources that these practitioners use when responding to those interpretations. These resources can, of course, be material artefacts, but they are also likely to be the specialist concepts and insights that are specific to different professional cultures.

Agency and responsibility

Working flexibly and responsively with expertise that is distributed across a system in order to improve the life chances of children calls for a high degree of professional responsibility. However, most of the professions that we were working with in the LIW study are characterised by strong external accountability and very little room for manoeuvre in professional decision-making. Indeed, social workers and teachers can sometimes be seen as vulnerable professionals, safeguarded primarily by the processes and procedures that shape their professional actions.

With this in mind, one of us has developed the idea of 'relational agency' to capture the agentic aspects of interpretation and response in collaboration with other professionals that is demanded by inter-professional work (Edwards 2005; Edwards and Mackenzie 2005). In CHAT terms, relational agency is evident in the ability to work with others to expand the 'object of activity' or task that one is working on by recognising and working with the resources that others bring to bear as they also interpret it. Relational agency also involves aligning one's own responses to that enhanced interpretation with the responses being made by other professionals.

Relational agency is a capacity that involves recognising that another person may be a resource and that work needs to be done to elicit, recognise and negotiate the use of that resource in order to align oneself in joint action on, for example, a child's developmental trajectory. It offers an enhanced version of personal agency and as a capacity it can be learnt. At the same time it can only arise in organisations that permit such expansive forms of practice.

Relational agency helps us to understand the negotiations and reconfiguring of tasks indicated by Engeström and Middleton (1996) by focusing on the capacity for undertaking these negotiations. It occupies a conceptual space between a focus on learning as enhancing individual understanding and the Engeströmian focus on learning as systemic change, and includes both. It fits squarely within CHAT readings of mind and world, by seeing mind as outward looking, pattern-seeking and engaged with the world in a process of internalisation and externalisation. Above all it can underpin an enhanced form of responsive professional practice for potentially vulnerable practitioners who find themselves working outside the safety of Sennett's bureaucratic shelters.

Organisational conditions for professional learning

Box 2.6 Expertise and responsible professional practice

Seeing expertise as negotiated task accomplishment is very much in line with those approaches to organisational development that emphasise outputs rather than clearly defined procedures. At the same time it implies an enhanced form of responsible professionalism, as practitioners negotiate their own ways towards desired outputs. Glisson and Hemmelgarn, writing about organisational climate and outcomes of US children's services in 1998, explain:

> process-oriented approaches emphasise pre-programmed activities which limit employee discretion and responsiveness to unexpected problems and opportunities. In comparison results-oriented approaches focus employee attention on the desired outcomes and require employee flexibility and discretion in the development of individualised approaches to reaching those outcomes.
>
> (1998: 416)

Their attention to individualising approaches reflects their concern that services should be tailored to each child. They argue

continued

vehemently from a strong evidence-base that front-line staff should be given the responsibility necessary to enable them to work responsively with children and each other.

There is a growing body of work on organisations that reflects the CHAT emphasis on the distribution of expertise across a system and our concern with how it is negotiated to offer tailored responses to the needs of vulnerable children. Boreham, for example, suggests that we should attend to the 'collective competence' of workplaces (Boreham 2004) and expand our definitions of competence to include both individual and collective competence. The intertwining of an individual capacity to negotiate task accomplishment and an organisational capacity to enable that to occur is also a major theme in Blackler's extensive CHAT-based analyses of organisational learning in, for example, information technology companies. He usefully argues (Blackler *et al.* 2000) that learning organisations should provide infrastructures for learning that acknowledge that collective learning involves tensions and unease and indeed these tensions drive forward change. Just as individuals need to be able to negotiate task accomplishment, so too do organisations and, as Baldwin has pointed out in his overview of social work systems as learning organisations, these negotiations should also include service users (Baldwin 2004).

Conclusion

The intertwining of learners, learning and the historically constructed social situation of that learning is central to the CHAT analyses we pursued. Inter-professional work involves working across systems to develop new practices outside the historically established practices of, for example, schools and children's services. Therefore, as well as learning how to work in new ways, practitioners can find themselves meeting frustrations in their home organisation as they try to work fluidly and responsively with children and young people and other practitioners. The tensions between individual professional action in new networks and the established practices of welfare bureaucracies are returned to throughout the chapters that follow.

Part II

What does the research tell us?

Chapter 3

The case studies

Introduction

In this chapter we describe the sites that were our longitudinal case studies. They are all quite different; for example, tightly bounded teams, a loosely coupled team with a specific task, and an emergent network. This chapter, as well as setting the scene for the chapters that follow, make it clear that policies for implementing inter-agency collaboration cannot be simply rolled out. The historical conditions and local aspirations of services and practitioners are central to shaping the development of new practices.

Selecting the sites

We explained in Chapter 1 that we selected case study sites that were moving from mass-customisation, that is, careful targeting of specialist provision, to co-configuration, that is, responsive interactions in the ways that professionals worked together to prevent the social exclusion of children and young people. To identify the English sites, a long list of local authorities was assembled on the basis of analyses of local authority approaches to prevention undertaken by the National Evaluation of the Children's Fund (NECF) (www.ne-cf.org).

Representatives of the authorities attended one of four regional workshops where we introduced the project and asked for expressions of interest in suggesting a case study site. These expressions were followed up by meetings with senior staff in the local authorities that responded, in order to ensure that the case studies being offered by the authorities were moving towards more co-configured ways of working. We selected expressions of interest in order to produce a range of types of local authorities, in both the north and the south of the country and with local services that were focusing on school-age children.

The final selection in England consisted of the following sites: two authorities in the North West, a unitary authority (Newhill) and a metropolitan borough (Wildside); a city in the Midlands (Castletown); a county in the South East (Seaside); and a unitary authority on the South Coast (Brookside). In Northern Ireland the sample was selected to provide examples of specific changes underway. There we focused on two multi-agency contexts: one involving two sites in a network of collaborating post-primary schools and one involving a joint project between a voluntary agency and a number of statutory agencies. Each of the seven case studies presented a very different context for the development of inter-professional working.

The findings presented in Chapters 4 to 6 are based on detailed work on data from the three English sites (Castletown, Seaside and Wildside) where we worked for eighteen months and that formed the main part of the study. However, the ideas presented in these chapters are also based on analyses of Brookside and Newhill, which had been pilot sites for the main study developments. The Northern Irish study was seen as an 'extension project' where we could explore ideas emerging in the English study in a different, and in this case highly complex, environment, it was therefore an important test bed for the ideas being developed in the English sites. In this chapter we provide short descriptions of each of the English sites. There is a slightly longer outline of the Northern Irish sites, as we do not discuss this project in detail during subsequent chapters. We then follow these outlines with an introduction to how we looked at sites as developing systems.

The description of the case study sites

Castletown

The local authority is a racially mixed city that has lost much of its manufacturing base. During the time of the case study there was a high degree of turbulence within the local authority as committees were reorganised and senior staff in the authority left and were replaced. The city was re-organising its schools into locality-based collaborating groups that would share access to local services. Because of the unanticipated turbulence, it regarded itself in danger of falling behind government expectations that they should move towards establishing local networks of services around schools.

The school that was selected by city officials for the Learning in and for Interagency Working (LIW) study was an established community school where it was expected that links with local welfare services would be strong. It was frequently referred to by local authority strategists as a school that represented the city's commitment to strong links between education services and other service providers. As a result, it had not been a focus for the local authority development activities aimed at setting up local collaborations, but it was expected that the school would be developing increasingly fluid ways of working. We found, however, that the school was evolving its own inter-professional practices in relative isolation from the local authority, and that the LIW project eventually provided senior staff in related local authority services with an important opportunity to engage with school staff to discuss future developments.

Importantly for the LIW study, the independence of the school from the local authority, its confidence in its practices and its position as the best example of working with other services among schools in the city, meant that the boundary around the school was constructed and controlled by the school. The study focused on the boundary and the work that occurred there. We were therefore not looking at the school, or the school's pastoral work, as activity systems. Instead, the negotiations of meanings and identities that occurred at the boundary between the school and local authority or voluntary sector services were our focus.

Participants in the six two-hour Developmental Work Research (DWR) sessions (see Chapter 1 and Appendix A) included the deputy headteacher with responsibility for work with other agencies, several teachers, the school counsellor, two education welfare officers, two educational psychologists, a senior social worker, an assistant social worker, representatives of local voluntary and community sector organisations, and a behaviour improvement project worker. In addition, the community police officer, the local school nurse manager and two local authority leads on school-community reorganisation each attended one session.

The first three DWR sessions were quite different from the last three. The first two sessions were not attended by the educational psychologists or the social workers, and during the two-hour meetings the boundary of the school was strongly defended by school staff. A psychologist joined the third session and consistently questioned the boundary and the impact that it was having on school staff. Interestingly, several teachers and the counsellor told the researchers, as they left that session, that they would be unable to attend future meetings. The final three meetings included the social workers and educational psychologists along with the deputy head, one and sometimes two teachers, an education welfare officer and representatives of voluntary and community services.

The reactions of some of the participants in Castletown demonstrate that DWR can be a personally challenging methodology as it questions assumptions about purposes and practices. In this case, although the teachers and counsellor had been introduced to the study by the team prior to the sessions, they had not anticipated its focus on questioning accepted ways of working. On the other hand, for the educational psychologists and social workers, the DWR sessions provided a space in which they could work on the boundary that was inhibiting the kind of fluid interactions they were hoping to develop with school staff, to mirror developments elsewhere in the city.

Seaside

Seaside is a large county in the South of England that has traditionally organised its services into a small number of distinct areas that, to a certain extent, remained independent of each other. Previous studies had established that this was a local authority with a high level of commitment to improving dialogues between service providers and users over the identification of need and formulation of provision, that is, it was clearly moving towards co-configuration. Initial contact was made with a senior officer who outlined the emergent strategy for meeting the demands of the *Every Child Matters* agenda, which confirmed this assumption.

In order to encourage practitioners from different professional areas to work together, a major transformation in the organisation of the workforce was initiated by the local authority. Sixteen Multi-Professional Teams (MPT) were created, each consisting of education-based professionals (MPT1) (educational psychologists, education welfare officers, behaviour support teachers, language and learning support teachers, ethnic language and minority achievement teachers), who each worked in collaboration with schools in particular geographical areas.

As a result, individuals who had formerly been located within their own professional groupings were now required to become members of inter-professional teams. Familiar patterns of line management were transformed and professionals became responsible to a manager who was not necessarily a member of their own professional culture. The former single professional groupings were disbanded and contacts, across MPT, between members of the same profession were signifi-cantly reduced or ceased completely. Halfway through the case study, these teams were expanded to include professionals from the Seaside Social Care service (MPT2). The teams were renamed as 'locality teams', and the number of teams was reduced to eleven. Senior officers of the local authority provided a briefing on changes that were taking place at the local level and suggested that we work with an MPT that was seen to be in an advanced state of development. Access to the MPT was facilitated by these senior officers who ensured that engagement in the project was seen as an important part of the work of the MPT.

The MPT1 that we worked with involved nine people, whereas MPT2 involved between fifteen and seventeen people, including a representative from the Children and Adult Mental Health Service (CAMHS) and a member from the school nursing team. We engaged with MPT1 when it had been working for eighteen months. They had made good progress in establishing understandings of the nature of each professional groups work in terms of both what they did and how they did it. Some practitioners felt empowered by working within the MPT whereas others felt isolated from their own teams.

In this established team it was possible to identify tensions. First, there was an emergent tension between being expected to be a generalist practitioner as a member of the MPT and sustaining and developing core expertise. Second, MPT1 felt it was not in a good position to engage with the complex systemic problems that they felt often underlay referrals of individual cases by schools and at the same time they were concerned that schools wanted the team to provide short-term input at the individual level. Third, both MPT1 and MPT2 in the study experienced difficulty in negotiating with services that were not represented in the team.

However, the most pressing and enduring concern expressed at the beginning of our work with MPT1 was to be found in the relationship between the operational and strategic levels within the local authority. MPT1 considered that their operational experience had helped them to make significant advances in the development of inter-professional working. However, the rules in their work systems that governed how they were able to collaborate were often seen to be obstructive. They felt that their strategic managers were responsible for these rules that, for example, established the lines of accountability for operational work. Thus a major tension emerged between the strategic and opera-tional levels. Strategy was seen to be making demands of practice but not listening to the operational level and learning from its experiences.

The boundary between operational staff and local strategists seemed to be very strong in Seaside, and this phenomenon was echoed, as we shall see, in the Brookside MPT.

Wildside

Wildside is a small metropolitan borough where, according to accounts in LIW interviews, employees enjoy harmonious working relationships. It has scored well in recent national inspections procedures and has a stable workforce with a high proportion of staff having worked there for many years. It was chosen as a case study site because senior local authority officers had expressed interest in developing the multi-agency working that existed, in line with the *Every Child Matters* agenda. There was therefore a willingness to engage in reflection and development, but a lack of clarity about how the necessary changes could be achieved.

This case study centred upon a group of professionals who were concerned with the wellbeing of children and young people who were looked after by the local authority. These are sometimes referred to 'Looked After Children', or 'LAC'; a more recent term used to define the same group of children is 'Children in Public Care' or 'CiPC'. The children concerned all have some type of court order to protect them and to ensure that their safety and wellbeing is paramount. In some cases they are entirely the responsibility of the local authority as they are adopted or fostered, while other CiPC may have the responsibility for their care shared between their parents and the local authority. These children are amongst the most vulnerable in the United Kingdom and their outcomes and prospects are the lowest on most available measures (Audit Commission 2004; Gilligan 2000; Mills 2004).

The grouping of practitioners working with CiPC were chosen as a case study as it comprised a mixed group of professionals, who all had slightly different roles in their work with CiPC. Importantly, they knew that they needed to improve how they collaborated as they did not meet and work together on a regular or sustained basis. These participants came from a variety of professional backgrounds and worked for a range of agencies as, although the core responsibility for CiPC lies with the local authority, other agencies, such as health, and other settings, such as schools, also have responsibilities; some of which have recently increased significantly.

The newly formed Children's Services in Wildside did not distribute staff into local multi-agency teams; instead, each agency remained autonomous. Two senior staff, one employed by the previous Education Authority, and one employed by the previous children's section of Social Care and Health, were tasked with developing a more integrated approach to service provision. However, the size of the authority and its long-term stability meant that work within the CiPC team was often facilitated by personal contacts and tacit understandings of the local system. Staff had recently become aware that by drawing so much on these resources it was possible that service provision may not be as strong as it could be. This topic became a major focus for the group's work in DWR sessions.

The participants in the six DWR sessions included three educational psychologists, an inclusions manager, two social workers, two teachers, an education officer with responsibility for CiPC, a nurse specialising in child protection in the authority and a quality assurance officer. Among the many issues addressed by practitioners in the sessions, a major discussion point was how to ensure that actions were taken quickly and fairly on behalf of the children and young people. A second recurring issue was the problem that some staff, and particularly social workers, had other statutory duties that meant they often could not attend critical meetings where decisions were made about plans for children. A third issue, tackled over time, was the apparently different priorities of the workers and agencies involved.

These three issues gave rise to the some contradictions in service provision that the strongly child-focused grouping wanted to tackle. The first was the difference in quality of service, which was often dependent on how well a practitioner knew the local system. The second, the difficulty that social workers had in attending the review meetings that were required by statutory regulations, meant that they could not easily contribute to these child-centred sessions. The third issue, which was common across all the case study sites, was the difference in professional priorities. For example, teachers focused on attainment and social workers on safety and wellbeing. These three contradictions, which were all centred on doing the best for a child, suggested that systemic boundary problems were less of a concern for practitioners in Wildside than they were for colleagues in Castletown and Seaside.

Brookside and Newhill

These two sites were the focus of pilot work in the six months prior to our work on the three main sites just described. We ran three DWR sessions in both of these sites with groups at different levels of organisational hierarchy. We therefore did not undertake the detailed analysis of learning over time that we carried out with Castletown, Seaside and Wildside. Nonetheless, there were some striking parallels across the two phases of the study.

Brookside, like Seaside, had created multi-agency groupings. In Brookside we worked with a newly created 'virtual' team comprising professionals from a range of services and agencies, which included social work, health, educational psychology, CAMHS and family support. Team members retained strong links with their home organisations, were not co-located and remained line managed within their own professional groupings. Practitioners, like those in Seaside, reported frustrations with inappropriate rules, which inhibited the development of inter-professional practices. In one example, a medical officer wished to take part in training provided for social care workers as part of the development of her understanding of the work that they undertook. However, the rules governing her continuing professional development meant she could only undertake training that was provided by health services.

In Newhill we worked with an established Youth Offending Team (YOT). The local authority was small with stable practices of the kind outlined in the description of Wildside, and with a similar propensity to work within established networks of inter-professional collaboration. The YOT was being charged with the need to work more flexibly with other services to support children. This involved them in seeing the young people they worked with as vulnerable rather than criminal. While this was not a new shift in focus, it was an additional challenge for those who had so far resisted this reinterpretation. Boundaries were therefore important in Newhill. In this case, there were boundaries within the Team, with newer appointments and the most senior staff in the YOT developing new inter-professional collaborations and middle-managers safeguarding the procedures that inhibited this more fluid way of working. In summary, the boundaries between the YOT and other agencies were maintained by the middle managers, while their colleagues struggled to open them up.

The Northern Irish sites

As we have already indicated, the two-year Northern Irish study was an extension to the English LIW project and started at the same time as the work in the three English main case studies. In order to reflect the particular situation of Northern Ireland we focused on two multi-agency contexts: one involving a network of collaborating post-primary schools that provided two sites for research; and one involving a joint project between a voluntary agency and a number of statutory agencies.

The schools' partnership included two Controlled (local authority) and two Catholic Maintained schools, a special school, the local Further Education college, alternative education provision, a behavioural support unit, professionals from the Education and Library Board (the local authority) and professionals from community and voluntary groups. One of the Controlled schools was an academically selective grammar school. Within the schools' partnership we focused on two research sites: one comprised the leaders of the partnership and examined their strategic role. For the second research site we concentrated on school-based Multi-agency Support Teams, which identified strategies for 'at risk' young people and engaged with agencies external to the schools, including social and welfare services and the Police Service of Northern Ireland (PSNI).

This schools' partnership is interesting for two reasons. First, in a divided society that has undergone a quarter century of political violence, the fault-lines provided by sectarian divisions run deep and are often reflected in institutional boundaries. Perhaps this is nowhere more evident than in schools where de facto parallel school systems exist for Protestant and Catholic young people. There is a small and growing integrated sector, but at the time of the study it comprised about 6 per cent of the pupil population. A variety of measures have been tried through education to promote better community relations. In the period of the peace process from 1998 onwards, the framework was provided by the Shared Future policy which encouraged attempts to build links across sectarian divisions. One potentially important example of this could be provided by collaborative links between schools seeking to make this particular institutional boundary more porous. However, concrete examples of this type of collaborative link were rare and, indeed, evidence on the impact of previous contact programmes between schools is decidedly mixed (O'Connor *et al.* 2002).

The second reason why the school partnership is of particular interest lies in a very different policy area. After the Second World War, Northern Ireland adopted a selective system of secondary education but, unlike the rest of the UK, retained these arrangements. After 1997 a series of research studies on the effects of academic selection (Alexander *et al.* 1998; Gallagher and Smith 2000), followed by a number of review group reports (Burns Report 2001; Costello Report

2004) led to recommendations that selection at age 11 years should be removed. This opened up an ongoing debate on the future of post-primary education that is as yet unresolved. The Revised Northern Ireland Curriculum offers the basis of one solution since it provides for a largely prescriptive curriculum up to age 14, but then requires all schools to offer a wide range of choice to all pupils. In practice schools will only be able to offer this choice if they work collaboratively with other schools. This possibility could allow for a diversity of school types, working collaboratively to provide wide choice to pupils.

It is obvious how the experience of a schools' partnership in Northern Ireland, involving a mix of local authority and Catholic schools, and a mix of secondary and grammar schools, has clear relevance for both policy debates. In fact the partnership we focused on for this study had evolved for more prosaic, if equally important, reasons, that is, a shared interest in establishing an improved educational environment for pupils across all the schools and in identifying a wider range of strategies for dealing with young people at risk of dropping out of school. Not surprisingly, the novel character of the partnership, in a Northern Ireland context, generated a lot of interest in their experience, but while the fact of their engagement was quite well known, relatively little was known about the manner and extent of their engagement.

The leaders of the Learning Partnership met regularly to review their collaborative programmes and establish processes to take the partnership forward, with the shared aim of creating an environment in which fewer young people would drop out of school prematurely. Our interest in engaging with this group was to examine the way they learned to work across traditional divisions and develop collaborative practice within their institutions, with these divisions effectively going three ways: across the religious divide, across the grammar/secondary divide and across the school/further education divide. All this was on top of the practical issues in finding ways to develop effective models of collaboration in a context where schools had traditionally valued their autonomy. In this site the research team worked with the principals of each of the schools or college and the advisory officer of the Education and Library Board.

The second research site within the schools' partnership focused on Multi Agency Support Teams (MAST) within the secondary schools. The role of the MAST was to identify pupils at risk of dropping out of school and identify specific measures to address their needs. Each MAST involved teachers, representatives of the Education and Library Board particularly those providing alternative education, and representatives of social service and welfare agencies. In addition, some of the schools had a representative of the PSNI in attendance. Over time the membership of the MAST extended to include a representative of a local community organisation. In this site the research team worked with a principal, two vice-principals, four school-based special needs coordinators, two education welfare officers, a year tutor, an education guidance specialist, local community development body representatives and a PSNI inspector.

We were aware of a number of issues facing the MAST groups as the fieldwork began. First, while the idea of MAST was common across the local authority area, there was a perception that the way they worked varied widely, as did their effectiveness. Second, a concern had been expressed about how to involve relevant agencies in the process, with the biggest problems appearing to arise for organisations that were not directly connected to education services. Finally, it was considered important to ensure that an appropriate repertoire of options was available to each MAST to meet the needs of specific pupils.

The third site and second Northern Irish case study was a collaborative project aimed at the needs of Looked After Children (LACE). The lead organisation in this project was a voluntary agency, but most of the other partners were drawn from statutory agencies, including the Department of Education, the Northern Ireland Office and the Department of Health Social Services and Public Safety (DHSSPS). Professionals from three major charities were also involved in the collaboration. The LACE project had been established in 2001 as a participative research project on the educational experiences of children and young people in care in Northern Ireland. Up to 2005, LACE had run a number of regional seminars, carried out an audit of services and initiatives addressing the needs of looked after children and developed training resources for work with young people and professionals. In addition, LACE had informed practice and policy development through the Children's Services Planning groups in three of the four Health Boards (McLaughlin 2002).

Following this work, LACE identified a number of areas that required development, including the roles and responsibilities of key agencies, inter-agency communication and the Looked After Children review meeting. In addition, it was felt that there was a need to establish baseline data and address the needs of young people with care experience who enter the youth justice system. In order to address these issues, the LACE Steering Group recommended that a strategic pilot project is conducted with at least two Health and Social Services

Trusts and with the education agencies in each of those Trusts, in order to advocate and to implement those systems and processes that would improve the educational outcomes for Looked After Children. The research site focused on the period when the Steering Group was overseeing these activities.

Multi-agency work involving voluntary and statutory organisations may be problematic for a number of reasons. One factor that we assumed would be important lay in the asymmetrical structure of the organisations, where the flatter, more 'democratic' structure of voluntary organisations often contrasts with the hierarchical and more rule-bound structure of statutory agencies. Prior to their involvement in this project the participants in LACE had found some difficulty arising from the different languages of their organisations and had even established a reference group to develop a common language for engagement.

Participants in DWR sessions were three representatives of voluntary sector organisations, one person from the Department of Education, one from the DHSSPS, one from the Northern Irish Office and two people from Health Trusts. The issues that the participants brought to the DWR sessions reflected a number of quite different concerns. On the one hand they were concerned at the flow of information from their meetings back into their host organisations and their ability more generally to lever policy or practice change in the host organisations. Related to this they were also concerned with the flow of information between the participating organisations. Given that the over-arching priority was to support professionals working with children in care, they were concerned also about maintaining stability of support for the children, while at the same time ensuring that an appropriately wide range of placement options were available. An issue that emerged as important related to succession problems when representatives of the participating agencies changed.

The Northern Irish work operated as a sounding board for the ongoing analyses from the smaller scale but more in-depth English studies, and continuously alerted the team to the shaping forces of history in the implementation of policy and the development of practices. Cultural Historical Activity Theory (CHAT) frameworks have the potential to direct researchers to placing their systemic and inter-personal analyses within broader socio-political changes, but perhaps this does not occur as frequently as it might.

All five English and two Northern Irish case studies were quite different, requiring the research team to follow the preoccupations of the participants while working within the CHAT frameworks that shaped the case studies. In particular we needed to identify where participants were placing their energies, either to defend or open up practices, this necessarily took us to analyses of power and control in settings. In the next section we introduce some of the ideas we used to understand these processes. We also return to these ideas in more detail later in the book: in Chapter 8 where we look at the implications of the study for organisations and in Chapter 9 where we discuss the theoretical contributions of the study.

Institutional analyses: the interplay of power and control

Box 3.1 The importance of beliefs about being a professional

As we indicated in Chapter 2, one of the defining features of the settings in which we have worked is distributed expertise. Joined up service provision means that the case of an 'at risk' child will rarely be the province of one profession but may entail professionals from education, social care, health and other agencies coalescing, negotiating and forming and reforming subgroups around the child's case. Therefore, issues of how expertise and specialist knowledge are claimed, owned and shared are extremely important and can be problematic. Alongside understanding how expertise is distributed between professionals, multi-agency functioning also requires an examination of beliefs about being a professional and about working with other professionals whose values, priorities, targets and systems may be different (Engeström 1992).

A model of description of the sites was developed with this understanding of the intertwining of these cognitive and affective factors in mind. We drew on both Bernstein and Engeström in this endeavour, but here focus primarily on analyses based on Bernstein's work.

The main starting points were as follows.

- We found that there was a need to refine a language of description that allowed us to 'see' institutions as they do their tacit psychological work through their discursive practices, that is, how they talk, interact and use resources. We needed a way of describing what were, drawing on Bernstein (Bernstein 2000), the 'pedagogic modalities' of the settings in which we were intervening. That is, we wanted to identify the institutional practices that would be sustained in those settings.

- One assumption of CHAT, which we discuss in more detail in Chapter 6, is that the development of systems occurs through their engagement with contradictions. We were therefore keen to try to identify points at which the communicative action of participants engaged with the transformation of the institution.

- Because we recognised that different social structures give rise to different ways of using language, which in turn mediate organisational priorities in different ways, we were aware of the importance of developing an approach to the analysis and description of our research sites that could be used to monitor changes that took place during our time with them.

From these starting points we developed an account of institutional structures as cultural historical products or 'artefacts', which play a part in implicit (Wertsch 2007) or invisible (Bernstein 2000) mediation shaping the practices that occur in them. In summary, our argument is that in order to understand how ways of thinking and acting are mediated in interactions it is necessary to take into account how the practices of a community, such as school and the family, are themselves structured by their institutional context (Abreu and Elbers 2005). This structuring is a process of continuous iteration. These practices are shaped by the social, cultural and historical circumstances in which interpersonal exchanges arise and they in turn shape the thoughts and feelings, the identities and aspirations for action of those engaged in interpersonal exchanges in those contexts.

From that standpoint, the relations of power and control within institutions, which regulate social interchange, give rise to different principles of communication. These principles mediate social relations and shape both thinking and feeling. They therefore shape the 'what' and 'how' of practice as well the 'why' and 'where to' concerns of professional learning. Understanding these processes seems, to us, to be an important part of understanding how professional learning occurs in different settings.

Bernstein's (2000) framework was designed to relate macro-institutional forms to micro-interactional levels and the underlying rules of communicative competence. He focused upon two levels: a structural level and an interactional level.

- The structural level is analysed in terms of the social division of labour it creates (e.g., the degree of specialisation, and thus strength of boundary between professional groupings).
- The interactional level is concerned with the form of social relation it creates (e.g., the degree of control that a manager may exert over a team member's work plan).

The key concept at the structural level is the concept of boundary, and structures are distinguished in terms of their relations between categories. The social division is analysed in terms of strength of the boundary of its divisions, that is, the degree of specialisation (e.g., how strong is the boundary between professions such as teaching and social work). The interactional level emerges as the regulation of the transmission/acquisition relation between teacher and taught, or the manager and the managed. The interactional level therefore refers to the pedagogic or learning context and the social relations of, for example, the workplace.

In Bernstein's framework, power is spoken of in terms of classification manifested in category relations that themselves generate recognition rules that allows the acquirer to recognise a difference marked by a category. This can be illustrated by rules that allow a professional to be recognised as belonging to particular professional group such as an Educational Psychology Service. Recognition is not simply a matter of finding out which service someone belongs to, but also refers to how forms of talk and other actions may be seen to be belonging to a particular professional category or grouping. When there is strong insulation between categories, that is, when each category is sharply distinguished, explicitly bounded and has its own distinctive specialisation, then classification is said to be strong. When there is weak insulation, the categories are less specialised and their distinctiveness is reduced, at that point classification is said to be weak. Professional groups, for example, may be more or less specialised and therefore differ in whether classification is strong or weak.

Bernstein writes of control in terms of framing, which is manifested in pedagogic communication governed by realisation rules that allow people to perform, in this case talk, in a way that is seen as competent. In doing so they realise difference that is marked by a category. Framing is relevant to studies of inter-professional work because it refers to the regulation of communication in the social relations through which the social division of labour is enacted. The principal features of these relations are distinguished by Bernstein (1981) when he refers to the selection, organisation (sequencing), pacing and criteria of communication – oral/written/visual – together with the position, posture and dress of communicants.

Bernstein's later work on discourse takes us further towards understanding the mediational power of institutions. Bernstein (2000) provides an outline of a key feature of the structure of pedagogic discourse with the distinction between instructional and regulative discourse. The former refers to the transmission of skills and their relation to each other, and the latter refers to the principles of social order, relation and identity. Regulative discourse is of particular relevance to the development of inter-professional practices as it communicates an institution's public moral practice, values beliefs and attitudes, principles of conduct, character and manner. It also transmits features of its local history, local tradition and community relations.

The language that Bernstein developed allows us to describe and position the discursive, organisational and interactional practice of the institution. Through the concepts of classification and framing, Bernstein provides the language of description for moving from those issues that CHAT handles as rules, community and division of labour to the discursive tools or artefacts that are produced and deployed within an activity (Appendix A). It, for example, allows us to investigate the connections between the rules the individuals use to make sense of their pedagogic world and how that world is structured and organised.

We used these principles to model each of the three main English case study sites in order to examine the development of inter-professional work. The models therefore needed to include the group of professionals who were involved in the DWR sessions, members of the wider local authorities and the clients who were to be served by emergent practices. The basic elements of the model were therefore:

- DWR group
- local authority
- clients.

Bernstein's (2000) concepts of boundary strength (classification) and control (framing) were applied to the model. Within each of the three main English case studies we looked at the following features:

- the strength of classification (horizontal division of labour) in the practices of professional agencies and control (framing) over the membership of these groups;

- the strength of distinctions in the vertical division of labour;
- the strength of the marking of hierarchy and the associated relations of control within this hierarchy;
- the strength of control over the regulative practice (matters of order, identity and relation).

The features of the practices within the DWR group were modelled as follows:

Instrumental or instructional practice*

Horizontal	Classification and framing

Instrumental or instructional practice

Vertical	Classification and framing
Regulative Practice	Framing

*Here we use the terms instrumental or instructional practice to refer to the pragmatic actions within practice.

In each local authority the vertical division of labour between participants in the DWR sessions and their colleagues in the wider local authority was also taken as a key feature of the research sites, along with the extent to which boundaries were maintained between the professions in the local authority. The control over the boundary relations between the DWR groups and the local authority was modelled as the framing of those relations. Here strong framing was taken as a boundary maintained by the authority; weak framing as a boundary relation in which the DWR group maintained control; and there was an intermediary position in which a relatively fluid two-way flow of communication was maintained. The features of the practices within the local authority were modelled as follows:

Instrumental or instructional practice

Horizontal	Classification
Vertical	Classification and framing
Control over boundary	Framing

The extent to which clients were classified as belonging to a particular category of need (strong classification) or as the 'whole child' (weak classification) was also noted. This was taken as the division of labour within the client community.

The overall model became:

DWR group

Instrumental or instructional practice	
Horizontal	Classification and framing

Instrumental or instructional practice	
Vertical	Classification and framing
Regulative Practice	Framing

Local authority

Instrumental or instructional practice	
Horizontal	Classification and framing

Instrumental or instructional practice	
Vertical	Classification and framing
Control over boundary	Framing

Clients

Instrumental or instructional practice	
Horizontal	Classification

Each aspect of this model was described for each of the three sites through data gathered through observations and interviews. A coding grid was developed for each aspect and the codings were independently validated by two researchers.

Conclusion

This Bernstein-informed framework for examining how organisations responded and have the potential to respond to changes in practices is particularly useful when considering the development of practices that necessarily cut across boundaries of expertise and institutions. We next return these analyses in Chapters 8 and 9 where we look at organisational implications and the contribution of the study to CHAT.

Chapter 4

What are practitioners learning while doing inter-professional work?

Introduction

The practitioners in the Learning in and for Interagency Working (LIW) study adjusted how they operated to fit with the service configurations that were going on around them while keeping focused on their work with children and their families. These adjustments reshaped their practices and their professional decision-making. Our aim was to capture the ideas that were being developed in these reshaped practices in order to make them visible, to share them and to subject them to scrutiny. Of course, the reshaped practices also had the potential to contribute to a reshaping of the organisational settings in which they were occurring, as revised practices often revealed contradictions between what was needed to accomplish inter-professional work and what the organisation was set up to do. In this chapter we focus on the ideas that were being developed and look at organisational implications in the chapters that follow.

Changing practices while changing practices

We elicited the ideas in the Developmental Research Work (DWR) sessions outlined in Chapter 1 and in Appendix A, and used an analytic protocol, described in Chapters 8 and 9 as the 'D-Analysis', to trace the development of the concepts that were revealed in practitioners' discussions of their current and future work in the workshops. These concepts usually emerged slowly over the six two-hour sessions. They were perhaps first pointed out in an early session, then worked with over subsequent sessions as people tried to make sense of them in relation to what they already knew. Finally there may be a moment of clarification and agreement that this idea was worth seriously embedding in expectations of practice.

The gradual emergence and refining of these concepts signalled their importance. Practitioners returned to the ideas, worried away at them and refined them in ways that reflected their use in the complex professional settings in which they were operating. Agreement on how every emergent concept could be taken into practice was not reached in every site. Instead, at times, we simply witnessed lengthy attempts at trying to fit the developing and obviously important ideas into current practices and expectations. These struggles were as important as the agreements, as they indicated topics that were seen as highly relevant by the practitioners and revealed a great deal about local constraints.

The concepts we will discuss in this chapter were the ideas that appeared and reappeared across discussions over the year of DWR sessions, and that clearly had value for the participants in their work. If we take 'knowing about the expertise that is distributed locally' as an emergent concept for taking forward inter-professional work as an example, this was usually pointed out in an early session, returned to frequently over subsequent ones as people thought about who might be involved in a local network and how it might be put into operation, and finally a way forward would be agreed that might involve creating or adjusting information sharing systems.

The concepts we discuss in this chapter were developed systematically in Castletown, Seaside and Wildside, and were then tested with a wider group of professionals from local authorities across England, and in cross-case comparisons with the Northern Irish cases. We therefore think that they have the potential to inform training programmes. However, we counsel very strongly against taking them as ideas to be taught. Rather they are ideas to be worked with and explored in relation to professional positions and practices. They have the potential to expand notions of inter-professional work and professional practice and are not offered as a simplistic curriculum for inter-professional work.

A quick word about methodology before we discuss the emergent concepts may be useful. One of Vygotsky's important contributions to understanding learning was his method of 'dual stimulation' discussed in Chapter 1. Vygotsky employed it primarily to elicit children's thinking while they undertook the tasks he set them. In brief, the way that children used cultural tools such as ideas and material artefacts revealed their current thinking and indicated where he should start to work with them to take forward their learning. In the DWR sessions, as we explained in Chapter 1, we provided the tools of activity theory to help people analyse their work. As they used those ideas with us, they revealed how they were thinking about the work they were doing and planning to do, and how the situations in which they worked enabled these developments. We suggest that dual stimulation is a powerful way of eliciting concepts in use in practices and will pursue that theme further in Chapter 9.

An overview of the main concepts in use

Box 4.1 The ideas in use to develop inter-professional work

Although there were differences in the time spent working on each of these concepts, in each setting there were concepts that were common across the sites. These were:

- focusing on the whole child in the wider context;
- being responsive to others – both professionals and clients;
- clarifying the purpose of work and being open to alternatives;
- knowing how to know who (can help);
- rule-bending and risk-taking;
- creating and developing better tools;
- developing processes for knowledge sharing and pathways for practice;
- understanding one's self and professional values;
- taking a pedagogic stance at work.

We will now examine each concept in turn.

What is striking about this list in its headline form is that it is not a blueprint for an accountability-led form of professional practice. Quite the reverse: it characterises practitioners who are working responsively to support children's wellbeing and as a result need to make informed decisions at the point of action. Also, because they are in the vanguard of these new practices, they need to be able to act on and reshape established institutional practices to ensure that they can accomplish their professional task of preventing the social exclusion of vulnerable children. This is an enhanced form of professional practice for most of the practitioners involved.

Focusing on the whole child in the wider context

Although in its headline form it appears quite bland, the idea is central to inter-professional preventative work. First, it is crucial to the diagnosis of vulnerability. The likelihood of social exclusion may not be evident unless practitioners are able to look across several aspects a child's life and build a picture of accumulated risk. Second, it is essential to the orchestration of responses to the diagnosis. Inter-professional practices are an attempt to move provision away from sequential referrals where a child is passed from service to service so that each service can, in turn, address a child's needs. Instead, they require services think in terms of parallel responses that wrap support around children and families.

All the practitioners agreed that this focus was important, and that the *Every Child Matters* agenda, which promoted this view, was a step change that could only be beneficial to children. However, this general agreement could close down discussions of important differences between participants about what constituted children's wellbeing. Once those differences were aired, participants were able to gain a broader understanding of a child's trajectory towards wellbeing, or in Cultural Historical Activity Theory (CHAT) terms an expansion of the 'object of activity'. It seems clear that it is important to dig beneath the platitude of 'whole child in the wider context' to unpack (i) how each practitioner is interpreting the idea and (ii) the preconceptions they hold about the interpretations of other professionals.

For example, in Castletown, one of the teachers felt that, even if the services outside the school were able to work responsively with the whole child, all that the school was doing was passing on 'bits of the child', and that the child with her problems still remained in school with the school having to deal with them on a daily basis. Her use of the term 'bits of the child' momentarily silenced the other participants to the extent that the teacher had time to reflect on what she had just said, retract and then consider how the social practices of the school had led her to use that metaphor. The discussion then stimulated a reconceptualisation of the local network to see how practices might be configured around a child's trajectory as the child moved from potential social exclusion to inclusion.

In Wildside, teasing out what focusing on the whole child meant for professional practice also required practitioners to think more overtly about inter-professional work as child-centred practice, where the following of immediate professional priorities had sometimes to take second place to the most pressing needs of a child. In both of these discussions practitioners were developing a rationale for decentring the procedures of their employing organisations, and for recognising the importance of following the child with the support of other experts.

In Seaside, the initial Multi-Professional Team (MPT) indicated that their whole purpose was to wrap support around vulnerable children, and that no more needed to be said. However, when children and families' workers joined the MPT, they brought with them some entrenched expectations about how the education specialists in the MPT interpreted the wellbeing of children simply in terms of academic achievement. These expectations shaped their somewhat negative interactions with their new colleagues and had to be unpacked in the DWR sessions before the MPT could move forward.

There were also tensions within professions. For example, the social workers in Wildside were aware that inter-professional preventative work did not have the standing within their profession that was accorded to more high-end child protection work, where a focus on the whole child in the wider context could be seen as a luxury.

The idea of focusing on the whole child, though central to inter-professional work, began to reveal important issues of professional identity as practitioners were seeing the need to move away from the security of established practices to follow children while working in parallel with other specialists. These identity concerns could not be buried, they needed to be faced and worked through if the level of trust needed for the exercise of relational agency (see Chapter 2) in professional practice was to be achieved.

Being responsive to others – both professionals and clients

In Chapter 1 we explained how we used the framework provided by Victor and Boynton (1998) to select local authorities where children's services were beginning to think about how to work in more responsively collaborative ways with each other, and with children and families. That is, these local authorities had recognised some of the limitations of targeting preventative services at neighbourhoods and were in addition considering, for example, how careful work with families could strengthen their capacity to overcome vulnerability and move themselves from risk of social exclusion.

This kind of work echoed what Victor and Boynton have called 'co-configuration' or a constant process of negotiation and adaptation to produce the 'product' that is needed. In the our study the 'products' we were examining were children's trajectories as they moved from risk of social exclusion to being able to take advantage of what society had to offer them. The potential participants in the processes of co-configuration were professionals with different forms of expertise and the children and their families.

Working in the responsive way characterised by co-configuration is likely to lead to the kind of relationships with caring 'prosocial adults' proposed by Masten and Coatsworth (1998), which can help to develop resilience. A CHAT perspective on resilience, however, goes further than promoting the kinds of sound interactions suggested by Masten and Coatsworth, by emphasising the need for children and families to be able to act on and shape the social situation of their development (Edwards and Apostolov 2007). As we illustrated in that paper, drawing on a study with voluntary agencies, a CHAT view of resilience involves children and families being partners with professionals in reshaping children's trajectories and the social conditions that are giving rise to them, and co-configuration is a helpful way of describing how practitioners and families can work together.

We are in no doubt at all that the professionals we encountered in the LIW study were working as caring prosocial adults with children and, when required, with their families. However, their energies while we were with them in DWR sessions were directed primarily to understanding how they might work with each other, and they only rarely engaged with the demands of how to work creatively with clients so that families might in time take control of their own trajectories. Practitioners recognised the need to aim at working with children and families in that way, but did not provide us with any evidence that it was an immediate focus for their work.

In Seaside, where an MPT was in the process of formation, and in Wildside, where we worked with a loosely coupled team focused on Children in Public Care (CiPC), the priority was to understand each other as professionals so that they could, in the longer term, work better with children. For example, in Seaside learning to be responsive initially involved learning more about each other's specialist expertise, and what mattered for each other as professionals when they worked with a child. This focus took them quickly to the organisational implications of these differences. These included, for example, the different thresholds for intervention across the professions; the need for them, as front line workers, to create ways of working together; and the need to push against the historically embedded social practices of their home organisations so that they might collaborate. As we shall see from other

concepts we discuss in this chapter, enabling inter-professional collaboration was a primary focus.

We were not surprised by the lack of attention to children and
families as partners in reconfiguring the trajectories of vulnerable
family members. Work done on 'participation' in the National
Evaluation of the Children's Fund (NECF) (Edwards *et al.* 2006) has
revealed that workers in statutory agencies found it difficult to
overcome the expectations of both services and those who used the
services that professional expertise involved putting people right.
There were examples of tailored support that worked with the
intentions and capabilities of families, but they were relatively rare.
Lack of attention in LIW to children and families as co-configuring
agents was also unsurprising because collaboration across the
professional boundaries is hugely demanding and particularly so when
home organisations are not keeping up with the demands.

It seems that we need to consider a two-stage process. Work is first
needed on inter-professional collaboration before attention can be paid
to involving children and families in the kind of ongoing and responsive partnership necessary for co-configuration work. In Chapter 2 we
introduced the idea of relational agency and will return to it in the
next section. In brief, a capacity for inter-professional relational agency
would seem a precursor to the kind of risky experience involved in
more responsive work with clients.

This assertion seems borne out by how working with parents wove
its way through the Castletown sessions. Castletown was not a team;
rather, it was a group of professionals who were attempting to find a
way of working together as a flexible system of distributed expertise
around an extended school. The school resisted what it saw as a potential erosion of its carefully constructed boundaries and established
social practices.

Good home–school links are uniformly presented as the bedrock of
a school's success and the Castletown school was no exception. 'Taking
the parents' perspective' was raised as a priority in the first DWR
session and became the focus of an extended discussion in the fourth
of the six sessions after participants had begun to understand how far
they needed to move if they were to have a functioning system of
distributed expertise focused on individual children.

Rather than working on how parents and carers might be brought
into that system, participants from across the professions argued
against family involvement on the grounds that they, as parents
themselves, would not want that degree of intrusion into their family

lives. As analysts it seemed to us that the participation of parents as partners in preventing social inclusion had not entered the collective consciousness of the group as professionals. Subsequent discussions with other groupings of education and welfare professionals have confirmed that while inter-professional work is an aim, the work that needs to be done to achieve inter-professional collaboration has delayed attention to partnerships with families.

NECF analyses have also suggested that these kinds of relationships are currently more likely to arise in the work undertaken by the Voluntary and Community Sector. However, schools in particular often have good relationships with families though the informal work of form tutors as well as through more formal systems of setting targets for children's achievement. It may be that the *Every Child Matters* agenda will increase the scope of the form tutor role to emphasise the more responsive and relational aspects of their work. This development is implied in the 2007 Treasury-DfES review of children's services outlined in Chapter 1.

Clarifying the purpose of work and being open to alternatives

Our CHAT framework is helpful here. In Chapter 2 and Appendix A we have outlined the terms 'activity', 'object of activity' and 'object motive', and explained that practitioners' interpretations of tasks are shaped by the activities in which they occur, and that they are drawn forward to undertake tasks in ways that reflect how they are able to interpret them. We gave a child's trajectory as an example of an object of activity and suggested that one way of looking at prevention was to see it as disrupting a trajectory that was aiming at social exclusion so that the trajectory began to reconfigure itself towards the benefits of social inclusion. We also argued that inter-professional work is central to prevention because it can help practitioners to see the complexity of a child's trajectory and open up a range of ways of responding to that interpretation.

In Wildside the focus on children's trajectories of wellbeing became increasingly enriched over the DWR sessions as different professional perspectives were brought to bear. In activity theory terms the object was expanded. But the expansion of the object of activity usually brings with it strains in the system. For example, existing rules or social practices need to adjust to accommodate new interpretations of the task, and often existing tools or strategies are found wanting. This was the case in Wildside where their development and enthusiastic embracing of a common assessment framework (CAF) was motivated by their growing understanding of the complexities of children's trajectories, and by the value they placed on their focusing on and following the child's trajectory as a common object of activity.

In Seaside, where there was a more formally constructed team, we saw an increasing capacity to work on and expand understandings of children and their needs within the team. This was driven by discussing dilemmas in current cases and focusing on the moral aspects of the work to be done. Forefronting professional values in the way that they expanded understandings of specific cases took this team towards questioning the rules that governed practices and thinking creatively about how they could encourage local strategists to listen to what they had to say about the new forms of practice that were emerging so that systems could be developed appropriately.

Expanding the object of activity therefore has considerable implications for the systems in which it occurs. As Engeström argues, it is likely to lead to changes at the level of the activity system, with revised rules, tools and division of labour (Engeström 2001). It is therefore unsurprising that established systems, such as the school that formed the core of the Castletown case, may wish to resist alternative interpretations of the task.

Resistance was strong at times. School-based participants, of course, brought the school's way of classifying children as 'participants in crime', 'silent sufferers' or 'high achievers' to the DWR sessions. In addition, the school had an internal pupil referral system that focused on behaviour and that was based on paperwork that included phrases describing behaviour as, for example, 'spoils lessons' and 'uniform offences'. When asked, school-based participants were clear that these classifications were not meant to travel beyond the school boundary. It was also clear in discussions that these descriptors did not connect easily with the meaning systems in the other professions represented in the DWR sessions.

These classifications appeared to trap some of the teachers. For example, the only way in which those teachers who wanted to rethink them as a result of DWR discussions could do so was by recalling other places where they had worked that had not used the same ways of categorising children. It seemed to the research team that the carefully protected school classifications impeded inter-professional work because, although they were clear, they were not open to expansion through collaboration with others.

The experience of both Wildside and Seaside would suggest that focusing on specific cases in structured discussions can help to expand understanding both of the object or task and of the ways in which other professionals are able to respond to aspects of these enhanced interpretations. Revealing the complexity of a task was therefore not a matter of making the job of one practitioner more complicated. On the contrary, it was an opportunity for eliciting and revealing the expertise available in a local system that could also be applied to the task.

The idea of relational agency, introduced in Chapter 2, can help us to prepare practitioners for clarifying their own interpretations, recognising how others are reading the problem, and becoming adept at working with the strengths that others bring to these enriched interpretations (Edwards 2005). It involves being clear and articulate about how you as a professional are interpreting a problem, how you might respond to that interpretation, and being able to recognise that other professionals will make different interpretations and offer different responses. Relational agency is therefore seen in the ability to work intentionally on the expanded problem with other professionals, taking the lead and withdrawing from it when appropriate. Not only is this way of working together likely to benefit clients; it also strengthens professionals as they undertake relatively risky work with vulnerable clients outside the safety of the established social practices of the home organisations. We now turn to what needs to be learnt in order to exercise relational agency.

Knowing how to know who (can help)

We have been suggesting that working in relational ways with other professionals in systems of distributed expertise can strengthen practitioners as they undertake risky responsive work with vulnerable children and their families. Our suggestions have underlined the professional decision-making of practitioners and started to unpack the ideas that underpin the capacity to work professionally on complex problems.

The idea that 'knowing how to know who' can also help to disrupt a child's trajectory emerged as an important concept in slightly different ways in each of the three sites. However, it was clear everywhere that simply relying on historical friendships and networks was an insufficient strategy for developing the kinds of child-oriented professional responses that were needed. This kind of reliance was insufficient for two reasons. First, it was difficult for practitioners who were new to a neighbourhood to function if networks were mainly personal. Second, old networks may not be appropriate for new and changing tasks.

The Wildside loosely coupled team was based in a local authority where there were exceptionally robust historically grounded inter-professional networks. The temptation to rely entirely on these networks was clearly strong for some practitioners. However, as the team became increasingly clear about the purpose of their work, they became impatient with the lack of precision and engagement with the object of activity offered by some of the people who were historically linked with the work of the team. For example, participants in the DWR sessions concluded that too many people attended team meetings with the result that there was sometimes confusion about what expertise was actually available. The development of an electronic CAF was in part a response to the need for clarity about what could be offered and how what was offered might contribute to the expertise available to support children.

In Castletown the emergent system of distributed expertise around the school was still developing while we worked there. The lack of clarity about the developing system increased the school practitioners' concerns about working more flexibly outside the social practices of the school. A recurrent theme throughout the DWR sessions was the school's isolation from existing and developing systems of expertise in the local authority. At the same time practitioners based outside the school were struggling with both knowing what resources were available from other professionals and the thresholds at which other professionals could take action.

When we compare Wildside and Castletown, two important issues arise. First, the Wildside team had a clear single focus in their work with CiPC, whereas the focus of the Castletown work outside the school was never clear. The idea of a child's trajectory gave coherence to discussions, but differences in forms of assessment and thresholds for responses were constantly returned to. The second difference between the two cases was that although there was agreement about a focus on children's wellbeing in both sites, in Castletown discussions focused on the difficulties in working together, how tools such as the CAF would not easily fit in existing systems, and how the school's practices needed to prevail. That is, there was a concern with the instrumental aspects of working together. In Wildside, in contrast, the focus on the child's trajectory was a reality. They could name specific children and, because of their focus on children, participants were able to think about how they might work together to develop alternative futures for them. The tools, both material and conceptual, that they developed in Wildside to enable them to work together could therefore be labelled as what Engeström (Engeström 2007b) has called 'why' and 'where to' tools, which would reflect their professional values and would help to take forward children's trajectories.

In the Seaside MPT it was expected that the team members would work together. Early sessions therefore focused on making expertise explicit and working out how they might work in relatively flexible ways, using mobile phone contact and so on. Like Wildside, ideas and artefacts that allowed a long-term view of a child's progress and the ongoing roles of other professionals were an important part of the team's development. For this reason explaining professional values was crucial, as shared values operated as a kind of 'glue' helping trust to develop and holding team members together as they looked forward and developed ways of working together.

Knowing how to know who is therefore not an instrumental skill that can be acquired on a training programme. Rather it arises in discussions of object-oriented activities in which expertise and values are clarified, and where it can be supported by tools, such as CAF, which harness the ways in which professional values drive the engagement of professionals with clients. Here trust is not the trust born of old well-established relationships, but of mutual respect as professionals oriented towards the same goals for children.

We are not alone in recognising the importance of 'know who'. Lundvall, working in the area of development economics, has long argued that 'know-who' is an important aspect of knowledge at work alongside know what, how and why:

> Know-who involves information about who knows to do what. But especially it involves the social capability to establish relationships to specialised groups in order to draw on their expertise.
> (Lundvall 1996: 7)

Lundvall, like the LIW team, argues that know-who is embedded and learnt in social practice, and cannot simply be codified into, for example, a register of names, though lists of names of local professionals are useful. Elsewhere we have suggested that what is crucial is a professional's capacity to work with a tool such as a list of names in ways that focus on propelling a child forward (a 'where to' use) rather than an opportunity to pass the child on (a 'what and when' use) (Edwards in press a).

Lundvall also argues that systems need to become more adept at learning from what is happening on the ground, that is, better at enabling vertical knowledge flows (Schulz 2001). This aspect of knowing who became a priority for the Seaside MPT. Once the team had developed ways of working together, it turned to the problem of how to inform local strategists about what they were learning and the organisational implications of the developing practices. Here they were faced with the double challenge of not knowing who the strategists were and not having appropriate tools for engaging with them. We shall pick up this topic in the next chapters. At this point we simply want to suggest that knowing how to know who can involve working across organisational boundaries and up organisational hierarchies, and perhaps the latter is the most challenging.

Rule-bending and risk-taking

Questioning rules or established social practices is one sign that a system is changing as a result of expanding understandings of the activity it is engaged in. We saw examples of rule-bending in both Seaside and Wildside, but not in Castletown, where the existing practices of the school were regularly reconfirmed in discussions of ways forward. Rule-bending is a sign that systems are beginning to deal with some of the contradictions that arise from the development of new responses to freshly interpreted problems, and in Castletown the resistance of the school was inhibiting the development of new practices.

Despite our seeing rule-bending and risk-taking as signs of the development of responsive practices, whenever we used these terms in discussions with participants, they were distinctly wary of the labels. Instead, they said they were simply making things work. Nevertheless, they regularly produced examples of how they were reshaping rules to enable them to do what was professionally desirable. In Seaside there were initial discussions of how rule-bending, in order to be responsive, might mean that some children 'fell through the net'. Yet the exploration of actual cases of rule-bending where, for example, a relatively low status professional made direct contact with another, higher status, professional, by-passing institutional hierarchies in order to respond to a child's needs, led to agreement that rules should be questioned if practice was to be driven by a focus on children's wellbeing.

However, knowing where to place a limit on rule-bending and risk-taking remained a discussion point throughout the DWR sessions in

Seaside. For example, practitioners were not always clear who made the rules, and what leeway they had in renegotiating them. Trust was also relevant here. Inter-professional trust was growing from analyses of shared values across professions when cases were discussed, and as a result some rule-bending at the operational level was possible. But the rule-making strategists were not part of these discussions with the result that practitioners were unsure of the values that drove those who were doing the strategy work. Their desire to talk with strategists about what they were currently learning and doing stemmed from their frustrations with some established social practices and the need to achieve some mutual understanding of values.

Similarly in Wildside considerable attention was given to how established rules did not always support emergent practices. Also, like at Seaside, there were times when operational staff felt it was professionally risky to rule-bend. Being able to rule-bend depended on the status of the professional: the higher the status, the easier it was to bend the rules. The link between power and rule-bending resonated across our later discussions with other practitioners. Yet we did see small moves being made by lower status practitioners who calculated risks and, driven by what they saw as children's urgent needs, took short cuts across communication systems to speed up responses. These were signs of systems that were changing, and like the situation at Seaside, a great deal depended on others recognising the need to respond positively to how rules were being nudged and the dynamics of work systems were being shifted.

In Castletown, there was arguably a need for rule-bending to reduce the time taken to support children, as within-school referral systems were frequently lengthy. Practitioners outside the school reported frustrations with the school's capacity to respond, compared, for example, with how local primary schools were able to work. However, rule-bending was dismissed by school staff as unnecessary and indeed too risky for vulnerable children who could regard school as their one 'safe haven'.

Rule-bending is a sign of both professional and organisational learning. It can also be a sign of the values-driven professional practice that we have argued is crucial to responsive inter-professional practice. It nonetheless presents a considerable challenge to organisations that are shaped by strong systems of accountability.

Creating and developing better tools

As practitioners expand understanding of the problems of practice, they not only find that existing rules can be unhelpful, they can also find that the resources or tools that they use restrict their responses to their fresh interpretations. Starting to look for other resources to support professional actions is, like rule-bending, a sign of learning while developing new practices.

We can look at the process of tool development in activity theory terms (Figure 4.1). In Wildside practitioners decided that they wanted to work in a more focused and responsive way with children, but current ways of communicating were inadequate (Stage One). Having identified the need for a new tool, they made the creation of that tool their priority and pooled their expertise in child-centred work to create an electronic CAF (Stage Two). Having created the tool they used it to work with children (Stage Three). In time, the electronic CAF became an expectation, or a rule, that was used in ways informed by practitioners' growing understanding of how to take forward children's trajectories (Stage Four). The creation of new tools is therefore both evidence of the exercise of professional judgement, and has an impact on the systems in which it is incorporated.

The beginnings of a similar process could be seen in Castletown. The different purposes and processes of the assessment systems used in and outside the school were regularly discussed in DWR sessions, with school staff arguing that the differences in assessment systems made it impossible for the school to be part of a local system of distributed expertise, and that instead it needed to continue to operate as a tightly bounded self-contained system. A breakthrough came as a result of per sistent work by one of the educational psychologists who

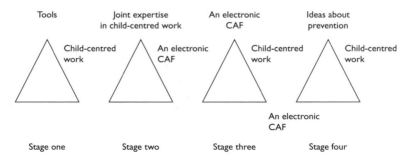

Figure 4.1 The development and incorporation of a new tool

consistently invited school staff to engage with the development of the local CAF to ensure that what mattered for the school was incorporated into the CAF.

A shift in focus from ensuring the wellbeing of children, to a focus on creating a tool that may enable that to happen, helped school staff to see that they could engage with the new local authority system and inform its development with the values of the school. That is, through becoming involved in developing the CAF, they were being brought into an activity in the new system. Here the CAF was operating as a potentially shared object that connected the school and local authority systems. We will look at the role of boundary objects in professional learning in Chapter 5. In time, the newly developed CAF could become a tool that was used in the school and eventually incorporated into the rules that shaped how the school worked with vulnerable children in much the same way as we have outlined in Figure 4.1.

The need to step back from longer-term focuses to create the tools that were needed also occurred in Seaside. Here it happened quite early on in the DWR process because members of the MPT found that, if they were to work as a responsive team rather than as sets of discrete professionals, they needed to distinguish between actions that were, for example, about passing on information about children, and those that ensured that relevant team members became involved in responsively supporting a vulnerable child. Here the tools were largely conceptual tools involving recognising the professional resources to be offered by others, and knowing how they might help move a child towards the desired outcome. Developing ways of knowing how to know who, and how to work in more relational ways across the team were priority tasks as the team came together as MPT1 and then expanded into MPT2 with the introduction of new staff to the team.

The Seaside example of tool creation is an important one, as we can all too often think of tools as simply material artefacts. As a result, conceptual tools, such as an idea that gives shape to practices, can be underplayed. The CAF developed in Wildside and under development in Castletown could be used in routine ways to simply record who had seen a child and who should see her next. Or it could be used in ways that wove together support around a child and brought her carers into an inter-professional process of co-configuring her trajectory. Without the conceptual tools that, for example, allowed practitioners to interpret the complexity of a trajectory or to recognise the potential in an assessment tool, the use of material resources can be relatively limited. Once again we return to the theme that inter-professional practice calls for informed professional judgement and a recognition of values-driven professional expertise.

Developing processes for knowledge sharing and pathways for practice

We have already seen how important knowing how to know who was as a prerequisite for relational inter-professional work, and in the previous section we saw how efforts were made to create tools that would enable people to work together. Discussions of knowledge sharing and ways of linking while taking action were, of course, connected to these developments, but were different because they focused on how practitioners could navigate the newly emerging local terrains of reconfigured children's services. The discussions arose from an increasing awareness that existing professional networks, which had developed in the past from working on different kinds of problems, were now inadequate and that new more fluid and responsive practices would need to be enacted in local systems that were themselves under transformation.

In Wildside, discussions about knowledge sharing arose when tensions between different professions and their priorities were made explicit. These discussions led participants to recognise the need to develop an electronic CAF. In Castletown, professionals external to the school argued for two-way flows of knowledge between the school and other services so that the school might be able to respond to feedback from external sources. In both Wildside and Castletown knowledge sharing was discussed as the basis for more collaborative, child-oriented and informed practice where practitioners learnt about the resources that were available across a locality and about the strengths and needs of the children with whom they were working. In Seaside, the emphasis on knowledge sharing related more to passing knowledge about changing practices upstream to strategists, and this will therefore be discussed more fully in Chapter 8.

When we spoke with participants after the series of DWR sessions had ended, it was clear that they felt that taking an outward-looking stance, and being able to recognise and use the resources available to them in their local systems were becoming increasingly important features of practice for many of them. For example, they enabled them to lever additional support for children and families at times when it was needed. Their feedback to us echoed findings from a King's Fund study (King's Fund 2001) and NECF (Edwards *et al.* 2006) that, because practice was running ahead of strategy in some areas, it was the practitioners themselves who etched new pathways across changing local landscapes in order to co-configure support around a child's trajectory.

Elsewhere, drawing on NECF (Edwards in press a), we have suggested that a sustained sequence of local meetings, where cases can be discussed so that expertise and other resources can be revealed, as they were in Seaside DWR sessions, can be regarded as springboards for starting local trails that may be useful in the future. Practitioners explained to the NECF team that even though the cases being discussed at these meetings may not be immediately relevant, they would always reveal information that may be useful in the future when working with other children. New terrains of practice are quite clearly opening up as services are being reshaped to enable more joined-up and flexible responses, and equally clearly practitioners need to be enabled to examine and explore them so they can help children and families to navigate them.

Understanding one's self and professional values

Here we move from looking outward and developing tools that enable collaboration, to begin consider the impact of inter-professional work on professional identity. We have already indicated how a sharing of values operated as a glue that kept professionals, who were operating with different priorities and thresholds, focused on children's long-term wellbeing.

While professional values were discussed in quite open ways, self-understanding unsurprisingly proved challenging. For example, one of the educational psychologists in Seaside slowly came to see that her role had been primarily focused on pupil attendance, and that, if she wanted to align herself with the team as it was developing more co-configured practices, fresh alternatives were becoming available for her.

In Seaside, MPT members worked hard to resist their being labelled by other professionals from outside the MPT as generic multi-professional workers, and had to work on understanding what they did stand for and could offer. New positions in new systems necessarily call for identity work, both with immediate colleagues and with those whose expectations are less informed. In Wildside, discussions of role and identity ran through all the sessions as this well-established team became increasingly reflective, using the tools of activity theory offered in the DWR sessions. In doing so they became increasingly aware of the need to emphasise specific expertise. It seemed that both new and established groupings benefited from attention to the expertise, individual priorities and the struggles of participants as they attempted to align themselves with other professionals.

In Castletown, identity work for the teachers was particularly challenging. They were being encouraged by discussions in DWR sessions, and a sharing of values there, to step away from the tightly boundaried social practices of the school, and to think about themselves as part of a fluid system of distributed expertise. This was difficult, and teachers who responded to invitations to expand their identities revealed a strong sense of feeling isolated in the school, when they saw more fluid inter-professional collaboration as the way forward.

The Castletown experience particularly highlights the vulnerability of individual practitioners who find themselves beginning to position themselves outside the established practices of their home organisations without the support of those organisations. We have suggested that a sense of relational agency, arising from good and focused links with other professionals, can help to strengthen a sense of purpose and effectiveness. However, as long as practices move ahead of strategies, professionals will find themselves brushing up against established practices in ways that are uncomfortable for both individuals and organisations. We return to this topic in Chapter 6.

Taking a pedagogic stance at work

The final emergent concept was a reflection of the growing sense of confidence and of intentionality or professional agency experienced by participants in both Seaside and Wildside. As they began to see themselves as drawing on and contributing to local systems of distributed expertise, they also began to see that they had some responsibility for informing them and ensuring that their potential contributions were explicit and readily available to others.

In Seaside, practitioners revealed how they took time to help colleagues with different professional backgrounds to complete paperwork so that it would trigger the right responses and release the resources that were needed when read by a social worker or mental health worker. Interviews in Castletown similarly revealed the importance of being helped to acquire professional 'multilingualism' when talking across professional boundaries. In Wildside, participants discussed how, once they had begun to unpack what was involved in current inter-professional working, they had taken lessons from the DWR sessions to other colleagues in the local authority and had worked individually with colleagues to help them see what was involved in collaboration. In Castletown one of the educational psychologists used the DWR sessions as a pedagogic space in which the school might be persuaded by counter examples to shift its position and join in the systems that were developing locally.

What all these examples have in common is that most practitioners had recognised the importance of being part of a system of distributed expertise, and maintaining the system involved giving mutual support in order to serve the best interests of children.

Another development in Seaside similarly reflected a growing confidence and sense of professional responsibility, but in this case the focus was not the strengthening of a system of practice-oriented distributed expertise. Rather, the frustrations with strategists that we discussed earlier in this chapter provoked efforts to take responsibility for working pedagogically with local strategists. Practitioners did this in order to mediate knowledge from practice 'upstream' to achieve appropriate institutional responses to changes in practices. The Seaside example, demonstrates that knowledge-sharing across professional boundaries is not enough and that there may be times when 'taking a pedagogic stance at work' will involve working pedagogically up local hierarchies. This point, we suggest, may be particularly important where inter-professional projects have been set up as local 'trailblazers'. But it is also relevant in situations, such as Seaside, where strategists believed, in good faith, that it was enough to initiate and roll out a strategy, without looking at the systemic changes that were required to maximise its impact.

An enhanced form of professionalism

The ideas outlined here were shared over the year that followed the DWR interventions, in workshops with practitioners and strategists across England. They were also explored in the data from the Northern Irish case studies, and were revealed again in follow-up interviews with participants in the DWR sessions. The ideas continued to be relevant, resonating with the experiences of those who were attempting to develop more responsive inter-professional practices.

Conclusion

Perhaps, one of the most important features of the concepts we have outlined is that they reflect a strong, informed and responsible form of expert professional practice. They capture capabilities that assist inter-professional work, but they are not representing a kind of professional hybridity where a multi-agency practitioner is all things to all people. The concepts that emerged from practitioners while they were discussing new forms of focused collaborations are important for professional practice regardless of the profession, but at the core of inter-professional work is a recognition of specific professional expertise. This expertise is arguably all the more important when practitioners are working outside the organisational social practices that sustain their status. Professional standing now needs to be earned in negotiations with other professionals and with clients. As a result, practitioners need to be clear about what they can contribute to local systems of distributed expertise.

Chapter 5

How and where are practitioners learning?

Introduction

The practitioners we worked with were learning to do inter-professional work while doing inter-professional work. What made that learning different from induction, for example, was that they were creating new practices rather than learning to make sense of established ways of working.

In this chapter we shall look at work-based learning: the particular demands of learning to do inter-professional work; how DWR sessions provided a kind of boundary zone between organisations where social practices could be critically examined and learning taken forward; how other resources have helped to develop inter-professional collaborations; and the inter-relatedness of professional and organisational learning.

Learning at work

The opportunities to develop practices varied. In the newly formed Multi-Professional Teams (MPT) in Brookside and Seaside there was some freedom to construct inter-professional practices that were driven by a developing shared understanding of child-centred prevention. In Castletown, where practitioners inhabited an emerging system of distributed expertise, while also maintaining a strong base in the social practices of their home organisations, reshaping organisational practices to work in new ways was often more difficult. However, in all the case study sites learning was helped by the opportunities to discuss the challenges of these practices in the Developmental Work Research (DWR) sessions.

Linking workplace learning with workplace practices is, for us, a crucial starting point. Like Hager (2004) we see practice as a process that coincides with learning. But importantly, in line with what Hager calls 'productive learning', linking practice with learning does not mean that learning is simply a matter of being swept along unthinkingly by the flow of processes and procedures. The learning we observed had much in common with Hager's description of productive learning which:

- redefines existing patterns and rules;
- involves the creation of new learning that simultaneously reshapes the environment in which the learning occurs;
- involves the social, cultural and political construction of individual identities;
- centres on holistic, whole person, embodied judgements.

(after Hager 2004: 15)

As we outlined in Chapter 2, professional learning for us is a process of sense-making and action that inextricably links professional judgements with professional identity and a sense of what one can do. We also recognise that when these judgements give rise to new practices, these practices will impact on workplaces, as the rule-bending and the creation of new tools discussed in Chapter 4 have illustrated.

However, let us first briefly examine some features of workplace learning in well-established settings where practices tend towards stability. Starting there will highlight some of the challenges in promoting workplace learning for newly emerging practices. One way into how work settings maintain particular ways of accomplishing tasks is to look at workplace talk. Talk reveals the categories used to identify and define tasks, and can therefore give us insights into the orientations and priorities of practitioners (Mäkitalo and Säljö 2002; Sarangi and Roberts 1999). For example, how teachers in Castletown talked about children as 'participants in crime', 'silent sufferers' or 'high achievers' revealed some of the options for action available to both teachers and pupils within the social practices of the school. By seeing some children as participants in crime rather than, for example, possible victims of crime, school staff were indicating how a label might help them categorise students so that they could be passed out of the school system and into the youth justice system.

Material artefacts also often carry the categories through which practice emerges. The within-school referral system that we discussed in Chapter 4, which required teachers to be alert to 'uniform offences' and 'spoiling lessons' and to record these problems on a paper form, worked as what Yates and Orlikowski (1992) have called a 'genre'. That is, a version of the referral form had become embedded within the timescales and social practices of the school to the extent that it in turn shaped those practices. For example, it carried the assumption that descriptions such as 'spoiling lessons' were self-evident and not open to interpretation or change.

Situated talk and situated use of resources not only reflect priorities and practices, but also give rise to them. Learning to work in established or stable systems therefore involves learning to use local resources in ways that sustain those practices. Eraut too has pointed to the underestimated power of institutional artefacts such as audit files, design specifications and handover notes in mediating and structuring work (Eraut 2007). Interestingly, when we asked the teachers in Castletown how professionals made sense of the terminology used in the referral form, they replied in unison that the form was not for external use. In other words, it was a genre that that helped to shore up the boundary between the school and other agencies.

Organisations that are not ready for change will cling to established genres. During the study the school revisited the referral form and clarified teachers' responsibilities in relation to different elements of the referral process. As a result, the form was more explicitly embedded within the school's system. This clarification was an example of how the school attempted to stabilise its practices. As we shall see, this attempt to stabilise its practices during a time of change provided evidence of a system that was resisting the learning associated with interagency work and led to some degree of frustration among some of the teachers.

As we indicated in Chapter 3, the link between talk and institutional practices is still being developed in CHAT research. In one important recent development, Wertsch has distinguished between explicit and implicit mediation in Vygotsky's writing. This distinction illuminates how institutional talk and genres, such as referral systems, mediate accepted understandings in workplace settings (Wertsch 2007). Explicit mediation, he suggests, involves the intentional introduction of what is to be learnt into a learning activity that is managed by someone who is designated as 'teacher', and therefore reflects what is common in formal education settings. Implicit mediation, on the other hand, involves knowledge being carried in the natural, that is the historically constructed, language of the situation.

Two features of implicit mediation seem to us to be particularly relevant to studies of workplace learning. First, because the meanings carried in the language are brought into use in the process of accomplishing a work task, they do not 'readily become the object of conscious reflection' (Wertsch 2007: 185). Second, despite not being open to reflection, meanings are open to change, that is, they can become increasingly sophisticated as the task itself reveals its complexity. In the LIW study, for example, practitioners' understandings of 'prevention' developed and terms such as 'a child's trajectory' took on enriched meanings for the professionals who worked with us.

These are not esoteric points for three reasons. First, workplaces rarely offer opportunities for conscious reflection to assist learning. Wertsch's observation may alert us to reconsider that situation. Eraut has come to a similar conclusion in his grounded analyses of what helps early professional learning in organisations and suggests that organisations should provide opportunities for feedback that assists learning (Eraut 2007). Second, people's propensity to seek meaning in and make sense of new experiences will mean that changing relationships between word and meaning can be evidence of both individual and organisational learning. For example, as teachers start to question the term 'spoiling lessons' and differentiate between different kinds of disruptive behaviour, their responses will simultaneously change. Entrenched organisational genres such as the paperwork used in the school's referral system can inhibit this kind of development and lead to contradictions between intentions for practices and the tools available to accomplish the tasks of practice.

The third, and perhaps most important, reason is that with the idea of implicit mediation Wertsch is providing a much needed link between the institutional priorities that are revealed in talk and the development of professional reasoning and action. That is to say, the idea of implicit mediation alerts us to how practices may be restricted by the way that institutional categories are used in practitioners' talk. For example, if we want to see children who are 'participants in crime' as children to be helped rather than punished, we need to reshape how we talk about them.

Box 5.1 New meanings are a sign of learning

Wertsch's insights also have implications for organisations. Those organisations that are able to recognise the learning that arises in practices as a result of changing relationships between word and meaning are, of course, likely to be places that enable professionals to make informed professional judgements that reflect their continuous learning. As we have already argued, such changes are likely to be relatively rare in organisations that are aiming at stability rather than learning, such the school in Castletown. On the other hand, they are particularly likely to occur in inter-professional work where increasing the complexity of interpretations of the task is a major purpose.

Pedagogic opportunities at the boundaries

As we outlined in Chapter 2, the DWR sessions we ran operated as places on the boundaries of established practices where people could look across professional boundaries, begin to understand the intentions and practices of other practitioners and re-position themselves in relation to them. In this section we unpack some of the processes that were occurring in these sessions and suggest some general principles about developing inter-professional practices.

There is an established body of research on boundaries in systems theory research (Midgley 1992; Ulrich 1983). Most of it builds on the work of Churchman (Ulrich 1988) who argued that boundaries are social constructions that define who is included and excluded from interactions and what knowledge (that is, agreed meanings) is considered relevant in those interactions. One consequence of Churchman's analysis is to encourage people to push out the boundaries to include more people within them, with all the threats to exclusive expertise, meaning-making and identity that this move might bring. We certainly saw examples of these processes in Seaside where the shifting of professional boundaries to build the new Multi-Professional Team (MPT) required, as we shall see, considerable attention to recognising expertise and negotiating meanings and identities.

Ulrich's development of Churchman's work has paid particular attention to the values that give shape to the boundaries. Again this strand of work is highly relevant to the LIW study where we found that once practitioners in the teams that we looked at were able to recognise just how much they shared professional values, they were able to work together on the common task of preventing social exclusion. Midgley's later analyses of how differences in values can give rise to differences in where boundaries are drawn and the marginalisation of the less dominant group are also relevant. Midgley draws on the work of Douglas (1966) for an anthropological account of what is going on at the margins in what he calls the 'gray areas in which marginal areas lie that are neither fully included in, nor excluded from, the system definition' (Midgley 1992: 6).

As well as encouraging us to examine the historical constructions of boundaries and to explore the boundaries themselves as sights of negotiation and potential instability, these analyses have strong practical relevance. Midgley *et al.*, for example, have used these frameworks to reveal how users of a housing service for elderly people were marginalised in the processes of service development (Midgley *et al.* 1998). Here the service users were given what Midgley *et al.* describe as a 'profane' status by service providers who wanted to exclude them from discussions about service improvement. In Castletown we saw a similar process at work, where all participants spoke at length, and with complete unity, about the need to exclude parents and carers from contributing to their children's common or inter-professional assessment.

Boundaries between organisations, professional tribes or service providers and users are therefore fascinating places, and we know far too little about what happens there. However, the DWR sessions, where professionals from different backgrounds met to discuss their work challenges, have provided us with the opportunity to observe and analyse what was going on. We shall now look in more detail at the learning that occurred across professions and some of the developments in professional identities that arose there.

Learning at the boundaries

As we worked with practitioners who had come together to develop their capacity for inter-professional collaboration, we found it increasingly useful to see the DWR workshops as boundary zones (Konkola 2001). In Chapter 2 we described boundary zones as neutral spaces on the boundaries of more than one organisation where the values and professional priorities of each practitioner are respected, where information can be shared and where trust can be built. Here we want to look at who was learning in those boundary spaces and what seemed to help their learning. What they were learning has already been discussed in Chapter 4.

Participants were all practitioners who were or were likely to be working together to follow a child's trajectory, giving support and putting in protective factors to lessen a child's vulnerability to social exclusion. As we explained in Chapter 2, this involved looking across the different domains of a child's life with the help of other practitioners in order to expand understandings of a child's strengths and vulnerabilities. To do this, practitioners needed to become more attuned to how other professions might primarily interpret a child, for example, as a victim of family disruption rather than primarily as a participant in crime. They also needed to learn how other practitioners would respond to those interpretations and to become aware of the resources they could bring to bear to support a child and how they might use them.

As they looked at what other practitioners gave priority to and how they operated, participants gained increasingly complex pictures of the children with whom they were working. In brief, practitioners learnt a great deal from each other, and in doing so developed increasingly sophisticated understandings of preventative practices.

But what helped inter-professional learning in the DWR sessions? The activity theory response is to look for potentially shared objects, that is, objects of activity or problems that motivated collaborations. Engeström's third generation activity theory (see Figure 5.1 and Appendix A) alerts us to the impact of sharing problems or tasks between systems. It was developed to recognise that participants from different systems bring different attributes to work on a common object or problem, which, in turn, is likely to lead to an expansion of the object and systemic learning within the collaborating systems.

In Wildside, the electronic Common Assessment Framework (CAF) proved to be a powerful shared object. Participants who were convinced of its value explained its importance to others and different professional perspectives fed into its development. Once this shared object had been shaped through this process of inter-professional

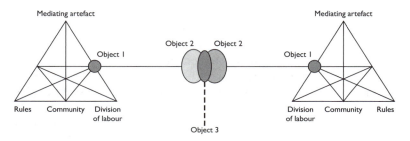

Figure 5.1 Two interacting activity systems (Engeström 1999a)

collaboration, it became a tool that was shared across professions and began to be integrated into the practices of these systems. However, we are aware that this was not the end of the story. As Peckover *et al.* (in press) observe, negotiating a CAF into established practices is far from easy.

In Castletown too the development of the local CAF was also offered as an object of activity that might be shared, when the senior educational psychologist suggested to one of the teachers that if she was concerned about how the CAF would reflect the school's priorities, she should become involved in the development of the CAF that was then underway. Here the potentially shared object was proffered as a way of bringing the school into the existing networked system of children's services that was already committed to co-configured practices.

The MPT in Seaside was more clearly a team, and the boundary that they focused on was the one between them and the local strategists and the lack of 'upstream' learning that was occurring. Nonetheless, in the early days of the MPT's development, orienting their energies on the problems and trajectories of specific children as shared objects and making explicit their interpretations, desired responses and current frustrations helped them to erode the professional boundaries that separated them as team members.

In both Wildside, where there was a loosely coupled team, and in Seaside, where a team was being created, we could see that expansion of the potentially shared object had been reflected back into the organisations leading to changes in the way they worked. In Wildside the CAF became a new tool and in Seaside collaboration led to the need to re-shape the rules that governed practice to enable more fluid and responsive work. In Castletown we observed a much earlier stage in work on a potentially shared object. Here the CAF was offered as somewhere where school teachers could engage with the priorities of other agencies while contributing to fashioning the object into a tool that suited their needs. In other words the educational psychologist, in offering this opportunity to the teacher, recognised that joint work on a shared object of activity could lead to mutual learning as well as a CAF that the school might find acceptable.

We also observed that some participants used the DWR sessions as opportunities to work pedagogically with colleagues. When that happened it tended to arise from discussing a contradiction that had been revealed through the use of the tools of activity theory on the accounts of everyday practice that were discussed in the sessions. In Castletown, for example, discussions of division of labour and the stress experienced by teachers in the school provided the opportunity for the senior educational psychologist and the senior social worker to discuss the possibility that, with its tightly maintained boundaries and increasingly complex problems to deal with, the school system might 'burst'. Although this was said with an emphasis on how much everyone had to learn, the structure of the DWR session provided the opportunity for contradictions to be faced and for people to say what might be unsayable in other settings.

This kind of work went with the grain of DWR and the dual stimulation methods on which it was based (see Chapter 2). These participants were using the sessions to open up the object, question the tools, rules and division of labour and take forward collective understandings. They were orchestrating the collective development of the meeting by appropriating the tools of activity theory and demonstrating how useful they were. They were also, very importantly, challenging the boundaries that others were sustaining. By pointing out inconsistencies such as the way that 'passing on bits of the child' was at odds with a declared focus on 'the whole child', these practitioners revealed for each other the need to rethink where boundaries lay and how permeable they were.

Identity work at the boundaries

In Chapter 2 we explained that we agree with Roth *et al.* (2004) that identity is not a stable characteristic, but is negotiated and accomplished within activities. But as Kerosuo (2003) has observed, boundaries associated with work are often unstable and can be uncomfortable places to be. Negotiating professional identity, that is, a sense of what one should and can do, at the boundaries of organisations while beginning to articulate new practices is particularly challenging. The call for a strong sense of what Gee has called 'projective identity' (Gee 2003), where identity work focuses on creating a sense of who one might become. Identity negotiations on or around boundaries are therefore often risky and demanding.

The work that practitioners did to sustain their professional identities and their sense of being competent actors varied from site to site, and depended very much on what were considered to be significant boundaries. These boundaries could change over time as was the case in Seaside. There a new boundary had been drawn around the MPT that separated them from other teams, from the schools they worked with and from the strategists who directed the implementation of local policies for integrated work with children. The identity work that we observed there over the period of the study started with the educational specialists negotiating their positions and professional identities within the new team, with these negotiations becoming more marked a little later when social workers joined the team and values and positions had to be explained more clearly. The DWR sessions were invaluable as places where these negotiations could be made explicit, differences confronted and collective meaning-making developed. As we have demonstrated in Chapter 4, learning between practitioners from different backgrounds was clearly happening in these sessions. Ways of understanding vulnerable children were expanded and words used within specialist professional discourses acquired enriched meanings as practitioners became aware of alternative interpretations of children's needs.

As the DWR sessions continued, we found that the MPT began to cohere as a team around discussions of *others* beyond the boundary of the team. These others included the schools, which were not always receptive to what the new MPT could offer, and, most significantly, the local strategists, who were not receptive to what the MPT could now tell them about what was involved in inter-professional work with vulnerable children. The new professional identities that were then needed, if the MPT was to influence schools and local strategy, had to include the ability to work pedagogically with others at the boundaries of the MPT in order to mediate the meanings they had developed within the MPT.

In Wildside, the loosely coupled team shared a strong focus on the trajectories of vulnerable children, and members were less preoccupied with boundaries and the need to negotiate identities. The team had been in place for several years, the local authority was small enough for people to know each other, and the team came together with a very clear focus on looked after children.

The situation in Castletown, however, was very different. There the DWR created a boundary zone where two processes were in play. First, the boundary itself was being contested. The school was working hard to sustain its historical boundary with other service providers and to contain preventative work within its boundary, at the same time as seeking ways of passing on some of the problems that could not be dealt with by the school to other specialist agencies. We have already discussed how institutional talk and genres such as referral forms helped to sustain the boundary and resist the changes being demanded by the reconfiguring of children's services locally. The carefully maintained boundary could, in turn, protect the established identities of teachers by also sustaining the social practices in which these particular forms of professional identity were negotiated.

Second, once the boundary was destabilised as a result of saying the unsayable in the DWR sessions – for example, by invoking the image of the bursting school – opportunities for re-positioning themselves in relation to the social practices of the school became a possibility for the teachers. We saw this happen in two ways in particular. One was the use of 'second stories' (Ryave 1978) where teachers could refer to another time or place to give an account of a practice that worked well but did not conform with what the school was trying to sustain. Here we see one of the teachers at Castletown recalling how she worked when employed in another city:

> I mean something that just . . . sorry, something that just came into my head is many years ago I worked in [name of city] for the child guidance service. And the way they worked it there was that the child guidance service – as it was then, not the psychology service . . . there were offices in each area. I think there were eight offices altogether. And each office then had its own schools and the schools referred to child guidance. In that team, I was a teacher in the team, we had weekly meetings where all the children that were referred by those schools were discussed with the paperwork obviously. That team consisted of psychiatrist, ed psych, social worker, teacher and I can see a couple of others but I'm not sure what agencies they were. So then the child is discussed, the presenting problem is discussed and it was decided at that weekly meeting which agency was actually going to be dealing with them, at that time, was going to initially. And then obviously the presented one would come back if it was felt, you know, there need to be more. I actually look back that on that system – it doesn't exist any longer in [the city] – but I looked on that system as being a very good one at the time.

This alternative could be discussed without directly criticising the current situation in the Castletown school, yet it also opened up the opportunity to consider other models of practice. The second story indicated that the teacher was beginning to distance herself from the defence of existing practices that marked the school's responses to suggestions that they worked more flexibly and responsively with other agencies.

The other phenomenon we observed in the boundary spaces created by the DWR sessions we characterised as 'balancing on the boundaries'. Participants could find themselves caught up in the discursive flows of the sessions. These flows might appear to be producing agreement; for example, that new forms of assessment should drive inter-professional work. We observed that some participants would then recognise that to go along with the flow of the discussion would, in this example, distance them from the accounting practices of their home organisations and lead them towards another, but different, set of socially sustained practices.

In other words, the DWR discussions would reveal new social practices or 'figured worlds' (Holland *et al.* 1998) for practitioners. These new practices would offer new variations of professional identity. For example, they might expect practitioners to consider a child's mental health alongside their curriculum performance. As these new opportunities for action were revealed, there would be some hesitation among some of the participants before they either explored those alternatives more fully, or retreated to the security of the established practices of the home organisation. In the following extract we see an example of balancing on the boundaries where one of the teachers who was most resistant to inter-professional work began to recognise that the local CAF was going to be put in place and began to toy with engaging with it, but then retreated:

> As for triggering a CAF. . . I don't think schools are important enough, does that sound bad? But I don't. Would all the other services take it seriously?

Box 5.2 Practitioners need support

These examples of second stories and boundary balancing have been given in some detail because our evidence suggests that working outside the safety of established institutional practices is exceedingly difficult for individual practitioners. That evidence leads us to suggest that efforts need to be made to shift institutional practices to enable inter-professional collaboration. It cannot be taken forward by the heroic work of strong individuals who are robust enough to sustain professional identities outside organisations.

The importance of how resources are used

We have already begun to discuss how a tool such as a CAF can help to mediate the professional knowledge that can be brought to bear on a child's trajectory. However, simply inserting a new tool such as an assessment framework into a system such as a school or an MPT does not guarantee that it will be used in the challenging and progressive way its designers had perhaps intended.

Box 5.3 The intertwining of ideas and artefacts

A Vygotskian approach to learning requires us to look at the use of tools as the intertwining of material artefacts such as assessment tools with the conceptual understandings that shape how the artefact is used. One consequence of looking for this intertwining is that it alerts us to what happens if a new tool is inserted into a system but the accompanying ideas are not introduced. For example, an assessment system can be used in so many ways: to filter, to reward, to ensure that procedures are followed and so on.

In Chapter 4 we also made much of how important professional values are for sustaining collaborations and in our discussion of boundaries earlier in the present chapter we have discussed how values can give shape to boundaries. Here we examine how values and professional knowledge interact with the use of the material artefacts such as lists of local experts, CAF, or mobile phones to take forward responsive multi-agency work.

As we indicated in Chapter 4, Engeström (2007b) provides a framework that helps us to distinguish between the different ways that everyday tools such as assessment proforma are used in professional practice. His starting point is the basic Vygotskian premise that how tools are used reveal how users are engaging with their worlds. While this is interesting when trying to gauge how a child is understanding number by observing what she can do with a numberline, it is equally fascinating when assessing how a practitioner is interpreting and engaging with a problem of practice.

In Figure 5.2 we can see that Engeström has distinguished between six types of tool use: 'what', 'who and when', 'where', 'how', 'why' and

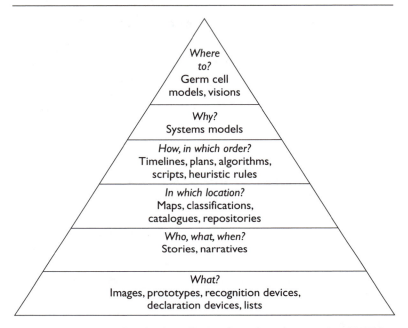

Figure 5.2 Epistemic levels of mediational artefacts (Engeström 2007b)

'where to'. For example, an assessment proforma may be used simply to identify a child's weaknesses as a 'what' tool. Or it may be used to map out who might next work with the child and when. A more complex use of the tool may involve some sharing of how and why people might work with a child and her family. The idea of a 'where to' use of a tool is particularly appropriate for thinking about co-configuration work around a child's trajectory from vulnerability to social exclusion.

Figure 5.2 gives Engeström's examples of the tools that might exemplify the different kinds of use, but it is important to remember that often the same tool can be used in different ways. Much will depend on how the problem is being interpreted and how the expectations and social practices of an organisation shape how a tool might be used. For example, each kind of use of a CAF can include the child and the carer, but the 'why' and 'where to' uses make it more likely that the assessment becomes the basis of the kind of discussion between child, carer and practitioner that would characterise co-configured working on a child's trajectory. Importantly, 'why' and 'where to' uses are driven by professional values and are open to being informed by the knowledge that everyone brings to the negotiations.

The term 'germ cell' (Figure 5.2) is a technical one within Vygotskian theory and refers to the key concepts in an area of knowledge, their relationships with each other and any tensions in those relationships. The germ cell is therefore always open to change as it is taken into use in the world. The idea of the germ cell, and the possibility that it might change, returns us to the challenges and importance of co-configuration work for professional learning.

When practitioners are working outside their professional shelters, existing professional knowledge comes into contact with the knowledge of other professionals and the experiences of clients, and will itself be reformulated. In other words, the professional knowledge germ cell, or the key concepts and their inter-relation, will be open to change and professionals will find themselves seeing something differently, in other words, learning something new.

The idea that professional knowledge can be pinned down and controlled by 'what' tools, such as the within-school referral form we have discussed, is seriously challenged by the potential for learning offered in co-configuration work. Here we see a comment from an education professional in Castletown who was responding to the idea of a CAF as a 'where to' tool in a DWR session and pointing out how the 'where to' use highlights its potential for preventing social exclusion rather than simply being a vehicle for dealing with crises.

> CAF seems to be . . . I mean potentially it's going to be a very powerful tool I think, and I like the way you talk about the sort of making it a bit more creative CAF, version number 20 or whatever. I think that . . . everyone who is working with young people should know what CAF is all about, should have an understanding of it. . . . And going further than that I think it would be really useful later on for parents to have the opportunity to find out about CAF, and not only at the point of crisis or whatever but actually to have understanding within the community there's such a thing as CAF.

The inter-relatedness of professional and organisational learning

We shall look at the challenges of co-configured inter-professional work for organisations in Chapter 6 and will tease out the implications for organisations in Chapter 8. Here we explain how Engeström's early development of activity theory inextricably connects individual and organisational learning through his idea of 'expansive learning' (see Appendix A).

Box 5.4 Expansive learning

Engeström's development of different kinds of tool use can be traced back to the influence of Bateson, the anthropologist, on his thinking (Engeström 1987, 2001). Bateson (1972) distinguished between three levels of learning. Learning I is sometimes described as conditioning and can be seen, for example, in rote learning. In Learning II people recognise and work with the rules and patterns of behaviour that comprise the context. Learning II can reveal unforeseen complexities that can in turn lead to Learning III where people start to question the context and to think about alternatives. Engeström sees Learning III to be likely to be a collective endeavour and compatible with what he terms 'expansive learning'. He describes expansive learning in the following way:

> The object of expansive learning activity is the entire activity system in which the learners are engaged. Expansive learning activity produces culturally new patterns of activity. Expansive learning at work produces new forms of work activity.
>
> (Engeström 2001: 139)

The idea of expansive learning can quite easily illustrated in an MPT such as that in Seaside where people were working in potentially shared activities within a single system or team. There the dynamic interactions between changes in tools, such as using mobile phones to contact each other, and in rules and the division of labour, such as ignoring traditional hierarchies of responsibility, occurred alongside an expansion of the object of activity, seeing children's trajectories as increasingly complex, and the development of their work practices. There we could see how individual learning was intertwined with changes in the work activity and we could trace how professional learning was mediated by increasingly implicit, yet fresh, assumptions about how resources might be used and how people interact. Wertsch's idea of implicit mediation (Wertsch 2007) was given substance in Seaside practices.

In Castletown the situation was more complex and therefore much more difficult for the participants. There we witnessed the beginnings of a system of distributed expertise stretching across a locality. Participants could potentially inhabit both the emergent inter-professional system outside their institutional boundaries and their well-established systems of their home organisations. However, the activity of preventing social exclusion was central to the emergent system, but not to the home organisation of the teachers. While we could begin to see that the emergent system might develop as an activity system, we were aware that much of the resistance to more fluid forms of inter-professional work arose because the home organisation that was the school was engaged in the activity of reaching attainment targets and felt that it had little choice but to focus on that.

Conclusion

In this chapter we have unpacked what we have seen as the main features of professional learning in the emergent practices we were studying. In particular, we have highlighted the importance of institutional genre, how boundary work offers both opportunities and challenges, and the intertwining of material and conceptual tool use. Finally, in keeping with our CHAT framework, we returned to the need to see how work systems shape possibilities for individual learning as well as for organisational change.

Chapter 6

What have been the challenges?

Introduction

In this chapter we examine the disruptive aspects of learning. In the Learning in and for Interagency Working (LIW) study we saw organisations resisting the learning that practitioners brought to them from interactions with other professionals, and we also worked in sites where their main purpose was to develop a new systems that could respond to the demands inter-professional work. We met practitioners who were initially reluctant to recognise the strengths and constraints of other professionals, and those who were eager to embrace the new insights that other ways of seeing the same child brought. We saw practitioners who, as we described in Chapter 5, 'balanced on the boundaries' in their conversations with other professions, and heard of others who were accused of 'going native' when they took ideas from these conversations back to their home organisations. The difficulties associated with professional learning are rarely simply cognitive, a result of a problem being poorly understood. They are more often than not contextual and personal.

We will start by examining the challenges faced by organisations when practitioners learn, in order to understand the complexities of organisational change. We shall then look at how learning through inter-professional collaborations and organisational responses to that learning are experienced by practitioners.

Organisations and change: an activity theory approach

So many studies of how people learn in the workplace focus on how people learn to adapt, adjust their values and become skilled at navigating current practices. Very few of these studies link workplace learning with organisational learning, by unpacking how organisations, or parts of organisations, respond to the learning of practitioners as well as enabling it. Engeström's work is so influential because it tries to do just that.

It was impossible to ignore what was happening in the work systems inhabited by the practitioners in the LIW study. The 2004 Children Act (DfES 2004), and the guidance that had led to it, were clear that that children's services were to refocus so that prevention became a higher priority (Dartington Social Research Unit 2004) and that this refocusing would necessarily involve the reconfiguring of services we outlined in Chapter 1. Therefore, while the professionals in the study were learning as they tried new ways of working, the systems in which they worked were also expected to change.

Changes within professional activity systems

As we explained in the first two chapters, the LIW study was framed by activity theory, which focuses mainly on how systems change. For example, Engeström's idea of expansive learning (Engeström 1987, 2001) takes a starting point that individual and organisational learning are intertwined and focuses on the learning that occurs at the level of the system. It captures the dynamics that arise when people who are engaged in an activity begin to recognise new complexities in the tasks they are working on, that is, they expand the object of their activity. These dynamics may be seen in how they begin to use familiar resources in fresh ways, develop new ideas as they use those resources, question the practices that get in the way of their work and begin to work with different people or the same people in new ways. Changes in relationships between, for example, resources, ideas, rules and how the work is shared out, are signs of expansive learning at the level of the activity system.

Box 6.1 Engeström's version of the zone of proximal development

Although these kinds of changes commonly occur in organisations, some organisations are better than others at accommodating the shifts: by encouraging an expansion of the object of activity and by responding to the outcome of that expansion. To describe this

---

continued

difference, Engeström takes Vygotsky's idea of the 'zone of proximal development' (ZPD), which was developed as a way of assessing a child's capability to learn, and uses it in relation to activity systems (Engeström 1987) in order to indicate the capacity of a system to learn and change. This version of the ZPD is a way of distinguishing between systems that are adept at learning and those that are less responsive: activity systems that responsively and dynamically evolve are seen to have an almost open-ended ZPD.

However, systems do not simply evolve: changes are stimulated by imbalances in the system and these lead to dynamic shifts of the kinds just outlined. Sometimes these shifts are barely discernable, as they arise from small tensions that occur. For example, lack of clarity over whether a form tutor or a head of year in a school makes contact with a child's parent may indicate a tension that may be resolved by a brief conversation, or it may be the first sign of a contradiction in a system where a new emphasis on attainment, which is the responsibility of the heads of year, is beginning to override the school's historically established emphasis on informal relations with children's families through form tutors.

According to Engeström's activity theory framework, changes in systems occur as a result of participants recognising and working with the contradictions in them. We shall look at his fine distinctions between different types of contradiction later in this chapter, but at this point just illustrate what we mean by contradiction with one of the most famous examples – from Leont'ev (1981). Leont'ev talked of contradictions in terms of a doctor in provincial Russia who sets up a practice to reduce sickness; however, if his work is to be sustained he needs the number of sick to increase.

Contradictions are to be found everywhere as few systems are so completely bounded that new ideas, resources or expectations are prevented from entering. When people first meet a contradiction – such as a new expectation that they will collaborate in parallel with other professionals to support a particular child, but at the same time are bound by rules in their workplace that are based on onward referral without continuous collaboration – they will feel frustrated with either the expectation or the rules.

If they are convinced, because of professional values, that parallel inter-professional collaboration is best for the child, they are likely to try to work on the rules in order to change them. In Chapter 4 we discussed rule-bending as something that practitioners said they had learnt to do to take forward inter-professional work. They also learnt to create new resources which, for example, helped to sustain inter-professional collaboration. These examples of creative responses are important because they help us to see that changes made by individual or small numbers of practitioners can shift systems. Indeed, from our perspective, if people do not try to adapt their work systems, then development in their systems will be limited.

Fullan's work on leadership from an organisational development viewpoint (Fullan 2001) has some echoes of Engeström's analyses. Fullan also recognises the dangers of constant equilibrium in organisational systems, the importance of 'disturbances' for their development and the centrality of moral purpose to organisational change. His starting points for this analysis, however, are the challenges these issues bring for leadership. He advises leaders to enable differences to surface, to guide people through them and to work through the ambiguities of complex problems. We would not disagree with Fullan's analyses of leadership, which takes the complexities of organisational cultures seriously. However, our starting point was the workplace learning of practitioners as they undertook new forms of work and how that might impact upon systems to ensure that learning continues. In our analysis we were interested in how the individual agency of practitioners can contribute to the shaping of systems and how systems might respond.

Il'enkov, a Marxist philosopher who contributed a great deal to post-Vygotskian theory, made the impact of individual action on the system very clear in the following extract:

> In reality it always happens that a phenomenon which later becomes universal originally emerges as an individual, particular, specific phenomenon, as an exception from the rule. It cannot actually emerge in any other way. Otherwise history would have a rather mysterious form. Thus, any new improvement of labour, every new mode of man's action in production, before becoming generally accepted and recognised, first emerges as a certain deviation from previously accepted and codified norms. Having emerged as an individual exception from the rule in the labour of one or several men, the new form is then taken over by others, becoming in time a new universal norm. If the new norm did not originally appear in this exact manner, it would never become a

really universal form, but would exist merely in fantasy, in wishful thinking.

(Il'enkov 1982: 83–4)

Box 6.2 Working with values when facing contradictions

According to the line we have been pursuing in this chapter, recognising tensions and contradictions and working creatively to overcome them is a good thing, as these endeavours will help to take systems forward so that they can deal with new demands, work more effectively and make the most of new resources. But this is not a question of instrumental modernity or progress for its own sake. Rather, the line also highlights the importance of values-led responsible professional action within organisations that may not yet have adjusted to new demands.

This situation was certainly the case for many children's services and schools at the time of the study. Practitioners working on the ground were constantly meeting these contradictions and developing professional responses as their practices raced ahead of the inevitably slower institutional responses of their work systems.

Changes at the boundaries of professional systems

We were not only looking at how the discomfort of contradictions can drive forward separate organisations such as schools or social work departments. As we indicated in Chapter 5, inter-professional work brought people together at the boundaries of their organisations or in new spaces outside the safety nets of the established practices of their workplaces. There, in their work with other professionals, they had to deal with different interpretations of children's trajectories, various ways of responding and incompatible priorities. In the Developmental Work Research (DWR) sessions, outlined in Chapter 1 and in Appendix A, practitioners wrestled slowly and carefully with these differences, often moving on to create new understandings that took forward their practices. Much as we would like to suggest that DWR should be the method of choice for exploring differences across professional boundaries, we know that is unlikely to happen.

Nonetheless, there are some principles that can be borrowed from DWR that will help.

In the National Evaluation of the Children's Fund (NECF) (Edwards *et al.* 2006) we looked at the processes at work in the local Partnership Boards that were made up of different services and charged with implementing the work of the Fund. We found that those Boards that took time in meetings to discuss argue and eventually reach tentative agreement over the purposes of the Fund were more likely to commission services that were responding to the needs of local children. A few Boards debated and wrangled over meanings from the outset. Others did it only when a government minister stepped in to divert 25 per cent of the Fund to just one issue, rather than allowing local Boards to set their own priorities. The outrage that his move instigated across many of the Boards meant that the purposes of the Fund became a topic for debate, requiring people to articulate their interpretations and values in relation to services for preventing the social exclusion of children. These debates were frequently mentioned as turning points in clarifying the direction of the Fund's activities.

The questioning discussions in what we termed 'developing' Boards in NECF shared many features with DWR. They focused on the object of activity, that is, what 'the prevention of social exclusion' actually was and, through taking seriously and questioning all the interpretations offered at the meetings, they expanded their understandings of it. These Boards were then in a strong position to set up commissioning procedures to provide the kinds of services that reflected these newly expanded understandings of prevention.

Making visible current understandings and practices, holding them open to scrutiny and keeping in mind long-term, relatively open, values-led goals such as the wellbeing of children, allowed understandings of prevention to be enriched by the different approaches to be found in the debates. On the other hand, those 'stable' Boards that saw themselves simply as groups of people who distributed the money without debating the purposes of the initiative, unsurprisingly, commissioned services that had a less direct match with the preventative intentions of the Children's Fund. Differences in understanding and priority can therefore be important and people need time to examine and discuss them; assuming consensus and rushing to action can, we suggest, be detrimental in the long term.

How discussions take forward organisational change

So far in this chapter we have been offering discussion and debate as a relatively unproblematic tool for surfacing differences and moving forward. By highlighting conversations we are echoing the discussion of institutional genres in Chapter 5 and the development of 'scripts' for inter-professional communication outlined in Chapter 2.

Box 6.3 Engeström's categories of collaboration

In Chapter 2, drawing on Engeström *et al.* (1997) we distinguished between:

- *Co-ordination*   where there is an agreed script or set of rules of working that co-ordinates the behaviour of each practitioner. Practitioners do not question or contribute to the script or develop new rules as a result of their work on their assigned tasks.
- *Co-operation*   where practitioners, instead of each focusing on carrying out their assigned roles, focus on a shared problem and try to find mutually acceptable ways to interpret and solve it. They do this without questioning or developing explicitly new ways of understanding the new script.
- *Communication*   where practitioners co-operate, but also question the rules that shape how they work on the problems of practice with others and so develop new scripts and understand their implications.

'Communication' can be quite challenging for organisations as it can lead to a disruption of organisational practices from within the organisation. In addition, as the new scripts associated with inter-professional collaboration for the prevention of social exclusion can arise through making explicit professional values, the questions can quite fundamentally challenge organisational precepts. The questioning associated with 'communication' is therefore quite ambitious and, if it is to be useful, needs to be incorporated into the practices of organisations.

In an analysis of how inter-organisational collaboration can stimulate organisational change Hardy *et al.* (2005) have gone some way to seeing how that integration can occur. They examined the role of conversations in constructing what they call a 'collective identity' among collaborators, through conversations that maintained the tensions necessary to ensure that competing views were played into discussions. The conversations led to shared understandings that could be conversationally integrated into the practices of the home organisation. We quote from the study at some length to do justice to their analysis:

> Our model has important practical implications for organisational actors attempting to develop effective collaborations. Participants first need to produce a collective identity through the establishment of both generalised and particularised membership ties. Practically speaking, the opening sequences of collaboration should involve conversations that connect the issue to potential participants and articulate specific connections between them. Generalised membership ties rely on the establishment and legitimation of a vocabulary from which participants can draw to explain their own and others' participation to each other and to their home organisations; particularised ties require discursive resources that can be used to describe and explain the relationships among participants.
>
> Once a collective identity is discursively produced collaborators need to shift the conversations toward the ongoing production of common and private constructions. Our analysis suggests that this can be facilitated by establishing formal procedures in the collaboration that focus on repeatedly articulating the concerns of managers in the home organisation; by building structures into the home organisations, such as teams, whose focus is integrating the learning occurring in the collaboration; by rotating membership in terms of who represents the home organisation and, where appropriate, by rotating or adding to the stakeholders represented in the collaboration; and by including in the collaboration process some formal joint analysis of the differences among participants' private constructions and between common and private constructions.
>
> (Hardy *et al.* 2005: 73–4)

Hardy *et al.* do not underestimate the work involved, particularly in ensuring that co-operative ways of dealing with conflict and productive forms of assertive talk are maintained. They therefore caution against taking the arguments they present as a set of expectations for organisational development, describing the collaborations they have outlined as ambitious and pointing out that 'such an investment is only worthwhile when the stakes are high' (ibid: 74). Arguably, the stakes for the professionals with whom we were working were high and much of benefit is to be learnt through creating structures and processes that aim at revealing and working with and on differences.

Working with contradictions to develop systems

The three main English case studies – Castletown, Seaside and Wildside – described in Chapter 3 were each different. We characterised the school in Castletown as a tightly bounded system and we focused on work at the boundary between the school and the system of distributed expertise that was beginning to become available outside the school. There we tried to capture struggles on the boundaries between organisations as they moved at different paces to make sense of the demands of the Children Act. The Multi-Professional Team (MPT) in Seaside was described as a new system that was put in place as a result of a dramatic shift in local authority structures and could be analysed as an emergent organisation in its own right. The Children in Public Care (CiPC) team in Wildside was an established team that was already well linked with local agencies, but was adjusting its work in the context of the 2004 Children Act. It could be seen as a discrete activity system in its work with looked after children, while recognising that members also had other organisational affiliations. We shall now examine some of the challenges that were presented as systemic contradictions in these sites in order to illustrate the kinds of contradictions we found and to examine any breakthroughs that arose to take the system forward.

In the analyses of processes in the cases, we drew on Engeström's (1987) distinctions between four types of contradiction.

Box 6.4 The four types of contradiction in activity theory

- *Primary contradictions* These are contradictions within elements in a system. The Russian doctor's conflict over the object of his activity mentioned earlier is one example, but there may be conflicts within rules, the use of resources and so on. For example, an assessment system may be a way of working flexibly with a family, but it may also have purposes associated with quality assurance or service agreement for the practitioner.

- *Secondary contradictions* These occur when a new element enters a system and leads to contradictions between the elements that pre-dated it. For example, the idea of 'prevention' entered children's services in the first few years of this century, requiring services to rethink how work was shared out, their service priorities and so on.
- *Tertiary contradictions* These arise when a system finds itself having to deal with a new and challenging object of activity that has been developed elsewhere. Tertiary contradictions are particularly pertinent to the development of services where ideas about how to disrupt children's trajectories towards social exclusion have been developed through interagency collaborations and are brought back to the home institution in the expectation that it will be able to adapt to accommodate them.
- *Quaternary contradictions* These represent contradictions between systems. They are also particularly relevant to the development of inter-professional work. For example, a children and families service may find it difficult to give priority to preventative work, while a school may expect the service to attend its multi-agency meetings and to engage with it in its preventative practices.

We found examples of each type of contradiction in the LIW cases. They were revealed in talk about work in the DWR sessions or in data gathered by practitioners with the researchers, which they brought to sessions in the form of short case narratives for discussion. We will use Engeström's distinctions as they help us to examine common elements in each example.

Primary contradictions

Recognising and working with conflicting understandings within systems of, for example, the rules and purposes of referral or the purposes of assessment were inevitable aspects of building what Hardy *et al.* (2005) have described as a collective identity through developing a shared language and understanding that allows practitioners to talk with each other.

Primary contradictions tended to be evident in talk while practitioners were discussing current practices in order to justify them. In Castletown, the school's referral system was presented as well-established and efficient, at the same time it was evident that teachers regularly took short cuts in the system in order to prevent the escalation of events for children. They also arose when practitioners were trying to make sense for themselves. For example, a practitioner in Seaside had to be persuaded by other participants that, despite her intentions, her work focused mainly on ensuring school attendance rather than more responsive engagement with families.

It seemed that the analysis of primary contradictions such as these were a very important stage in questioning practices and opening up discussions that then allowed participants to move on to think about contradictions between elements in the systems.

Secondary contradictions

Welfare services and schools are accustomed to receiving ideas or resources from government that can lead to contradictions between, for example, the rules and divisions of labour that pre-dated them. One of the challenges of policy implementation is that these ideas and resources can enter systems and disappear. They become adapted to existing practices and, instead of being tools for changing practices, they become rules to comply with, with minimal disruption to what is happening. The idea of a secondary contradiction is helpful because it requires us to look at the contradictions between existing aspects of a system that arise when a new element is introduced and to see how a system might respond to an idea by working on the contradiction rather than by ignoring it.

In Wildside, for example, a newly agreed focus on parallel and flexible support for children, coming from discussions of prevention, gave rise to concerns about changes in management style. Discussion of the assessment systems needed for this more flexible way of working revealed a contradiction between (i) the 'common-sense' style or implicit rules that pre-dated the increased emphasis on prevention and (ii) a new demand for a more prescriptive approach to how documentation was dealt with.

Secondary contradictions do require some resolution if the system is to respond and develop. In the case of Wildside, the contradiction between management styles and expectations was discussed at length in DWR sessions to reveal underlying differences between the need to tick boxes and the need to focus on children's long-term wellbeing. Eventually guidelines were developed to ensure that these concerns were addressed.

Tertiary contradictions

These are more challenging to organisations than other kinds of contradiction because they arise as a result of an attempt to re-orient or give a new purpose to their work that is brought into the system from outside. In the case studies, the new object of activity was 'the whole child' as she or he was helped to reshape their developmental trajectory away from potential social exclusion towards inclusion.

The LIW study did not produce any simple examples of practitioners who worked with other professionals outside the social practices of their home organisations and brought back new ideas that they then tried to integrate into the old system. This could have happened in the Castletown school, but the school was so resistant to recognising and working on contradictions that the fresh ideas were dismissed at every opportunity. Instead the frustrations and contradictions remained at the boundaries between the school and the other services, and were consequently experienced as deeply personal and uncomfortable by the school-based professionals who recognised them.

In Seaside, the local authority had pre-empted any slow development of organisations in response to the new object of activity by completely disrupting existing systems and practices and instead setting up MPTs. Each team was quite tightly boundaried, as members struggled to understand each other and work on their team's complex objects of activity. Although the new object of activity was not negotiated into these systems, practitioners had little choice but to create it themselves as work on the complexity of children's trajectories was their *raison d'être*. The refining of the object of activity involved a parallel refining of other elements in the system. The Wildside CiPC team had not experienced an equivalent disruption, and was instead able to accommodate the new focus on the whole child, and deal with the systemic contradictions that arose.

In both Seaside and Wildside there was therefore evidence of practitioners recognising that there had been quite profound changes in the object of activity as a result of government demands, and their systems needed to respond. They responded in several ways. For example, they created new tools that enabled them to work with the most appropriate people for each task. In Seaside they discussed ways of approaching each other and identifying the expertise needed for each case, while in Wildside they developed criteria for attendance at team meetings because they found that too many people were attending and work was not moving forward.

The change in the object of activity arising from changes in external expectations of how practitioners should work led to shifts in the division of labour and the rules that underpinned working together. These, in turn, stimulated the changes in thinking and practices that were outlined in Chapter 4 and point to the importance of engaging practitioners with the purposes of work if practices are to develop.

Quaternary contradictions

Contradictions between the aims and purposes of different professional organisations were evident everywhere. They were glaringly obvious in the frequent discussions in Castletown about the different and conflicting goals of schools and social services advanced by some of the teachers. They were to be found in the traces of professional tribalism that produced the initial wariness of social workers about working with educational professionals in Seaside. They were not absent from Wildside, but were dealt with by the creation of the electronic assessment framework that ensured different goals were made visible and seen as relevant for the children.

The implications of contradictions for organisational development

These contradictions have been described in some detail because they offer a framework for organisational analysis and may be helpful in recognising that organisations can be open to change and self-regulating. They also suggest that resistance to recognising and dealing with contradictions is likely to prevent organisational development.

Contradictions of the kind outlined need to be recognised, interpreted and worked on if they are to be useful for shaping organisational development. Here trust and power are relevant. In Stage 3 of the LIW study we experimented with DWR sessions to see whether sessions that involved local strategists, senior managers and front-line workers were effective in revealing what was going on as systems responded to the 2004 Children Act. We compared these events with the sessions that involved only strategists or only front-line workers. Our conclusion was, like that of Engeström *et al.* (2003a), that relationships of power in the mixed status sessions can impede the development of ideas within sessions if the participants are not used to working together to solve problems.

However, where there is trust, power distinctions are less important. Differences in status between participants within the Seaside and Wildside teams were recognised and ultimately informed the development of ideas. In brief, contradictions cannot be surfaced without trust, evidence and a willingness to see them as an important element in the development of responsively managed organisations. When these three elements are in place, arguably all that is needed is the time to discuss the evidence of contradictions and consider their implications for the organisation and its values-led development.

The challenge to organisations of co-configuration work with clients

In Chapter 1 we introduced the idea of co-configuration and compared it with mass-customisation. The distinction between these two ways of organising work and relating to those who use services highlights an important challenge for welfare services. In summary, mass-customisation can describe the kinds of carefully targeted services that have been so much a feature of local interventions aimed at improving conditions for discrete groups in specific neighbourhoods. These targeted services can, of course, become co-configured over time by being responsive to local need. This ongoing reshaping happens as practitioners adjust their provision on the basis of feedback, and work hard at ensuring that the service offered best fits what is wanted. These adjustments, although they are a form of responsive co-configuration, can be characterised as service-led and have long-been recognised as good sensitive practice.

An alternative and more institutionally challenging form of co-configuration can be seen as client-led work. In this type of co-configuration the individual trajectories of vulnerable children are negotiated and constantly configured with parents, the child and the relevant practitioners (Edwards and Apostolov 2007). This co-configuring of individual trajectories, rather than of service provision, reflects some of the intentions of recent work on the 'team around the child' in England (Siraj-Blatchford *et al.* 2007), where teams of professionals work together to set up care plans for children. In some

English local authorities there is an emphasis on involving parents quite centrally in these negotiations. Where the problem being worked on is vulnerability to social exclusion, the gradual independence of the family and its networks can be part of the planning that occurs, so that the child's trajectory towards inclusion is helped by a strengthening of the family and its support networks.

This idea of a trajectory that helps people move away from dependence on the caring professions echoes the contradiction experienced by Leont'ev's Russian doctor whose livelihood depended on sickness. Working with service-users to help them become independent of the service does not always mesh with organisational targets. However, perhaps the biggest challenge for organisations is the flexibility that client-led co-configuration demands of workers within organisations. For example, if social service systems are to contribute to flexible client-led inter-professional negotiations, they need to develop ways of prioritising cases that take into account how other services are identifying their priorities and are working to strengthen families.

In the LIW study, as we indicated in Chapters 4 and 5, we found considerable reluctance across all sites to engage with parents or carers as partners in co-configuring children's trajectories. In Chapter 4 we suggested that perhaps the professionals needed time to discover how they might work together before tackling new and flexible partnerships with parents. However, the challenges involved in negotiating expertise with clients, rather than asserting it through an organisationally sustained position as professional expert, may be also part of the problem. This is an organisational problem. Although negotiating expertise may seem to be a personal challenge for individual practitioners, their employing organisations need to be in a position to support them as they negotiate and respond to the outcomes of the negotiations.

Engeström (2005) has started to tackle how organisations develop a propensity for flexible work outside their established boundaries. He recognises the difficulties of what he calls 'distributed work' and sees 'the shape and implications of spatio-temporally distributed work and expertise' as 'fragile and open, literally under construction' (ibid: 324). He offers two new concepts that are intended to reflect purposeful work under these conditions. He describes these concepts as 'immature' and presents them in order to open up the field for further theoretical work.

Both concepts operate at the level of the collective, which may be, for example, an organisation or a work unit. First is the idea of 'collaborative intentionality capital' as 'an emerging form of organisational assets', which enables an organisation to encourage collaboration on complex tasks beyond organisational boundaries. The second tentative concept, 'object-oriented interagency', suggests a slightly more interactional focus. Engeström sees object-oriented interagency as a form of 'connecting and reciprocating' while 'circling around a complex object' and 'dwelling in' the object, that is, maintaining a long-term relationship with it (ibid: 333) and being sensitive to changes in it. Although these concepts are directed at a general management readership, they are particularly relevant to the work of organisations where practitioners need to be alert to the changing needs of children as they develop, meet fresh problems or begin to engage with the opportunities available to them.

Central to both of Engeström's concepts is the idea that activities can be taken forward by what he calls 'future-oriented' envisioning, which give direction to the smaller scale steps that are taken to develop the activity. These ideas resonate with LIW findings that have highlighted how an open-ended concept such as a child's wellbeing, combined with an articulation of professional values, can give shape to the smaller steps that comprise inter-professional collaboration in the activity of supporting the child.

But we can see from Engeström's tentativeness about these two concepts that we are some way from understanding what is involved for organisations in a shift towards more flexible and negotiated forms of work. Also, we should not underestimate what may be lost if this kind of work develops. The relatively rigid bureaucratic structures of most statutory sector welfare organisations have had an important role to play in sustaining the professional identities of the practitioners who work in them and undertake often risky work with clients.

It is little wonder, therefore, that much of the co-configuration that has occurred so far in welfare work has been service led, involving slight adjustments to aspects of service delivery. Organisations and practitioners are in relationships that are mutually sustaining. Disrupting that inter-dependency can be risky for both parties. Sennett gives some hint of the risks involved:

> The rigid large scale bureaucracies which developed at the end of the nineteenth century provided an institutional architecture in which dependence became honourable, to which the learner could become loyal. Static institutions provide, unfortunately, a framework of daily trust, a reality which has to be acknowledged in

thinking about efforts in our own time to take these institutions apart.

(Sennett 1999: 19)

Client-led co-configuration can remove practitioners from the safety of the stable practices of their organisations. It can also present their organisations with challenges to their practices when the implications of negotiations with clients need to be addressed.

Practitioners and change: the individuals in activities

Earlier in this chapter we compared the LIW focus on the implications of practitioners' learning for organisations with Fullan's (2001) focus on leadership and organisational change. We particularly pointed to how individual practitioners can nudge work systems towards change by seeing things differently and by then trying to act differently. We also said that the LIW study identified (i) the occasional impact of values-led individual professional actions within organisations that had not adjusted to new inter-professional activities and (ii) that practitioners were constantly meeting contradictions, as their practices raced ahead of the inevitably slower institutional responses of their work systems. We now turn to how these contradictions were experienced by individual practitioners.

They were experienced slightly differently in the three case study sites because each site reflected a rather different organisational response to the 2004 Children Act. The most dramatic response was creating the Seaside Multi-Professional Team. This had involved re-organising the division of labour and the rules of working to produce a multi-professional work unit. In Seaside, practitioners found themselves placed quite abruptly in a new social space without established practices. Indeed, it was a place where traces of old practices, such as levels at which decisions about children could be made, were meeting new ideas about practice that called for quick responses to children's needs, and it took time for the new practices to settle and for practitioners to feel at home in them. Removed from what Sennett (1999: 19) called their familiar 'institutional architecture', practitioners in Seaside found themselves having to leave their old ways of being and navigate practices at the same time as the practices were being developed.

The challenges they faced were considerable, involving them in recognising the purposes and rules in the new inter-professional activities, and in finding their own position within them. From the beginning of our time in Seaside, practitioners worked hard at understanding what the new team would mean for them as professionals. There were huge concerns about becoming 'generalist' multi-professional workers and losing touch with their 'home' teams. These worries were not resolved by the end of the year, leaving the practices and Sennett's idea of 'loyalty' to the unit potentially unstable.

Interestingly, as the Seaside MPT began to gel as a working unit, through a sharing of professional values and the development of a common sense of purpose, it began to direct its energies at labelling the boundaries around it. These were the boundaries between the team and the schools with which it worked and particularly the boundary between the team and the local strategists at the level above them in the local authority hierarchy. Team members argued that the strategists seemed to be deaf to what they were trying to tell them about how inter-professional work might be sustained. It seemed at times as if the team managed to maintain a collective identity through the tried and tested process of identifying 'outgroups' against which a common sense of purpose could be generated.

Wildside offered a quite different set of experiences for practitioners. There had been no disruption of the division of labour. Instead, an existing team was expected to work in slightly different ways while retaining an established focus on 'Looked After Children'. A well-established local authority, Wildside was also relatively small, with good systems of communication and high levels of trust among practitioners who also knew each other. Practitioners' subject positions did not need to be asserted and worked out in new practices; links with home organisations were assured as the team's work was just one part of each member's workload; and although practices shifted as result of new assessment tools there was no need to negotiate unknown terrain in the ways that the Seaside practitioners had done.

However, the more explicit focus on inter-professional work demanded by the 2004 Act was helped by acknowledging what had hitherto not been extensively discussed in the Wildside team. Topics included misunderstandings that arose when home organisations and their management systems operated as silos preventing collaboration, implicit power differentials as a result of differences in professional status, and lack of sympathy for the priorities of other professionals. Each of these issues got in the way of responsive practice and each was brought out into the open in the DWR sessions. But there was no strong sense of uncomfortable struggle or a destabilising of professional identity in Wildside. Rather, this case study offered an example of a responsive system of distributed expertise where professionals were able to work fluidly with each other and with children.

In Castletown the efforts of several of the school staff were focused on avoiding disruption to the division of labour in the school and any identity struggles that might ensue from inter-professional collaboration. At the same time, other participants in the DWR sessions – educational psychologists, social workers, education welfare officers, voluntary sector workers and health professionals – were bemused by these attempts at resisting change and constantly pushed the most outspoken teachers into questioning their purposes. There were therefore frequent struggles in the DWR sessions that were reflected in later interviews with those teachers who were not convinced by their colleagues' resistance to inter-professional work. These non-resistant teachers found themselves experiencing significant conflicts in the motives for their work: student attainment as supported by existing school practices, and student wellbeing as supported by the system of distributed expertise that was developing outside the school.

Conflicts in the motives for practice are hugely challenging. In Chapter 2 we discussed how motives are embedded in the object of activity and revealed in how we interpret the purposes of our work. It is therefore extraordinarily uncomfortable to be, for example, a teacher whose professional values direct you towards seeing the purpose of work as developing children's wellbeing, while working in a school where practices sustain pupil attainment as the purpose of the school's activity.

The three case studies exemplify different responses to inter-professional work: complete disruption of the old system and creation of a new one in Seaside; gentle adjustment to a well-functioning system in Wildside; and complete resistance to change in Castletown. These responses, in turn, presented practitioners with different challenges: the need to negotiate new subject positions within newly configured practices in Seaside; the opportunity to surface differences that might impede the development of practices in Wildside; and the discomfort of conflicting motives for some of the practitioners caught in processes of disruption that marked the DWR sessions in Castletown. However, in each of these cases the understandings and actions of individual practitioners were crucial for taking forward the systems in which they worked. As a result, they all experienced the pressures of systemic change quite personally.

Box 6.5 Practices were outpacing institutional responses

The practices and the learning that we were examining were part of a major shift in policy for work with children and families. Practitioners had little option but to move forward, however slowly, and engage with what the new policies requested of them. Standing still and hoping that the juggernaut would pass was not an option. Yet as we have seen, developments in practices were frequently outpacing institutional responses to them. Practitioners were therefore in the vanguard of unavoidable changes and bearing the brunt of the contradictions between old rules and new responses that emerged at almost every turn. At the same time they needed to sustain their senses of themselves as responsible functioning professionals. It was a stressful time.

We are therefore certain that the emotional or affective aspects of changing organisations and practices should not be down played. Vygotsky was quite clear that emotion cannot be filtered out of analyses of how we act in the world. For example, he argued that if emotion were ignored:

> thought must be viewed . . . as a meaningless epiphenomenon incapable of changing anything in the life or conduct of a person.
> (Vygotsky 1986: 10)

In the last year of his life, Vygotsky developed his ideas on the importance of emotion with a new unit of analysis, namely, *perezhivanie* (Vygotsky 1994: 339). Perezhivanie can be equated with lived or emotional experience and was, for Vygotsky, relevant to the formation of consciousness and how we engage with the world.

Perezhivanie has been largely ignored in the development of post-Vygotskian theory. However, it was refined in the writing of Vasilyuk (1991) when he introduced the notion of 'experiencing', which involves living through personal crises in creative ways in order to restore meaning to life. Vasilyuk's examples of critical situations are often quite dramatic. Nonetheless, the attention he paid to the discomfort of personally experienced contradictions and the questioning of meaning in activities provides a useful counterweight to seeing learning new practices as simply various combinations of the cognitive and the behavioural that are shaped by context.

Kozulin, in his review of the English translation of Vasilyuk's book, suggests that it combines Vygotskian ideas about learning as processes of making sense and meaning as we engage in the world, with 'Western studies of the psychodynamics of the unconscious' (1991: 14). By making that connection between thinking and the unconscious, Vasilyuk has helped us to see that coping with change is not simply a behavioural response, but also involves a relatively slow process of working through contradictions or 'crises' and gaining new forms of mental equilibrium that enable functioning.

Conclusion

The process of working through crises and the repositioning involved, in turn, leads to our interpreting the world differently. New meanings then become clear as we engage with others to work with and reflect on those interpretations. As esoteric as this analysis might sound, it has direct bearing on the need to attend to how people gradually make sense of the contradictions they face and the new meanings that arise as they work their way through them and discuss their experiences with others. In this chapter we have attempted to tease out some of the inter-related challenges that arise when individuals find themselves in the forefront of systemic change.

Part III

What are the implications?

Chapter 7

Implications of the LIW study for the learning of individual professionals

Introduction

It is now almost commonplace to discuss the times we live in as 'post-social' (Knorr Cetina 1997: 5), where individualisation is the emergent theme and where the complex structures of bureaucratic organisations are being broken down into small units with flat hierarchies and negotiable social practices. These work systems have become more open with, as Sennett puts it, 'febrile' boundaries and mixed work forms. The argument goes that these more fluid systems are also unlikely to operate as 'institutional suppports' (Sennett 1999: 21) that sustain professional identities. Instead, professionals are obliged to negotiate their expert identities with their 'publics' (Nixon *et al.* 1997: 5) whether these are other practitioners or clients.

In this account of being a professional in late capitalist society, the old certainties have been eroded – with the result that practitioners inhabit what Giddens (1991:151) has described as 'a runaway world' that cannot be predicted and controlled. Consequently, professionals need to be reconciled to managing their way forward, recognising that trust from and for others is tentative, and yet moving responsibly and optimistically towards long-term goals imbued with values that may sustain the common good.

In this chapter we discuss some of the tensions facing professionals who work in organisations that are starting to accommodate the responsive practices and negotiations that are eroding institutional certainties and calling for new ways of thinking about professional identity.

These tensions included:

- working alone in relatively high-risk responsive interactions with vulnerable children outside the safety net of long-established organisational procedures;

- recognising the expertise of others and making explicit their own expertise in mixed work systems, and needing to negotiate that expertise with children and families;
- negotiating expertise while working on shifting tasks in a 'runaway world';
- negotiating reciprocity in professional collaborations when inter-professional trust is offered tentatively;
- undertaking long-term planning with children and families in a world marked by uncertainty;
- undertaking new forms of work that demand extensions to the knowledge-base of the profession.

The main tension underpinning this list is between individual professional responsibility and the shifting work systems in which it is to be exercised. If these systems were to offer rigid support for professional action, they would inhibit the reciprocity needed to, for example, put in place timely protective factors that may prevent children's social exclusion. Yet if work systems do not offer some way of sustaining the informed purposeful, or agentic, action of professionals, practitioners may become vulnerable as they negotiate ways forward with children and families. We shall explore the implications of this core tension and shall focus particularly on what it means for being a decision-making professional in situations where expectations of professional responsibility are high, yet professional authority and knowledge are negotiable.

Being a professional in interagency work

Throughout this book we have emphasised how individual and organisational learning are intertwined. Our present focus on individual practitioners and their learning is therefore premised on recognising that the learning of individual practitioners occurs in organisations that co-evolve to enable the practices that develop. However, the new forms of professional practices we tracked were racing ahead of the systems in which they were located and were driven forward by practitioners who, despite being placed in the potentially risky situations of responsive action outside their familiar specialist work teams, were invigorated by the opportunities for professional decision-making that arose. That decision-making was always responsibly oriented towards the long-term good of children and, as we have outlined in the previous three chapters, could lead practitioners to questioning and bending procedures or rules that impeded necessary action.

> ## Box 7.1 The importance of values on inter-professional work
>
> A strong theme in Chapters 4 to 6 has been the relationship between professional values and the development of the long-term open-ended goal of children's wellbeing. This value-laden goal allowed practitioners to overcome tribal differences and to recognise how small steps that drew on specialist expertise or forms of rule-bending were ultimately contributing to achieving it. Values therefore gave cohesion to discrete practices and helped them to move in the same direction. The importance of values seemed to signal a revitalised professionalism. Practices were not being given shape entirely by paperwork and procedures, artefacts such as Common Assessment Frameworks (CAF) were still work in progress at the time of the study; instead, much depended on the informed judgements of practitioners. As a result, it seemed to us that the inter-professional work we observed was an enhanced form of professional practice that was shaped by beliefs and a sense of professional responsibility to other professionals and to clients.

However, while the practitioners could all affiliate with the idea of working towards children's wellbeing, their motives for doing so varied. That is, for each profession the reason why they were doing this work was different. They were filtering their responses through the priorities of their professional cultures. Nardi (2005) has criticised studies of collaboration because of their tendency to focus on *how* it is achieved rather than the motives that give shape to participation. She draws on Leont'ev's idea of 'object motive' that we outlined in Chapter 2 and argues that more attention needs to be given to *why* people engage in collaboration and what are their 'passionately held motives' (ibid: 37).

Nardi's argument is as follows. When trying to understand collaborative work we should temporarily separate the object of activity (in the LIW context that might be a child's trajectory) from the motives for engaging with it in order to pay distinct attention to the 'why' of action. There are several implications arising from her suggestion.

First, if object and motive are not aligned in the same way for each collaborator, attention needs to be paid to aligning the different motives of, for example, a teacher and a social worker as they work with the same child. In other words, it is not enough to focus only on *how* they work with a child, exchange information and so on, we need also to examine *why* they are working with the child.

A focus on the why of collaboration, and Nardi's suggestion that we should recognise the variety of motives that might lie behind a single object of activity in collaborative work, takes us back to the idea of perezhivanie, as a process of working through contradictions (Vasilyuk 1991) (see Chapter 6). By recognising how contradictions are experienced we can begin to see the personal nature of the ambivalences that need to be worked through by practitioners who are caught up in collaborations to improve the position of vulnerable children. These professionals are driven forward by the passionately held motives that are intrinsic to their interpretation of the object of activity, but they also need to respect the motives of others and to align their work with them. As a result, they find themselves experiencing the contradictions that are bound to arise as they, for example, hold back to let the motives and priorities of other professions dominate.

A second implication of recognising the multiplicity of motives in collaborative work relates back to the importance of having a relatively open-ended, and perhaps indeterminate, goal, such as children's well-being, that can be acceptable to everyone involved. Children's well-being was a cohering goal in many of the discussions we had with practitioners, yet it was rarely unpicked in any detail. We were not surprised by the lack of specificity. Engeström has observed that in complex work environments direct connections between workers and those objects that carry the collectively developed object motive of systems, such as working on illness in hospitals, are often hard to discern, but are nonetheless important.

When teasing out the relationship between the small action steps that practitioners take and what he terms 'future oriented' envisioning, Engeström (2005) argues for maintaining a close relationship between longer-term goals and day-to-day actions. For him this is the key to engaging agentic, or purposeful, practitioners with the long-term goals of the systems in which they work, so that their collective agency, that is, sense of purpose, moves their organisations forward:

> Human agency gains unusual powers when future-oriented activity-level envisioning and consequential action-level decision-making, come together in close interplay.
>
> (Engeström 2005: 313)

Pickering (1993, 1995) has also emphasised the importance of long-term goals for understanding how practices remain focused yet develop over time. Pickering's analysis has a more individual focus than Engeström's and he explains the relationship between immediate practices and distant purposes slightly differently, working with a more individual notion of human agency that he sees arising through practices that are connected with long-term goals:

> we should see the intentional nature of human agency as itself temporally emergent, albeit on a longer timescale than the details of practice.
>
> (Pickering 1993: 598)

Box 7.2 Having a sense of the short and long term

Both Engeström and Pickering are seeing the temporal dimension of intentional action as central to their analyses and the longer-term goals as ways of stabilising activities so that they might connect over time. Discussions with practitioners in the LIW study suggest that the distinction between immediate activities and longer-term intentions is helpful. In that way an activity, such as a collaboration between a teacher and a social worker to reintegrate a child into a school after a complex family breakdown, might be seen as part of the longer-term activity of ensuring her wellbeing. A sense of the longer-term activity allows the social worker and teacher to orchestrate their responses with that long-term agreed intention in mind. In other words, the why of collaboration gives shape to the how.

The longer-term analyses offered by Engeström and Pickering also highlight the way that any problems being worked on can change and can assume a life of their own as they move ahead of practitioners: a phenomenon that is instantly recognisable to professionals who work on children's trajectories in order to divert them from potential social exclusion. To capture that experience Engeström, echoing Giddens' (1991) description of the complex 'runaway world' of high modernity, labels these as 'runaway' objects, which call for collaborative and negotiated responses that may not be predictable. Here again the *why* of action within an activity becomes a crucial aspect of dealing with unpredictability as the object of activity is followed and responses woven loosely together.

In Chapter 5 (Figure 5.2), we outlined the importance of keeping in mind the long-term purpose of how practitioners worked with the tools of inter-professional work, by drawing on Engeström's idea of 'where to' tools (Engeström 2007b). There we gave an example of how a CAF might be used to prevent social exclusion rather than simply be a tool for dealing with a crisis. Preventative work necessarily involves the long-term view and the ability to use tools in 'where-to' ways that recognise that over time children and their families will take control over the trajectories that are currently being co-configured.

Being a professional within the work systems examined in the LIW study was hugely challenging, yet as we have already noted quite invigorating. It involved frequent informed and purposeful actions in activities that had meaning for the participants. Yet there were considerable concerns about the potential vulnerability of professionals as they worked outside the well-established practices of their home organisations that had in the past simultaneously protected them and constrained them.

Being a resourceful practitioner

In the previous section we positioned the professionals with whom we worked within broader social changes and indicated that they needed to be both self-reliant and alert to the expertise that other professionals might bring to the task of disrupting children's trajectories of social exclusion. In this section we examine what is involved in working with the expertise that is to be found across open and fluid systems of potentially collaborating professionals by examining the concepts of *distributed expertise* and *relational agency* and their implications for professional learning.

The understanding of learning and action in the workplace that underpinned the LIW study was outlined in Chapter 2. There we explained that, for us, professional learning involves being able to interpret work tasks and to respond to those interpretations in increasingly informed ways. It therefore includes being able to recognise, access, use and contribute to the knowledge that is embedded in the social practices and resources of the workplace.

This framework for understanding learning begins to reveal the potential for enhancing learning that inter-professional work can offer practitioners who work outside established work systems. For example, a social worker and an educational welfare officer will create a much richer picture of a child and her world if they do it together than if they do it separately. At the same time they will together offer a more broadly informed set of responses to that picture and will be able to draw on a wider set of resources to support their actions than if they worked entirely independently. While this kind of collaboration is likely to benefit children and their families, it is also likely to benefit the professionals involved by, for example, strengthening responses and sharing responsibility.

Distributed expertise

Distributed expertise captures the idea that different professionals offer different kinds of expertise to the co-configuring of a child's trajectory. That expertise will include both specialist knowledge and the material resources that sustain that knowledge in action. In fluid and responsive forms of inter-professional work it is helpful to recognise that expertise may be distributed across a neighbourhood or local authority and that practitioners can contribute to it, draw on it and engage with it.

The idea of distributed expertise that was developed in the LIW study builds on Engeström and Middleton's (1996) description of expertise as the discursive construction of tasks and solutions rather than individual mastery of specific areas of relatively stable activity, which was given in Chapter 2. The Engeström and Middleton line is particularly relevant to a study of new practices arising in response to new policies for work with children. It suggests that that professional knowledge is not a stable body of knowledge simply to be acquired through participation in accepted practices. Rather it can be reconstructed in an ongoing dynamic that takes into account historic values as well as new problems to be worked on. Expertise, as described by Engeström and Middleton, is therefore the capacity to learn, act on and transform the problems of practice. However, it is not, in their terms, an individual capacity, but is integrated into the dynamics of work systems as learning systems.

The LIW development of distributed expertise does not deny that expertise can involve a strong individually held knowledge-base and experience in interpreting and acting in specific situations. However, it tries to add to that understanding by incorporating Engeström and Middleton's attention to the conditions in which it is brought into play and by highlighting the processes of negotiating its use in complex work situations that may be shaped by multiple motives.

The LIW focus on expertise as distributed is very much in line with standard sociocultural analyses of work systems, which see intelligence as a resource distributed across people and which is accessed by participants in the systems. Bruner, for example, has talked about the extended intelligence of research labs (Bruner 1996). It also recognises that cultural tools, whether they are material – for example, an assessment system – or conceptual – for example, specialist knowledge about dyslexia – are loaded with intelligence, which can turbo-charge the purposeful actions of the resourceful practitioners who can recognise their potential and work with them.

Working with the expertise of other practitioners to co-configure enriched responses to professional problems involves recognising local expertise and knowing how to bring it in to play. One problem to overcome is mutual incomprehension. During the LIW study we talked with practitioners about the extent to which they felt they needed to become professionally multi-lingual if they were to recognise and encourage into action the expertise of other professionals (Edwards 2004). In one of the responses to our question an educational psychologist, who is married to a clinical psychologist, described how the ability to speak the language of clinical psychology had helped him to engage Child and Adult Mental Health Services (CAMHS) with the children who needed them. It enabled him to 'press the right buttons' when making requests for help with children.

We would suggest that this ability to talk quickly and meaningfully across professional boundaries is even more important in the more open-ended fluid work we were beginning to see emerge. Of course, with the language will come the concepts and an increased sensitivity to how other professionals are seeing children.

Box 7.3 Helping others to recognise your expertise

Distributed expertise as a set of resources that is developed and assessed by local practitioners should therefore counteract concerns that inter-professional work involves creating the new generalist inter-professional worker and an erosion of expertise. Quite the reverse, the idea of distributed expertise requires practitioners to become more adept at identifying and articulating their own expertise so that it can be recognised by others. It also requires them to develop skills that might be seen as core or generic to inter-professional working because these skills enable practitioners to work across professional boundaries.

Relational agency

These core or generic attributes can be captured in the idea of relational agency that we introduced briefly in Chapter 2 (Edwards 2005; Edwards and Mackenzie 2005). Relational agency is a capacity for working with others to strengthen purposeful responses to complex problems. It is helpful to see it as a two-stage process within a constant dynamic. It involves:

- working with others to expand the 'object of activity' or task being working on by recognising the motives and the resources that others bring to bear as they too interpret it;
- aligning one's own responses to the newly enhanced interpretations, with the responses being made by the other professionals to act on the expanded object.

We suggest that it can be learnt and, because it involves working alongside others towards mutually agreed outcomes, is particularly relevant to the work of practitioners who may feel vulnerable when acting responsively and alone without the protection of established procedures.

Relational agency is particularly relevant to inter-professional work to prevent the social exclusion of children, because its starting point is that the practitioners need to recognise the complexity of a child's trajectory before responses can be considered. As we have argued throughout this book, the full extent of vulnerability may not be apparent unless practitioners can look across different aspects of a child's life. In addition, as they examine a child's trajectory through the lenses offered by other practitioners, they also need to be sensitive to *why* other professionals are engaging with the child (Nardi 2005), as joint interpretations and responses will involve recognising their motives.

The framework for understanding collaboration offered by relational agency is therefore quite different from versions of networked support that are based on the interpretations of a single professional who then asks for the support that she considers most appropriate for her interpretation.

In one account of using others as resources for work in that more narrow way, Nardi *et al.* (2002) discussed the emergence of personal social or 'intensional' networks in work systems. They described them as the hidden underpinnings of organisational structures that enabled work to be accomplished. Arguing that in new organisational systems 'It's not what you know, it's who you know', they traced the formation, maintenance and activation of networks in what they describe as network, which benefited both individual workers and their organisations. In that study, networks were presented as usefully resource-laden but needing nurturing so that they could be accessed to accomplish the work identified by the netWORKER. However, no attention was paid to expanded interpretations of complex objects as a prior to identifying the resources needed to work on it. We suggest that the emphasis in relational agency on jointly expanding the interpretation of the object adds a useful dimension to understanding inter-professional work and how it might be supported. So let us now turn to some of the implications of a joint focus on the object of activity for professional learning before examining what is involved in aligning responses to it.

Stetsenko's work (2005) on relationships between the acting subjects and their objects of activity (see Appendix A) is a useful starting point. It helps us to see how enriched interpretations of the object of activity can enhance practitioners' learning and inform their future interpretations. Stetsenko was not writing about collaboration. Rather, she was trying to tease out the dynamic that exists between the interpreting subject and the object of activity or problem of practice that is being interpreted. This is an important focus for the development of activity theory, but it is also of direct relevance to understanding how working across professional boundaries can contribute to the learning of practitioners through a dynamic between subject and object.

For Stetsenko, the focus on the transaction between subject and object presented an opportunity to bring human subjectivity into activity theory; indeed, a human subjectivity that 'is laden with practical relevance and agency' (ibid: 83) as people's interpretations are always purposeful. Her argument goes as follows: as someone works on an object, the object itself works back on them and impacts on their subjectivity and how they in turn approach the object. Recognising a dynamic between subject and object is not a new insight, but Stetsenko turned the spotlight on it in order to pay attention to the intentionality and agency of actors within activities.

We have suggested (Edwards 2005) that, in the context of inter-professional work, when more than one person works on the object of activity the transactional relationship between subject and object can be quite powerful as:

- practitioners may expand, that is, transform the object through exploring and contesting its meaning, and so come to understand it better;
- they may also transform themselves because new meanings made with other professionals will bounce back and shape how they next interpret and approach the task.

Stetsenko's argument therefore connects easily with relational agency's focus on the interpretation of the object. For example, joint action by a counsellor and a welfare manager in a school, on a child's phobia of school, involves bringing to bear two professional subjectivities and two sets of conceptual tools on the problem and so expands interpretations of it. As one practitioner in the Seaside MPT team put it 'when two or three of you are working on a child's trajectory as an object, we bring to bear different mindsets'. As we have just indicated, when the object is expanded through bringing to bear these different mindsets, it can work back on the mindsets of the practitioners and these may in turn be enriched by the interpretations of the others.

We could see these expanded mindsets at work in the case study sites as practitioners began to use the enriched understandings of children's lives that working with other professionals had provided. These complex interpretations called for complex responses. We therefore now turn to the learning involved in recognising and accessing the expertise of others and in aligning responses to complex interpretations.

The framework for examining learning that we have been using sees professional action as resourceful task accomplishment. In other words, having interpreted a task and its demands, practitioners identify and use the resources available to them to accomplish the task, whether it is the re-integration of a child into school after a period of exclusion, or helping a child in the care of the local authority to consider all the educational opportunities available to him. These resources may be material, such as exercises that allow the student to catch up on the curriculum that has been missed; they may be embedded in the practices of a setting, such as a gradual resumption of a full curriculum; they may involve drawing on the expertise of others, such as when a child's social worker calls on the experience and know-how of the child's form tutor to jointly explore education options. In our discussion of relational agency we are focusing on the expertise of other practitioners as a resource, but working with the expertise of others may also include access to other material resources.

The first step in aligning motives and actions for resourceful practice is knowing who to work with. This was a problem that vexed many of the practitioners in the LIW study. Knowing about and working with the expertise of others is a preoccupation of other professionals too. Lundvall, developing the idea of the learning economy, has long argued that we should consider 'know-who' to be as important as know-how, know-what and know-why when looking at knowledge at work. He explains, as we have already noted, as follows:

> Know-who involves information about who knows to do what. But especially it involves the social capability to establish relationships to specialised groups in order to draw on their expertise.
>
> (Lundvall 1996: 7)

Arguing that know-who is embedded and learnt in social practices and cannot simply be codified into a register of names of people who can be called upon, his description of know-who as an ability to 'draw on' expertise resonates more with the Nardi *et al.* (2002) notion of netWORK and of the expertise of others as a resource to enhance one's own performance than it does with the reciprocity of relational agency. Nonetheless, the labelling of know-who is helpful, indicating that knowing how to know-who is a useful professional attribute.

However, relational agency at work is not simply a matter of identifying and selecting the expertise necessary for responsive inter-professional work. How that expertise is brought into play and is mutually aligned needs to be negotiated. Engeström and Middleton's account of expertise as the 'discursive construction of tasks, solutions, visions, breakdowns and innovations' (1996: 4) captures the challenges of these negotiations.

Relational agency can help us to understand the negotiations and reconfiguring of tasks indicated by Engeström and Middleton by giving us a framework for looking at what is involved in recognising expertise and negotiating actions. The LIW study showed that material tools such as assessment systems can help with recognising expertise and mobile phones can help with accessing it. Being professionally multi-lingual in the way outlined in the discussion of distributed expertise is also another useful attribute.

However, there is still work to be done on identifying what is involved in negotiations. We suspect that being able to give and ask for reasons for actions, to explore the many purposes of multi-professional work, is important and intend to pursue that hypothesis in other studies. While we are some way from identifying exactly the skills involved in recognition and negotiation, at the very least it seems to involve being able to take an outward looking stance and engage with the motivations of other professionals.

Shotter has been grappling with similar issues when thinking about responsive practices more generally. His idea of 'withitness' thinking (Shotter 2005) has developed from his long-held interest in relationships in human action. Withitness thinking, Shotter explains, is a form of reflective interaction where new possibilities of relation are engendered and new interconnections are made. It is an expansive practice that presupposes openness to the other as a source of learning and repositioning. He contrasts 'withitness' thinking with 'aboutitness' thinking. In aboutitness thinking, the other person is an object of consciousness and not another consciousness offering responses to which we in turn respond.

Know-who that embraces 'withitness' thinking seems to involve ongoing and unchoreographed movements of action and withdrawal based on constantly revised interpretations of a changing object of activity and a respect for the expertise and motivations of the other actors. It seems to echo aspects of Engeström's tentatively offered concept 'object-oriented interagency', which we discussed in Chapter 6. Engeström sees this as a form of 'connecting and reciprocating' while 'circling around a complex object' and 'dwelling in' the object, that is, maintaining a long-term relationship with it (2005: 333).

There are also some echoes in relational agency of the work of Hakkarainen *et al.* on reciprocity and mutual strengthening of competence and expertise to enhance the collective competence of a community (Hakkarainen *et al.* 2004). However, relational agency is more directly concerned with the interactional and the relationships that comprise a distributed system of expertise. It therefore connects with Billett's attention to relational interdependence (Billett 2006), by arguing for greater attention to agency or intentionality in explaining relationships between individuals and others in working life.

Box 7.4 Having an outward-looking stance

Seeing other professionals as part of local systems of distributed expertise is, we suggest, a prerequisite for exercising relational

---

continued

agency across professional boundaries. From there it is small step to working with the expertise of others in co-configuring children's pathways out of risk of social exclusion. This work involves an outward-looking stance, 'withitness' thinking and attention to know-who. As well as being an enhanced version of practice, it offers a very different view of being a professional from the individually responsible practitioner who is obliged to draw on their own resources.

We are aware that this focus on collaboration and enhanced professional practice is not entirely new. In 1994, for example, Hargreaves speculated on the impact of government reforms of English schooling on what he termed 'the new professionalism' of teachers. The parallels are quite striking. The long-established bureaucratic structures that shaped teaching were destabilised by the national reforms, but Hargreaves argued that, rather than de-skilling teachers as so many feared, the reforms had given rise to fresh and valuable ways of thinking about professional action and the principles that underpinned them. In particular there were signs that they were leading to a stronger sense of collaboration and reciprocity in the practices of teachers. Hargreaves was not undertaking a CHAT analysis, yet one can see in the picture he painted that the erosion of stability brought about by the reforms had led to changes in how work was shared out, new discussions about the purposes of schooling and new ways of working together.

Knowledge in practice

The destabilising of practices and the knowledge embedded in them that Hargreaves witnessed in English schools in the early 1990s paralleled the background to the changes in practices we observed in the LIW study. This kind of disruption can be quite threatening, leading to fears of loss of expertise and de-skilling. So far in this chapter we have argued that the reverse occurs. As practices are called into question, practitioners are obliged to articulate what matters to them. As a result, professional values and motives are disentangled from the rules and procedures that have sustained them in the past. We have particularly argued that having a long-term imprecisely articulated goal for practice, such as children's wellbeing, can give direction to newly emergent practices.

In this section we look at how professionals engage with knowledge and suggest that freeing professional knowledge from rigid rules and procedures so that it becomes open to negotiation and reconfiguration can be beneficial for practitioners. One starting point is that professional knowledge is not easily parcelled up into sets of behaviours that can be practised and polished into acceptable performance. The contexts of professional work are rarely that predictable. The other starting point is that professional knowledge needs to be seen as renewable as it incorporates the use of new tools and responds to new demands as a result of changes in society and the knowledge generated elsewhere. We shall take forward the second point in this section.

In a recent study of professional learning among accountants, computer engineers, nurses and teachers carried out at the University of Oslo (Jensen 2007), the Norwegian research team found that each of these groups were aware that they needed to continuously renew their knowledge-base. This was particularly true of the computer engineers, but also of the others who talked of upgrading and updating their knowledge and of needing to relate to changes in the rules and laws that shaped their professions. The researchers drew on the work of Rheinberger (1992) and Knorr Cetina (1997) to see knowledge as open, question-generating and unfolding as professionals engaged with it.

There seemed to be a dynamic between their professional commitment and the knowledge they encountered so that the practitioners worked on new knowledge, attempting to overcome lack of clarity and driven forward by trying to fill gaps in understanding. Knorr Cetina and Jensen both work with the idea of a 'structure of wanting'. For Knorr Cetina this occurs when experts engage with knowledge and experience a 'lack' (1997: 12) that arises because knowledge is always unfolding as they work with it and because of a commitment or desire to grasp what is important for practice in an ever-unfolding process of interaction with knowledge.

Jensen and Lahn (2005) have illustrated these ideas in their account of how a commitment to nursing during training grew alongside engagement with the knowledge-base of nursing among nursing students in their study. They argued that when external social ties were being weakened, in the way we outlined at the beginning of this chapter, they are being strengthened among some professionals through commitments to abstract and open-ended knowledge projects. These are complex ideas that deserve more attention than can be given here. Nonetheless the processes of knowledge-seeking identified in the

Norwegian study are worth pursuing in a discussion of learning for inter-professional work.

Box 7.5 The need for discrete knowledge

One conclusion arising from comparing the four professional groups (Jensen 2007) is that when knowledge fields were weakly framed and involved a range of disciplines without clear boundaries to the knowledge-base, it was difficult for practitioners to find their way, to identify what was important to work on and to connect with professional knowledge in the way that the nursing students in the 2005 study had done. Jensen suggests that a challenge for those who want to encourage professional learning is to create a knowledge infrastructure that does not oversimplify but that identifies themes or areas where it is useful to do work and to ensure that these themes or fields connect with the desire or engagement that reflects professional values.

Jensen does not look at inter-professional work, but her conclusions about having boundaries for expertise connect with what we have been saying about distributed expertise. Inter-professional work puts the spotlight on professional expertise and the response, in our view, should be a strong affiliation with the discrete and unfolding knowledge-base of a profession. This strong affiliation to the knowledge-base and values of discrete professions, in turn, needs to be set alongside developing a set of attributes that enable the exercise of relational agency in systems of distributed expertise.

We are not suggesting here that these discrete knowledge-bases stand still. Indeed, we have been saying throughout our account of the LIW study that inter-professional work and the conversations that occur on the boundaries between professions will provoke useful questions about the discrete knowledge resources of each profession. Indeed, work on knowledge and boundaries within the field of organisation science suggest that these kinds of questions are essential for innovation and organisational adaptation (Carlile 2004; Heracleous 2004). The trick seems to be to sustain a clear framing of the field while being open to new ways of working with the knowledge that makes it way into it.

We have so far emphasised the kinds of professional knowledge that can be articulated and publicly scrutinised. But we do not underestimate the power of more locally and historically situated forms of knowledge such as what led to people in a particular housing charity to be reluctant to work with social services, or what resources a community arts project might be able to bring to a child. One aim of the study was to examine what needed to be learnt by practitioners if they were to be able to access and work with this more situated knowledge. We have therefore offered the ideas of distributed expertise and relational agency as ways of conceptualising how the knowledge of, for example, the community arts worker might be recognised and mobilised by a teacher.

During the study, the Developmental Work Research (DWR) sessions were sites where local knowledge was shared. Practitioners learnt from each other about how local agencies operated, the resources that were available in neighbourhoods and so on. All of this was useful information, but it was heavily situated and therefore of little use when practitioners moved to a different local authority. One of our aims as researchers was to work with practitioners to reveal the principles and concepts embedded in these discussions. These concepts were discussed in Chapter 4 and were clearly seen as relevant by practitioners in other parts of England.

The DWR sites were also places where learning across professional boundaries occurred. This learning involved practitioners in learning from each other about their professional motives, what procedures were necessary in their service, what their practices were intended to achieve for a child, what they would expect of parents and so on. This learning could also be seen as situated in particular local services, but there were also more universal aspects to it, so that social workers and teachers, for example, learnt to be more aware and tolerant of each other's priorities. The receptivity to the views of others that this kind of learning demanded was revealed as an important attribute. We summarised it earlier in this chapter as being outward looking, and in Chapter 4 we saw that practitioners regarded being able to 'take a pedagogic stance at work' was important for successful inter-professional collaboration. Inter-professional learning of this kind could inform their work, enabling professionals to align their practices with those of others and opportunities to learn from others were welcomed.

While practitioners were happy to acquire situated information or enrich their understandings of children by engaging with other practitioners, moving knowledge through organisational hierarchies was more difficult to achieve. We shall examine the difficulties involved in moving knowledge that has been refined in practice upstream or vertically though local authority systems to inform strategy in Chapter 8. In the present chapter we shall focus on knowledge work on the boundaries between practitioners and children and their families. We have already indicated that we had very few examples of practitioners involving families in co-configuring their own trajectories in partnership with professionals, and that practitioners did not seem ready to push forward to develop these practices.

There were examples of placing parents in 'profane' spaces on the boundaries (Midgley 1992) where their views were likely to be discounted in the basis of their own neediness. The knowledge that they did bring, when it was recounted by practitioners, was also recast in categories that reflected professional work systems: a high achiever, a poor attender, a homeless child and so on. The co-configuring of children's trajectories out of risk of social exclusion should lead ultimately to independence from the services that hover at the ready to give support. If that is to occur, practitioners also perhaps need to examine how the expertise of families can be recognised and then mobilised and how to weave that knowledge into their interpretations of children's trajectories and the range of responses available to them.

Again the problem of recognising and working with lower status knowledge is not unique to the kind of work we studied. Yanow has outlined the marginalisation of peripheral workers in organisations, their closeness to the field and the extent to which the knowledge they bring is overlooked (Yanow 2004). Her examples include the knowledge about sheep grazing after Chernobyl that was held by shepherds in the North of England and the poorly articulated, yet important, understandings of local rock conditions among dam builders in Denver. In both examples, quite disastrous outcomes could have been avoided if this kind of expert knowledge had been sought and had informed decisions. The classic study of the depth of this kind of knowledge and how it is articulated and shared is Orr's work on the photocopy repair men who shared their knowledge through stories about what happened in practice (Orr 1996).

Yanow argues that when these situations arise, two different knowledge systems are in play: one she terms 'rational-scientific-technical', which is accorded the higher status, and the other she calls 'know-how' (2004: 21), which is local and often tacit. These distinctions are not new. However, Yanow's argument that these two kinds of knowledge are incommensurate helps to clarify one of the learning challenges for professionals who are attempting to work with children and families to co-configure their trajectories.

Box 7.6 Respecting the expertise of families

We suggest that, in co-configured work to prevent social exclusion, professionals cannot afford to ignore the local knowledge of families as they negotiate ways forward with them. Part of the expertise of professionals in these situations needs to be the ability to enable families to reveal and work with their own expertise, perhaps through factual stories about the children concerned. This way of working will involve respecting and, at times, privileging the non-specialist expertise of families and it adds to the risk of working outside the safety of rigid organisational procedures.

The view of learning that has been driving our analyses is commensurate with a respect for local knowledge. We indicated earlier that the framework for examining learning that we have been using sees professional action as resourceful task accomplishment, we then went on to discuss the related processes of interpretation and resourceful action that shape task accomplishment. The local knowledge of the children and families who are ultimately to take over the task of configuring their own trajectories out of risk of social exclusion needs to be brought into those processes, and the threats to professional status that might accompany these negotiations need to be recognised.

Implications for training and professional development

Booker, writing about the 2004 Children Act and the subsequent integration of children's services, makes the important point that too much of a practitioner focus on 'getting things done' (2005: 138) can mean that useful debates and differences are 'smoothed over' and too little attention is paid to 'working through'. Our analyses would suggest the Booker is absolutely right. Drawing on Oakley's work on policy development (2003), Booker argues that common narratives need to be developed locally if children's services are to allow autonomous decision-making through, in his example, flexibly networked teams. Although we are not suggesting that teams offer a better model for inter-professional work than the other options outlined in Chapter 1, we do agree that the professional decision-making necessary for responsive practice is best served by being located within understandings of common narratives aimed at regularly debated long-term goals.

These narratives take time to develop and involve some quite profound reflections on professional stereotyping, the purposes of professional action, the nature of different professional expertise and how that expertise might be negotiated with others including children and families. In Chapter 5 we discussed the boundary spaces where this kind of learning can occur. In this chapter we have attempted to indicate some of the personal challenges for practitioners.

Conclusion

Our conclusion is that training and professional development for inter-professional work needs to be mindful of the extent of the demands being made on practitioners and to put in place systems of supervision and support that enable them to work through contradictions and take advantage of the new opportunities for action that arise.

We would also suggest that training and professional development programmes should distinguish between:

- the boundaried expert knowledge of discrete professional groups;
- the generic skills involved in being able to work within systems of distributed expertise;
- the local knowledge, whether from other practitioners or from children and families, that can inform the interpretations and responses that shape their practices.

In making these distinctions it would be important to recognise what each brings to resourceful task completion, and what is involved in engaging with them.

Chapter 8

Implications for organisations involved in inter-professional collaborations

Introduction

In this chapter we consider the implications for organisations involved in inter-professional collaborations from the study as a whole. Our premise is, as we have argued throughout this book, that individual and organisational learning are inextricably connected in processes of expansive learning (Engeström 1987, 2001). Put simply, individual change is unlikely without organisational change and *vice versa*. This assertion calls for an understanding of the relationship between the two.

In Chapter 3 we outlined a way of thinking about organisational change that built on the work of Basil Bernstein. In this chapter we take that analysis further to link it with the way practitioners in the study talked about organisational change. The chapter concludes with a consideration of the implications of these analyses for organisations.

Individual and organisational learning

Cole (1996, 2003) has argued that we need to exercise some care when thinking about the idea of context when considering individual change within organisational change. He identifies two possible forms of reference. He equates one to the term 'environment' and suggests that this refers to a set of circumstances, separate from the individual child, with which the individual interacts and which are said to influence the child in various ways (Cole 2003). He sees this notion of context as separable from person and to be of limited value. His second account of context is related to a dictionary definition 'the connected whole that gives coherence to its parts'. Cole proceeds to adopt an understanding of context that captures this sense of a process of weaving together. He acknowledges that at times there is a need to separate context and person for analytical purposes but suggests that the reality is one of inseparability.

Engeström *et al.* (2003a) add to this view of mutual constitution of organisational and individual features by arguing that historically formed aspects of an organisation and the immediate social actions of individuals co-construct each other. They both shape and are shaped by each other:

> Historical analysis implies a broad institutional and societal framework and a long time perspective. Situated analysis implies focusing on the here-and-now, typically on what can be captured on tape in a given situation or single encounter. Acknowledging that the two are mutually constitutive only opens up the challenge: How does this mutual constitution actually happen and how can it be empirically captured?
>
> (Engeström *et al.* 2003a: 286–7)

Institutional analysis

Wertsch's (2007) development of the idea of implicit mediation was introduced in Chapter 5. It carries with it the suggestion that cultural constructions, such as institutions, mediate engagement with the world. We became interested in how practices of power and control, as witnessed in the principles of social regulation in institutions, mediate relationships between participants. This issue is all the more pertinent when studying inter-professional work that by definition involves the transformation of such principles of social regulation.

In Chapter 3 we introduced a tentative model for the analysis and description of settings in which multi-agency working develops. This model referred to the group of professionals who were involved in the Developmental Work Research (DWR) sessions (see Appendix A), the wider local authority and the children and families who were to be served by emergent multi-agency practices. We explained how Bernstein's (2000) concepts of boundary strength (classification) and control (framing) can be applied to the model and we used the terms instrumental or instructional practice to refer to the actions of practice.

In the Learning in and for Interagency Working (LIW) study we were interested in how practices of power and control within each local authority connected with how participants in the DWR sessions made sense of their working relations. We therefore examined evidence gathered in the sessions and in interviews to understand institutional relations through assessments of the following strengths:

- classification, that is, the strength of professional boundaries when the work was shared out, in the practices of professional agencies;
- control, that is, the framing that occurs in the regulation of communication in the social relations that govern the social division of labour between workers;
- distinctions in the vertical division of labour, that is, differences between layers in organisations;
- control over the regulative practice, that is, matters of order, identity and relation.

In the local authority, key features were:

- the vertical division of labour between DWR participants and their colleagues in the wider authority;
- the extent to which boundaries were maintained between the professions in the local authority.

In order to understand better the institutional mediation that was occurring in each local authority, the control over the boundary relations between the DWR participants and the local authority was modelled, somewhat awkwardly, as the framing of those relations. As we explained in Chapter 3, strong framing indicated a boundary maintained by the local authority, weak framing represented a boundary relation in which the DWR participants maintained control and there was an intermediary position in which a relatively fluid two-way flow of communication was maintained. The extent to which clients were classified as belonging to a particular category of need (strong classification) or as the 'whole child' (weak classification) was also noted. Being alert to how children were classified was an indication of the division of labour when working closely with children and families.

Each aspect of this model was described for each site through data gathered through observations and interviews. A coding grid was developed for each aspect (see Table 8.1 for examples). The codings were independently validated by two researchers.

As we noted in Chapter 6, the Multi-Professional Team (MPT) in Seaside was a new system that was put in place as a result of a dramatic shift in local authority structures and could be analysed as an emergent organisation in its own right. The Children in Public Care

Table 8.1 Example of coding grids applied to a model of description

-	1 C--	2 C-	3 C+/-	4 C+	5 C++
Seaside	x				
Wildside	x				
Castletown				x	

Model Feature – Division of Labour (Vertical)
Exemplar interview question – How hierarchical is the management in your work?

Coding
1. C -- = All members of a 'flat' team
2. C++ = Strong hierarchy (director, deputy director, principal, senior, junior)

(CiPC) team in Wildside was an established team that was already well linked with local agencies, but was adjusting its work in the context of the 2004 Children Act. It could be seen as a discrete activity system in its work with Looked After Children, while recognising that members also had other organisational affiliations. We also noted how attempts were made to coordinate services in the wider local authority as well the form of any recent disruption in the order of the local authority. These features are given in Table 8.2.

Table 8.2 Features of the local authorities

	Seaside	*Wildside*	*Castletown*
Co-ordination of agencies and agents	Perceived lack of response to operational staff views (at several levels)	Strong strategy	No strategy that impacted on case study site. Strategy developing within rest of LA
Disruptions	Several major re-organisations Radical localisation of services		Recent leadership changes and reconfigured systems

At a very general level there were stronger values of classification (boundaries) and framing (control) of what might be termed the instrumental or instructional practice (the what and how of practice)

in Castletown and progressively weaker values in Seaside and Wildside. In addition, a consideration of the nature of the regulative or moral and attitudinal aspects of practice in each site suggests strong framing in Seaside, weak framing in Castletown, with Wildside occupying an intermediary position. Thus, in Castletown the instructional practice (which is strongly classified and highly framed) predominates over the weak regulative discourse. Whereas in Seaside the relatively weak boundaries, witnessed in the weaker values of classification of the instructional practice, are embedded in the regulative practice through which common values and meanings have been the object of much of the early work of the team. In Wildside an intermediary position is seen in the embedding of the instruction and regulation. We found these distinctions helpful, not least because of the increasing evidence we gathered during the study of the importance of professional values and passionately held motives that ensure professional engagement with the object of activity, which we discussed in Chapter 7.

We created a crude typification of the three main English case studies by applying Bernstein's model of the embedded features of pedagogic practice in which instructional practice (I) and regulative practice (R) are mutually embedded but in which one may predominate.

In this way we arrived at condensed codings of what may be seen as the historical legacy presented at the moment when we started to engage with groups of professionals at each site.

As we explained in Chapter 2, we carried out six two-hour DWR sessions over one year in each of the three sites (Appendix A). As we explained in Chapter 1, sessions were comprised of the practitioners who were working together or were moving towards working together. We used ideas derived from activity theory to stimulate their reflections on the contradictions that emerged when they, for example, examined how the histories of their work had shaped the present and potential for future work.

Seaside   i/R The regulative aspect is predominant

Castletown   I/r The instructional/instrumental aspect is predominant

Wildside   I/R An intermediary/balanced position

Figure 8.1 The structure of pedagogic practices in the English case studies

We developed analytic protocols in order to analyse the talk in the DWR sessions. David Middleton, a member of the research team, proposed an approach to analysis that focused on the forms of social action that are accomplished in talk and text and the sorts of communicative devices that are used. The particular focus of what became known as the 'D-analysis' grew out of a concern to examine the emergence of what-it-is-to-learn in settings as the participants developed their inter-professional work, across the three sites. Stages of learning-related talk were identified and used to code the talk in the sessions.

1   *Deixis – indication, pointing*
    This stage involves making a start on a topic during a conversation to draw the audience's attention towards a particular problem.
2   *Delineation and definition*
    This involves a reaction to what has been said in the conversation indicating that sense is being made. When another person moves on to explain the point from their own perspective by a) acknowledging and qualifying that point, b) explaining further that point by drawing on their local context, or c) emphasising a different view, that may serve as a basis for expanding the conversation to explore what has just been seen as important.
3   *Deliberation*
    This involves narrowing down the thinking process towards reaching an agreement. This is actioned through either giving or asking for consent in the conversation by a) building a consensus by evoking local situation/knowledge, or b) building a consensus based on general knowledge.
4   *Departure*
    A departure could be seen as a shift towards a qualitatively different stage in communicative interaction. At this stage we can see progress in the group's conceptualisation of the problem.
5   *Development*
    This involves finding a tool from within the previous conversation that enables people to discuss a solution to an identified problem and moving the conversation to a more 'action'-oriented level. In this way the conversation reaches the level of 'recognition' of a particular issue. (After Middleton *et al.* in press.)

Sequences of communicative action were analysed in the transcripts of the sessions. Some sequences progressed to departures, others remained at other stages. Related sequences were identified and these were grouped into strands of talk that wove their way through the progress of the each series of sessions. These strands witnessed the progression of learning through and with talk in the sessions. A learning strand was defined as a narrative that focused on one and the same concept and was developmental in its nature, that is, there was a movement from recognising towards proposing an action. These strands revealed the ideas in use as people developed their new ways of working and have been described in Chapter 4. Each sequence prepared the way or the one that followed either in the same session or in subsequent ones. At the end of the project, participants were interviewed about what they gained from the experience and showed that the concepts captured by the D-analysis and outlined in Chapter 4 remained relevant for them.

Vertical learning

We will now look at a specific strand of communicative action that was identified at Seaside. In part, this strand relates to the distinctions between horizontal (cross-profession) and vertical (across levels of hierarchies) learning that Edwards and Wiseman (2005) noted in their analysis of data collected during the National Evaluation of the Children's Fund.

We would like at this point to distinguish between our use of the term 'vertical' and the more commonly used Vygotskian idea of vertical learning. Our use refers to learning that results from moves up, and sometimes down, the management hierarchies of an organisation, so that we can use the term 'vertical' interchangeably with 'upstream' or 'downstream'. The more classically Vygotskian understanding sees learning as taking place in the vertical movement between everyday experience of the world and engagement with historically culturally formed concepts that Vygotsky termed 'scientific'. In that sense ours is a more local or situation specific understanding.

Figure 8.2 depicts a summary of this strand of evidence. A tension was identified and was subsequently explored and elaborated. Departures and developments occurred and were then resisted before new tools were ultimately developed and implemented.

The tensions in vertical relations (between operational and strategic levels of the organisation) were initially discussed in terms of the ways in which each level was organised. Participants, who were all members of the MPT, indicated that the categories that were used to organise staffing were at variance with each other. This extract from a DWR session illustrates:

Strategic resources and development which have still been structured in exactly the same old education, welfare, EP . . . system and have not moved as far as the multi-professional team integration have at the operational level. So the people who are going to be looking at development and resources have been up until now structured still in the very old system.

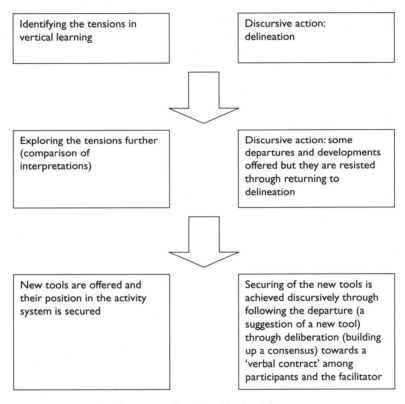

Figure 8.2 The development of a strand in Seaside

The initial act of pointing (deixis) to a particular tension was reaffirmed at another moment some time later in the same session:

Yeah, because we're dealing with very senior people who are making the overall strategy of the multi-professional team. You've got people who are operational on the ground floor level who are working hard to move further and further towards it, and you've got one layer which somewhere is, I don't know what do they do.

This tension is subsequently delineated in that a specific problem is identified. The concern identified in the next quote is that of the pressure to conform rather than complain or argue against strategic directives:

> It's very hard in that context to actually be a lone voice and say actually, you know I do think this. . . . But it can . . . the pressure of being seen to agree with your peers is actually very strong.

An interchange follows about the personal characteristics and experience that might be useful in alleviating this tension. Here there is a sense of the need for managing disagreement:

> Speaker A: But you see I've done this for so long I feel quite happy to be out as a single voice saying, no I think that or whatever.
> Speaker B: But that's the key . . . it takes an awful lot of confidence and experience to be able to do that. And it's a very uncomfortable place to be.

The facilitator then tried to consolidate the outcome of the interchange. This was further refined by two participants:

> Facilitator: So professional confidence is something you need to work on.
> Speaker C: Mmm, but I don't know how you can acquire that other than by doing it and. . .
> Speaker D: Time. . .
> Speaker E: And experiencing the tension and stress and still hanging onto what you think.

The focus on refinement of the problem area began to shift to consideration of the kind of developments that could be initiated. This process was prompted by remarks about the difficulties experienced by operational staff when they tried to contact strategic managers. The experience of rapid change and reorganisation appeared to have exacerbated the problem:

> Speaker D: I think, well I would, I mean it's sort of, I suppose initially you're kind of trying to clarify who the people are, I mean

that's one of the things. I think when Speaker A just said a moment ago it feels as if there's someone's sitting in an office making decisions and kind of rolling things out. I think one of the issues, it does feel very much like that and [unclear] that kind of identifying kind of who those key players are initially. And I think that's one of the things that . . . part of it is a process of waiting because there's been so much change upon change, kind of waiting for things to kind of get to a point of bedding down a little bit and actually being formalised so that you can get to a point and so, oh okay so so and so does that, so and so does that, so that we can then kind of maybe get to the point of putting structures into place around that organisation is my kind of [unclear].

A member of the research team then interjected by comparing aspects of the vertical challenge with the developments in the learning from each other (what we are calling horizontal learning) that had taken place. In Seaside the development of horizontal learning had taken place through an initial focus of the regulative (social order, relation identity) aspects of the team practice:

Research team member: That's very interesting because that's parallel to what you've done within the team isn't it, because your first phase of working was a lot of who does what, who are you, what are you doing, let's sit down and just have a cup of tea and chew that over and get to know and get to trust you, get to understand you a bit, but also know what you're doing and how you do it. And you're saying, you need that with the people who are developing strategy.

At this point the session moved to a discussion of concrete proposals for action. Speaker D reaffirmed a specific need and formulated a proposal for action:

Speaker D: Yeah, we need to just know who the game . . . who the players are in the game because that just feels so far removed that you don't even know where they are or anything. That's how I feel about it. I would like somebody, each of the people at the development level having a responsibility to be a link for each of the localities. So that they if you like came to locality meetings or some locality meetings and then fed what was being said in those back into and across the development strategy meetings up at

County Hall where they live. So it was actually somebody who is [unclear] strategy who has a link with each of the locality teams and is responsible for hearing what it was that they were saying and they could then, where they get together and actually feed what was being said sideways.

This proposal was resisted. Speaker D appears to think that strategic level professionals should adopt what might be thought of as a transmission-based pedagogy with operational staff. The appeal for a form of dialogic practice that has been discussed and formulated by her colleagues is seen as unrealistic. Again the concern is raised that professionals working at the operational level do not appear to disagree with strategic proposals for action:

> Speaker E: I think strategists need to talk with you rather than talk down to you. Because I've been to so many presentations when, you know you're given this, it seems like an unreal world that they're talking about and it doesn't fit with the reality on the ground at all. And you just go away at the end of it thinking this is rubbish. Um, but nobody really disagrees too much at what they're saying.

Speaker E extends what might be seen as a cynical view of the context in which strategic level professionals are working. She speculates that rapid turnover in the allocation and designation of responsibilities compounds the problem that was being progressively redefined in discussions over the series of DWR sessions:

> that some of these strategists, what appears to be on a weekly basis, these people that work in strategies leave their posts and move onto [unclear]. So have we actually got anybody rolling out strategy that actually invented the strategy in the first place (laughs). And if not, are they just are they just trying to roll out something that they don't believe in?

A very similar finding has been reported by Yanow who discusses a 'double periphery' in which a community of practitioners acts across both a horizontal, geographic periphery and a vertical, hierarchical periphery:

> In principle, these workers develop knowledge in interaction with clients and customers that could be valuable to the organisation,

were it but to learn from them. Instead, the 'local knowledge' they learn in acting across these peripheries is discounted, if not disparaged, by more centrally-located managers and executives.

(2004: s9)

Organisations that want to develop new forms of work clearly need to be mindful of the dangers of ignoring the need to genuinely learn from emergent forms of operational practice as they develop their strategic thinking and policy.

Resistance

The entire sequence reported above stretched over four meetings in the period February to June. Although the elements of the development are represented, the sketch of the strand outlined above does not fully capture the frequent movements between the different phases of learning encapsulated in the D-analysis. The learning is characterised by several types of movements and transitions that were accomplished within each specific sequence and across the whole strand of sequences of communicative action in the workshops. The participants worked through a number of issues related to vertical communication with strategists. They began by outlining the problems they experienced in the communication with strategists and negative implications the problems entailed for the team's everyday work. As the communication developed, there was more focus on exploration of these problems, which were motivated by the wish to share understanding and interpretations of the problems with colleagues. In this respect the workshops served as a boundary zone for professionals where they did not have to focus on the immediate detailed procedures of their everyday work but could explore the problems and reflect on them.

The analysis of this strand demonstrates that the participants began by identifying the tension they had experienced in the communication with strategists. Among them were the tensions between the new and the old rules (the operational staff believed they were working within the new rules whereas the strategists were still operating within the set of old rules). There was evidence of resistance in acknowledging that they too were responsible for the communication problem. Within a number of mini-sequences, different tools were offered that could potentially improve communication with strategists. These included the identification of a 'link strategist' who could attend monthly meetings. However, these suggestions were resisted by some members of the MPT who, instead of discussing these tools, further changed the discussion towards further exploration of the problem, thus, returning the conversation to where it initially started. There then followed a series of proposals for action that were intended to alleviate the difficulties being experienced in the vertical communication and learning between operation and strategy. At each point when a concrete proposal was formulated, there was a move away from action on the part of the individuals who would have been required to act had the proposal been implemented. This resistance to change arose when participants in the DWR sessions understood that they should make changes in practice and organisation but could, or would, not engage with the processes of making those changes.

Our current thinking on this kind of response is influenced by the Russian writer Vasilyuk (1991) who discussed such examples of inner resistance. His work directs attention to the affective dimensions of change that are too often under-theorised in studies of the development of new forms of professional practice. Engeström's (2007a) latest interventionist research, for example, shows that whilst individual practitioners were happy to construct new models and tools for changing their work they appeared reluctant to proceed with implementation.

This resistance to the construction of new professional identities presents a challenge to the overly cognitive orientation of much research based on activity theory. As we outlined in Chapter 6, in the last year of his life, Vygotsky turned his attention to 'perezhivanie'. It can be seen as close to the idea of 'lived or emotional experience' and is a concept that directs attention to the emotional dimensions of professional identity and practice in settings where new forms of multi-agency working and new configurations of professional expertise are emerging.

There is an interesting parallel here with a new wave of research in work-based hospital activity that focuses upon the intersection between power and identity as this emerges in explicit acts of resistance to habits, conventions and associated protocols (Bleakley et al. 2004; Bleakley et al. 2006).

Iedema (2007) and colleagues have explored everyday practices embedded in, and often frustrated by, organisational structures such as power relationships in communication between nurses and surgeons in constructing the operating room lists. They report that 'nurses are positioned between competing organisational discourses that privilege time and efficiency and the hierarchical dominance of surgeons' (ibid: 223). However, nurses still challenge surgeons' traditional and hierarchical right to determine the order of the operating list.

In his analysis of the all too frequent failure of teamwork in the operating theatre, Bleakley (2008) calls for a consideration of the notion of ethical courage (or parrhēsia), which he suggests is required to breakthrough established patterns of authority that are apparent in work-based talk. His research exposes ethical tensions and injustices arising from power and legitimacy issues. His particular focus is the rituals that formulate the ethos of the collective household that is the anesthetic room, operating theatre, and recovery room:

> Where patient safety is linked with effective interprofessional clinical teamwork, the movement to interprofessionalism cannot be forced by introduction of protocols but depends upon prior values change, or a change in ethos, to promote sustainability. Collaborative teamwork in the operating theatre is frustrated by conventions of hierarchy and these affect the ethos of practice. Paradoxically, forms of resistance to these conventions – exercised by those lower on the status hierarchy such as nurses, and expressed as voices speaking rhetorically – may act to reinforce divisive professional interests – Unidirectional culture change, involving building new practices for patient safety, will be difficult to establish and harder to sustain if it is enforced, offers unwelcome colonisation, or attempts to build on a values quicksand. Values and attitudinal change are foundational, where they precede and form behavioural and performance change.
>
> (Bleakley 2008: 268)

Our work is not alone in pointing to the importance for organisations of practices of vertical learning and in the consideration of ways in which the regulative features (social order, identity and relation) of practices may need to be a particular focus of attention when seeking to counter what appear to be very prevalent affective dimensions of resistance to change at personal and organisational levels of analysis.

Yanow (2004) adds to our own conclusions through a reminder of the power of the language that is used to describe participants in complex organisational development. The suggestion is that organisations should rethink the terms of address that they use when trying to ensure that effective and efficient vertical learning takes place:

> In order to escape the pitfalls of denigrating peripheral workers' knowledge and modes of knowing, organisations – executives, managers, and others alike – need to learn to see organisational life 'multiculturally', not in a race ethnic or other trait sense, but

in a work practice and knowledge system sense. The implications for organisational knowing and learning are broader than the treatment of the peripheral border-crossing workers. The language of 'end users' objectifies people, like the copier operators. The language of 'customer' and 'client' maintains boundaries that are conceptual alone, despite systems-theoretical arguments for open systems and permeable boundaries. The esteem in which technical expertise is held, and the concomitant denigration of local knowledge, contributes further to organisational processes that are patronising and demeaning, and which ultimately do not serve the organisation, or its employees at all levels, well.

(Yanow 2004: s23)

Awareness of structure and boundaries and their implications

We will now move to consider the relation between the communicative action that took place and the historically given structures that shaped and were shaped by the practices of participants in our study. Over the run of DWR sessions many structural transformations were witnessed.

The historical legacy of the Castletown school meant that it was strongly boundaried and professional practices within the school were highly controlled and remained distinct from practices outside it. A move to multi-agency working and thus a weakening of the school boundary was most likely to be achieved through external influence on the values that sustained the school's boundary, the relatively weak regulative practice of the school. Our analysis of communicative action within the sessions revealed how an educational psychologist, based in the local authority, worked consistently on these values in the sessions and strengthened the regulative discourse.

In Seaside, the focus of talk in the sessions was on the rules and practices of communication within the instructional practice. Participants became frustrated by the contradiction between existing rules that were maintained by the local authority and the new emergent tasks and practices of multi-agency work. They had already established a strong regulative practice before the DWR sessions started. On the basis of this background they examined the contradictions in the instrumental aspects of their practice and began to bend, or even break, the old rules. The strong boundary between the MPT and the local authority was maintained by practices of communication in which instructions, that is rules, were formulated and transmitted by local authority strategists who were, in turn, unresponsive to ideas formulated by operational staff. The D-analysis confirmed that the boundary between the work-shop group and the local authority was the focus of the communicative action in the workshops.

In Wildside, the wellbeing of children and young people was the primary concern for participants in the CiPC team. There were no strong barriers between the group and the local authority, and although the categorisation of professional agencies within the authority remained strong, the learning focused on ways in which multi-agency work could be co-ordinated through strategic tools such as an electronic assessment system. These tools were the focus of much of the communicative action in the Wildside sessions.

Box 8.1 Connecting Bernstein with an analysis of communicative action

This, Bernstein-influenced, approach gives some insight into the shaping effect of institutions as well as how they are transformed through the purposeful agency of participants. To summarise the process we:

- modelled the structural relations of power and control in institutional settings;
- theorised these relations as cultural historical artefacts, which invisibly or implicitly mediated the relations of participants in practices;
- analysed communicative action from the DWR sessions in terms of the strands of evidence of learning in and for new ways of working.

This process provided empirical evidence of the shaping of communicative action by organisational structures and relations. One implication of this is remarkably simple. The development of new ways of working is contingent upon the institutional arrangements that are in place in a specific organisation. In other words, one size does not fit all and the notion of 'rolling out' a policy through a central initiative which requires uniform implementation across a broad range of organisational structures ignores the specificities of patterns of communication and learning that will be shaped by local organisational arrangements.

Building cognitive trails and networks for learning

The need to understand local organisational landscapes calls for an account of how local practitioners navigate within and across the boundaries and relations of control that structure settings. An important mechanism through which development takes place in specific settings is through the creation and use of what Cussins (1992) has termed cognitive trails. These are in some ways comparable with the songlines of the indigenous Australian peoples (Chatwin 1987). Cussins explains that trails mark the environment as they are enacted. This description echoes the confidence pathways that are linked with gossip circles in the work of Knorr Cetina:

> Confidence pathways create a form of organisation that cuts across technology groups, institutes and experiments, linking individuals who say they have learned, through experience, to appreciate each others' opinion, work, assistance or style of thinking.
>
> (1997: 202)

These pathways can create 'trust cohorts' that 'outlast collaborations'. But, she argues, a second mechanism for binding individuals together is the 'evaluative, personal discourse of technical gossip' (ibid: 203). This gossip:

> mixes report, commentary, and assessment regarding technical objects . . . It often involves evaluative assessments of physicists' work intentions and competence, but may also relate to groups or whole experiments (significant 'theys').
>
> (ibid: 203)

For the professionals in our study, the development of new cognitive trails was a key element in learning to work with distributed expertise. It involved building knowledge about the kinds of skills and expertise other professionals can offer and a confident understanding of how to access others' expertise, what we described in Chapter 4 as knowing how to know who (can help). In workshops practitioners questioned the extent to which these cognitive trails could work informally or needed to be formalised through tools such as meetings, referral processes and information-sharing databases.

Importantly, accessing distributed expertise is also dependent on professionals being able to understand the rules within which other professionals' practices are embedded. Effective cross-boundary collaboration is predicated not only on knowledge of what other professionals do but also why they operate as they do. Contradictions emerged in the multi-agency activities in our research sites because of contrasting professional values and also because different professionals were working to divergent targets, statutory guidelines and thresholds of concern. As Brown and Duguid note there are important distinctions between information and knowledge:

- knowledge entails a knower, but information may be independent of persons;
- knowledge is harder to detach and transfer than information;
- knowledge requires assimilation, digesting, while information can merely be held (2000: 119–120).

We observed that practitioners were striving to move from information exchange to shared knowledge formation as the following quote from the second DWR session at the Seaside site shows:

> At Multi-Professional Team meetings, we seem to have more of these dialogues I suppose. But before we had the multi-professional team working I would find people would leave copies of notes for me. For example, speech and language had been into the school they would leave a copy of . . . or the schools SENCO, Special Needs Coordinator, they would give me copies of all 'this child had an assessment in speech and language and this is a copy for you', you know. So I never actually got to see the person on the other end, I didn't know who they were, where they were based, how they were working. But now when we have the meetings we're all together, there's a bit more of this immediateness about it, you know, time, it's almost like short cutting the time factor.

Box 8.2 Learning in knowledge-laden practices

On the basis of our findings, it is clear that whilst information is of considerable importance, it is not sufficient to manage the transforming objects of work on its own. It was in collaboration within the sites that information held and acquired by various participants was shared and new knowledge was acquired on the basis of the information and mutual interaction. This implies that processes of professional learning must be a central concern for organisations.

Toiviainen (2003) has distinguished between learning in networks and learning to network. Engeström *et al.* (1995) similarly argue that learning and knowledge creation are constituents of expertise. They contrast the view that tasks in which expertise is needed are well defined and analysable as well as stable and unchanging with the understanding that expertise is acquired by negotiating and combining cognitive tools, rules and patterns of social interaction from the multiple contexts in which the experts necessarily operate. They conclude that practitioners must move across boundaries to give and seek help and to find information and tools wherever they happen to be available.

This suggestion, in turn, raises questions about the ways in which collaboration can be brought into play in complex organisations. Puonti (2004) notes that synchronisation is a particular challenge for collaboration, and she discusses it as a flow between sequential and parallel collaboration. The extract from our data shown below provides a glimpse of the ways in which one of the sites struggles to find a way of synchronising their actions:

> Speaker A: Because I think that in a sense there needs to be . . . my concern is that at the moment we've got a lot of children who are being seen by more than one person. And when they're open cases or not open cases [inaudible] is a long-term one. But I think that there was still . . . there . . . unless we know . . . unless you know that X is seeing that child why would you contact her to actually discuss it? We haven't got a system by which children . . . we are making sure that children are being seen by more than one person and those people are connecting together. [talking together]
>
> Speaker B: We use the, don't we use the SENCOs in schools to kind of. . .?
> Speaker A: Well I think there's still quite a few. And certainly because . . . certainly because educational welfare of course the SENCO may not know. And so it can be coming from a variety of different sources. And I'm not sure that actually we still make sure that, or SENCOs think that they need to tell us that somebody else is seeing the child.
> Speaker C: But people would ask. I mean if I was asked to see a child just came out of the blue I would be able to . . . I would ask who else was involved immediately and then make the calls before I did anything.

Speaker D: And you've seen people recently and said, right I want the EP involved.

Speaker C: I've come to find you, yeah.

Speaker D: A sees people and says to the school, right the EP needs to be involved and I go to see her. Or you, or you mention them to me. So. . .

Speaker C: It's quite immediate, A. Within seeing a child [talking together] school contact me straight away and I contact the student in 24 hours.

Temporality is a particular and important aspect of collaboration. The challenge is to manage time collectively, and to synchronise actions that have different priorities as dictated by the core tasks of the divergent participants (Puonti 2004). Puonti provides the following distinctions between sequential and parallel collaboration shown in Table 8.3.

Table 8.3 Sequential and parallel collaboration (Puonti 2004: 81)

Sequential Collaboration	Parallel Collaboration
Isolated, individual efforts to collaborate	Common social ideology as a basis for collaboration
Restricted information exchange only when necessary	Legislation modified to enable functional information exchange
Interaction between authorities only when needed	Liaisons with 'other' agencies to increase personal contacts, shared projects
Separate training for each authority provided by the respective administrative sectors	Shared training courses for authorities
Executive assistance as the standard form of collaboration	Collaborative operations and multi-organisational projects as standard forms of collaboration

We observed movement on all these dimensions across the three English sites. The DWR sessions that focused on the operational processes provided a forum for the shift from sequential to parallel collaboration. An early indication of this movement is seen in the following quote from the second session held at Seaside:

Because I've got open communication with a group of people, group of professionals I've got very easy access to their knowledge. I really don't know what happened before. . . . You know quite often I will pick up a child and you know you get a gut feeling and it's not just . . . there's something more than and then I will speak to the EP to see if they've seen the child, and we share. So it's communicating, and I suppose it's professional sharing and a lot more quickly perhaps than they would have done before.

These findings point to the importance of the analysis of process as well as outcome in organisations, particularly as they embark on periods of significant change and development. This suggestion is echoed by Glisson and Hemmelgarn's (1998) study of the effects of organisational climate and inter-organisational co-ordination on the quality and outcomes of US Children's Services systems offers noteworthy findings in respect to rule-breaking. They conclude that efforts to improve Children's Services provision should focus on developing positive organisational climates that are conducive to practitioner improvisation.

They argue that, while high quality services are characterised, in part, by forms of process-orientation that ensure availability, comprehensiveness and continuity, 'process-related requirements for quality service are not necessarily related to outcome criteria' (ibid: 416). In short, rigid approaches to procedures risk limiting 'employee discretion and responsiveness to unexpected problems and opportunities'. Their analysis indicates that improved outcomes for young people are strongly related to practitioners' 'tenacity in navigating . . . bureaucratic hurdles . . . to achieve the most needed services for each child' (ibid: 416).

Box 8.3 Organisational climate for responsive practices

We would argue that organisational climates that allow for rule-bending have much in common with the climate needed for co-configuring services around a child. That is, they are predicated upon highly responsive, highly personalised case work and customised relationships between professionals and young people that emphasise the need for client participation in planning and decision-making. Moreover, these climates are driven by results related to children's wellbeing, rather than by rigid adherence to prior formulations of practice.

This kind of responsive case work arose during the second DWR session at Seaside when participants identified differences in the organisational structures and regulations between social care and education. They were concerned that some referrals from education to social care were difficult to effect. During the discussion two professionals (one from education and the other from social care) decided to explore the possibility of working on a referral together. As a result, the education professional learnt some of the social care terminology, which helped her to complete the referral forms and follow the most effective procedures.

When reflecting on this collaboration, both professionals recognised that they shared similar professional values. They understood that they were driven by the same concerns for better services and outcomes for children and their families and recognised that the best way to achieve them was through a faster and more efficient referral process. Thus, by learning to share a professional tool (a referral process) they began to develop professional understanding and trust. In this manner, the team identified changes in procedures that could bring about a more flexible and responsive approach.

Hybridity

In order to refine an understanding of organisational, discursive and transmission practices in such situations, new understandings of concept formation that emphasise the complex nature of concepts need to be deployed. An important part of the challenge is to show how written and spoken hybrid discourse, which can deal with the complexity of inter-professional work, arises and to investigate the consequences of its deployment. This feature has been noted by Engeström *et al.*:

> In their work, experts operate in and move between multiple parallel activity contexts. These multiple contexts demand and afford different, complementary but also conflicting cognitive tools, rules, and patterns of social interaction. Criteria of expert knowledge and skill are different in the various contexts. Experts face the challenge of negotiating and combining ingredients from different contexts to achieve hybrid solutions.
>
> (1995: 320)

In response to the challenge of studying new and emergent expert practices, an understanding of hybridity (Sarangi and Roberts 1999)

Table 8.4 Tentative typology of hybridities

	Weak control over professional behaviour (F--)	*Strong control over professional behaviour (F++)*
Strong categories of professional (C++)	Switching between specialisms	Collections of distinct specialists
Weak categories of professional (C--)	Generalists 'melting pot' that may be given coherence through a strong regulative practice	Success of generalists (people)

may provide an important opening for the development of an understanding of changes in discursive practice as different activity systems are brought into different forms of relation with each other. We outline the kinds of professional hybridity that is reflected in talk in Table 8.4.

The strong boundaries around the professional categories and the strong control over professional behaviour in Castletown maintained the practices of individual specialists. At Wildside there were weak boundaries around the professional categories in which professionals were situated in the workshop. They were more in control than their peers in Castletown. However, in Wildside operational professional practice witnessed strong boundaries between services and their professional values coordinated by strategy resulting in a coordinated collection of specialists in the field. In Seaside the weakened professional boundaries and relations of control that had been weakened through rule-breaking and rule-bending gave rise to a collection of workers who drew on the primary strengths of their colleagues when they recognised the need for their expertise. The early days of this development are witnessed in the following statement from Seaside albeit with a cautionary note that whilst operational practices were giving rise to new forms of identity there was something of a dissonance with strategic structures:

But the key difference, which we have tried to broadcast is that basically everyone is a Children's Service worker. People are responsible for the whole child, you're not responsible for this bit of a problem that is presented in relation to this child or this family. And so there is an overarching responsibility. That's taken a while for people to really get to internalise, and I'm not sure we've completely achieved that yet. But within the leadership team it has taken time for people to stop thinking of themselves as Education or Social Care people. . . . So, sort of completely integrated philosophy is tempered by that I think.

This move was not that of the dissolution of professional expertise. The following statement attests to the recognition of the need to retain in-depth skills, knowledge and understanding:

We might not see our colleagues from one month to the next, so we don't have their support but we have the support of the multi-professional team. So to be honest since I've been part of the multi-professional team I haven't really taken too much notice of the other educational welfare officers because I see myself I suppose more a part of the multi-professional team. And they're all in . . . I mean my educational welfare officer colleagues are all in their teams as well. I mean we all got together yesterday because we had a training day and that's quite unusual. You know it's nice to catch up because obviously we can talk about our particular discipline, which we can't do so much in the team.

This recognition of the need to retain professional strengths is set alongside the emergent attributes of relational agency outlined in Chapter 7:

I mean I've found it's a learning curve because I've found out more about other members of the team and what they do, which has actually helped me as a professional. . . . So that has actually helped me in my professional development and it's helped me to feel more confidence as well because I can say to a family, well I think perhaps, you know, you need support from such and such and, you know, I can follow that through and get that support for you. And then when that all works I think, yes!

The development of this way of working also helps organisations needing to destabilise their categorical knowledge. This is knowledge that constrains action to possibilities afforded in gaze of the single professional acting alone. We saw many examples where new ways of working gave rise to shifts from what Engeström has called stabilisation knowledge to possibility knowledge:

Stabilisation knowledge is constructed to freeze and simplify a constantly shifting or otherwise bewildering reality. It is used to turn the problematic into a closed phenomenon that can be registered and pushed around rather than transformed. It commonly takes the shape of fixed and bounded categories, but also narratives may be used to stabilise. Stabilising categories often become stigmatic stamps on objects, both human beings and things. . . . Possibility knowledge, on the other hand, emerges when objects are represented in fields with the help of which one can depict meanings in movement and transformation. One traces transitions of positions in a field, which destabilises knowledge, puts it in movement and opens up possibilities. In this sense, possibility knowledge is agentive knowledge, the instrumentality of agency at work.

(2007c: 271)

As we indicated in Chapters 6 and 7, the emergence of this agentic collaboration between actors is a form of what Engeström (2004) has called collaborative intentionality, which he argues constitutes a new form of capital and is a central feature of organisations that are successful in developing multi-agency working. The agentic collaboration between the practitioners involved in the sites we studied provided valuable assets for the organisations involved:

They perform a dual job in that they solve very complex problems and also contribute to the reshaping of the entire way of working in their given fields. They are very cost-efficient in that they do not require the establishment of new positions or new organisational centres. Indeed, these formations tend to reject such attempts. Rejection and deviation from standard procedures and scripted norms are foundational to the success of such amoeba-like formations. Their efficacy and value lie in their distributed agency, their collective intentionality. In this sense, they suggest the notion of collaborative intentionality capital as an emerging form of organisational assets.

(Engeström 2004: 28)

Learning to work on a shared object of activity

Our study investigated how practitioners actually learn. It was clear that the professionals we worked with did learn from their mistakes and successes, but that, in the context of outcomes-driven management that also emphasised procedures, they felt that collective reflection on the process had not been very common. Ways of talking about and explaining what they did and how they did their own forms of professional work were, however, very important. They were central to how participants in the DWR sessions came to rethink their viewpoints. They were also relevant to how professionals were able to explain the working procedures of their own 'home base' organisations and enable other professionals to understand, adjust to and work with them.

It appears, at times, that tools cross boundaries more easily than people. However, from our analyses of the English case studies it seems that boundary crossing may be easier when the participants work in physical proximity. If nothing else, this increased the likelihood that discussions of process and the renegotiation of objects can occur.

As Engeström *et al.* (2003b) note, significant change is not made by singular actors in singular situations but in the interlinking of multiple situations and actors accomplished by virtue of the durability and longevity of objects. This calls for a conscious expansion of attention beyond the subjects, to include and centre on the objects of work and discourse.

Conclusion

In conclusion, our study suggests that implications for organisations include the following:

- organise in a way that allows strategy to listen and learn with operation, beyond the rhetorical consultation;
- build collaborative intentionality capital that allows for the development of possibility knowledge;
- support the development of structures that derive their rationale from process as well as outcomes;
- analyse rule systems for the future rather than letting legacies of the past dominate;
- develop awareness of structures and boundaries and their implications and structure the division of labour (vertical and horizontal) to align with new demands;

- organise for regular purposeful reflection oriented to surfacing underlying tensions in practices and the development of new tools for new tasks;
- develop ethical courage and terms of address that support rather than inhibit vertical learning;
- articulate what needs to be worked on and changed as well as focusing on outcomes.

Chapter 9

The implications of the Learning in and for Interagency Working Project for cultural historical activity theory

Introduction

The Learning in and for Interagency Working (LIW) study was funded in Phase III of the Teaching and Learning Research Programme (TLRP). TLRP is under the remit of the UK Economic and Social Research Council (ESRC). Therefore, as well as enhancing under-standings of twenty-first century society, studies have a responsibility for developing social science. The LIW study has reflected both the societal and the social science concerns of the ESRC. We have so far largely discussed the former. In this chapter we turn to the latter and the contribution we think that the project might have made to the 'work in progress' that is Cultural Historical Activity Theory (CHAT).

The aims of the study

Two of our six research questions were focused specifically on metho-dological developments. These were:

- How might the methodology of Developmental Work Research (DWR) be developed to capture the emergence of the responsive inter-professional working we were looking at?
- What is involved in studying the learning that occurs as people engage in new ways of working?

As we remained alert to these questions, other methodological ques-tions arose from, for example, our relationships with the practitioners in the case studies and evidence of the importance of boundaries as sites for action. In this chapter we reflect on these and other methodo-logical issues we met over the four years of the project. They are as follows:

- Using DWR in a research study;
- Developments in operating DWR sessions;
- The analysis of the discourse in DWR sessions;
- Revealing concepts in use in the analysis of discourse;
- Attending to the relational and the distributed nature of expertise;
- Boundaries as a focus of research;
- Analysis of institutional effects;
- Engaging research participants in the research process.

Using DWR in a research study

This sub-heading may seem a little odd to CHAT researchers. For us, DWR is a research methodology that reflects the view that social science should enable people to make the world a better place, through enhancing their understandings of their actions and their implications. Vygotsky's view of mediation and intentional action, one of the starting points for DWR, underpins that view of social science. The following extract from his writing indicates the importance of people being able to act on and knowledgably shape their worlds as well as being shaped by them:

> The person, using the power of things or stimuli, controls his own behaviour through them, grouping them, putting them together, sorting them. In other words, the great uniqueness of the will consists of man having no power over his own behaviour other than the power that things have over his behaviour. But man subjects himself to the power of things over behaviour, makes them serve his own purposes and controls that power as he wants. He changes the environment with the external activity and in this way affects his own behaviour, subjecting it to his own authority.
>
> (Vygotsky 1997b: 212)

While Vygotsky was looking at relationships between people and their worlds, DWR, as we explain in Apppendix A, is more focused on systemic change. The following two central precepts for DWR reflect the more recently developed focus on collective or systemic transformation so strongly evident in much of Engeström's work:

- changes in systems and how people are positioned in them are driven forward by the contradictions that exist in them;

- these contradictions need to be recognised and worked on within systems for changes to occur.

In other words, a recognition of our capacities to transform our worlds by working on them is at the core of the version of CHAT developed by Engeström (2007a). Of course, the processes of transformation may be smoother in some situations than in others because of economic and other social conditions.

As we indicated in Chapter 1 and in Appendix A, DWR draws on Vygotskian ideas of dual stimulation where participants are given the tools, or stimuli, of activity theory to work on and understand their working lives so that they might be better able to shape them to the tasks they see as necessary. In the case of LIW, this task would be working responsively on a child's trajectory. DWR is therefore, by definition, an interventionist methodology where researchers work with research participants to reveal contradictions and to promote the use of the tools of activity theory to enable practitioners to work on the contradictions.

From what we have said so far, DWR could be seen as a particularly powerful tool for a change agent rather than a researcher who is, for example, looking for patterns and theory building. However, we had two reasons for selecting DWR as a methodology. First, we were examining emergent practices. We were looking at what was happening at the time when practitioners were learning to work in new ways. We therefore needed to capture their sense-making as they took forward the newly expanded objects of activity that arose in their work across professional boundaries. At the same time, we needed to capture the systemic contradictions that these fresh interpretations of the purposes of work and the resulting emergent practices brought to the organisations in which the practices were developing. We were not setting out to change the systems as the primary purpose of the research. Rather, in the context of a TLRP study, we wanted to find out about what was being learnt and what made that learning possible or limited it. This takes us to the second reason for working with DWR.

We were aware that, by stimulating practitioners' thinking about the purposes and practices of their work in the DWR, we were also intervening in their work systems. We saw that an advantage of DWR was it allowed us to make that intervention an explicit element in the study. There are two implications arising from being explicit about our potentially disruptive role in the study. First, it became important to evaluate how DWR worked as a methodology that could elicit the concepts that were buried in practice and that had a broad relevance for practitioners elsewhere who were engaged in similar activities. As we have already explained, we found that the concepts outlined in Chapter 4 were indeed of lasting relevance to DWR participants and to other practitioners in other settings.

The second aspect was that by recognising that DWR would accelerate awareness of new forms of work, we were not obliged to hide the extent to which we were intervening in the worlds we were investigating. This issue is of broad interest to social scientists. Giddens, for example, has encouraged us to recognise the impact of our practices as researchers on the field of study, seeing one of the virtues of social science to be its capacity to impact on the world it attempts to reveal, sending it 'spinning off in novel directions' (Giddens 1991: 153). Chaiklin, writing from a CHAT perspective about what he terms 'a science of societally significant practices' (1993: 398), has pushed us a little further. He argues that we need to move on as researchers from systematic investigation and analyses, though these are important, to:

> continue building our tools for understanding individuals engaged in meaningful practices in a way that acknowledges and builds the human values contained in those practices, and with a view for these ideas to be potentially incorporated as part of the practice.
> (ibid: 398)

For Chaiklin, this view of social science research demands a different relationship between the researcher and the object of research study. We return to these points and their implications for, for example, negotiating entry into research sites, when we discuss working with research participants later in the chapter. At this point we simply want to highlight the tensions that arose as we worked with an interventionist methodology while undertaking an investigation. Our solution as a research team was to keep a firm hold on the theoretical tools we brought to the study in order to maintain some distance from our potential position as change agents. Our focus was therefore on the ideas about practice and the conditions of practice that were emerging, and on the tools and their usefulness in examining practices. In the sections that follow we discuss the development of these research tools.

Developments in operating DWR sessions

The LIW study benefited enormously from close contact with Engeström and his colleagues at the Center for Activity Theory and Developmental Work Research at the University of Helsinki. The Helsinki team were at the time working on 'New forms of expansive learning at work: the landscape of co-configuration', which they describe as 'an intervention study' and which is outlined in Engestrom (2007c). They had been using DWR in their work with practitioners from different settings within the health service for some time and had, for example, examined problems of differentials in power and status within DWR sessions and the discursive construction of under-standings (Engeström *et al.* 2003a), all of which were issues we tackled in the LIW study. In this section we reflect only on the specific techniques that were used in the sessions and that are outlined in Appendix A.

Because we were using DWR in a research study that involved on-going analysis and cross-case comparisons of the three English sites, the sessions were held every two months to give time between sessions for the analytic work. This frequency was far less than the arrange-ments in place in most of the Helsinki projects, where the intensity of the engagement is usually important. But apart from that difference, we very much followed the Helsinki processes and experimented with the ideas they were developing when working with people who were not always from the same work setting. We shall look at three of these processes.

Mini-labs

These were suggested to us by our Finnish colleagues as a useful way of familiarising participants with the analytic tools of activity theory through, for example, worked examples of the histories of the site, enabling them to get to know each other and allowing them to have extensive discussions on the objects of activity and the values embedded in them. They differed from the sessions which followed later in the sequence because they permitted an initial gentle explora-tion of ideas and differences and the opportunity to get to grips with the main features of the activity theory analyses they would be doing. Though it varied slightly from site to site, the first two sessions in the series of six were close to what the Helsinki team term mini-labs and the subsequent four sessions focused much more on revealing and discussing the contradictions that arose from the data.

We found this gentle introduction very useful, perhaps particularly so as we had not negotiated entry into sites as change agents. Rather, our purpose, from the participants' point of view, was to help them understand the practices they were taking forward. Part of our pay-back to them was to leave them with the analytic resources of CHAT so that they could continue to analyse and develop their work.

The presentation of data in the DWR sessions

We were anxious to ensure that the voices of the participants were heard in sessions and that they did not simply react to evidence brought to them by the research team. We did this in two ways: the first involved the team in selecting the evidence to be represented, while the second depended on practitioners bringing case studies to the team so that they could jointly prepare the presentation of evidence.

In previous projects using DWR we had become accustomed to combing interview data and earlier DWR data with the same partici-pants to select statements that either contained a contradiction within them or that revealed a contradiction when held alongside another statement (see Chapter 6 for definitions of contradictions in activity theory). These statements would then be represented to participants as mirror data stimuli for their analyses of the contradictions they were facing in, for example, a rules-object relationship. We continued with this practice, but began to augment it with video clips from previous DWR sessions. Again this work was already part of the repertoire of the Helsinki team, who also use video clips of interviews. However, we found that the English participants were not happy about our filming interviews, while the problems of taking the presentations to a range of different sites where we were dependent on local technology meant that we eventually limited the use of video clips from previous sessions.

The second strategy, of asking participants to present edited accounts of the challenges they were facing and how they overcame them, was more successful, but needed to be handled carefully. In Seaside, for example, an education welfare officer and an educational psychologist gave a concrete account of how they jointly interpreted a child's problem, had to act quickly and therefore had to bend some of the rules to trigger the child's move to another school. The presenta-tion of concrete cases is a powerful strategy, therefore it can be quite threatening to practitioners who are cautious about change. In Castletown, a case study example from an education welfare officer working with another school that described how she had acted quickly and, with that school's support, circumvented the established referral system, invoked strong negative reactions from teachers in the main Castletown school. The school-based practitioners declined to engage with the possibility of working in that way. This response was important data for the study, but potentially uncomfortable for the practitioner-presenter.

When practitioners presented case accounts, they therefore needed the backing of the researchers. This backing occurred through our working together to develop brief accounts that contained key elements, undertaking analyses jointly so that the practitioners could deal with questions and, as the Castletown experience showed to be necessary, taking joint responsibility for the analysis so that the research team could step in to deflect any adverse reactions.

Preparation

The planning of the two-hour DWR sessions was therefore important. We spent around four hours planning each session as a small team, having all undertaken an initial analyses of the data on which we were drawing. Having identified the contradictions to be the focus of the session, we selected the mirror data and ordered it in a way that allowed the contradictions to emerge. The next step was to prepare PowerPoint presentations that reflected the decisions in the planning meetings, and to send extracts of these to the relevant participants to gain their agreement to use evidence they had provided. We would then take the presentation to the sessions, start off as planned and then work increasingly responsively as the session progressed, moving around the presentation and often abandoning it. Flip chart paper was an important resource as we frequently found ourselves modelling and remodelling work systems in DWR discussions. We also took pre-prepared activity system triangles, which we stuck to walls of the session rooms and could use to remind people of the analytic tools they could use.

The most important aspect of the preparation was the research team's familiarity with the data and their understanding of the contradictions to be found in them. We are aware that too little work has been done on the role of the facilitator in DWR sessions. Engeström *et al.* writing about their DWR work with medical and health practitioners and patients have concluded

> in such studies, researcher interventionists make themselves
> contestable and fallible participants of the discourse, which means

that their actions also become objects of data collection and critical analysis.

(2003a: 313)

We would agree. Our careful hold on the theoretical tools we brought to the analyses of evidence is only part of the solution to the problems of interventionist research. In the next section we discuss how we developed and used analytic protocols for examining the discursive construction of the concepts underpinning the practices discussed in the DWR sessions. However, even attention to the detailed preparation of protocols does not entirely deal with the demands of studies, which in Chaiklin's terms require us to recognise how we engage, as researchers, with the 'moral and political content' of the practice under investigation (Chaiklin 1993: 396).

The analysis of discourse in DWR sessions

We regard the development and application of the D-analysis, outlined in Chapter 8, as one of the major contributions that this study has made to the current approaches to data analysis within the cultural–historical tradition. As much of the research in CHAT moves to asking questions concerning progressively more complex networks of activity systems, there is a need to develop forms of analysis that can capture change over time and across settings.

The English LIW study presented three analytical challenges:

- it was a study of multiple sites (we worked over time with five services for children and families with complex needs);
- it was also multi-centred (there were five universities) employing university-based research officers and three senior practitioners seconded from the three case study sites in the main element of the study;
- having used a top-down analysis based on Cultural Historical Activity Theory (CHAT) concepts to select material used in the DWR sessions, we needed to move to a 'bottom-up' comprehensive analysis of the organisation of communicative action in those sessions in order to identify evidence trails of work-based learning in each site.

We discussed how we used the D-Analysis of communicative action in Chapter 8. Here we outline how we introduced the analysis to the research team once the six workshops in each site had been completed. The analysis brought into focus the communicative devices that participants used to recontextualise their working practices and their ongoing enquiries into them as they participated in DWR sessions.

The D-Analysis protocol (see Chapter 8) was designed to focus the analytic attention of the research team on the emergent distinctions that mattered for participants as they worked with the mirror data presented to them in the DWR sessions. This protocol provided a shared unit of analysis for examining the sequentially organised session talk over one year. It allowed the research team to remain close to the specific data in each site and to identify distinctions that made a difference for participants in learning to do multi-agency work. We were able to track the emergence of what-it-is-to-learn as an analytic focus across sessions at each site and to compare all the audio-visual evidence of interactions in the DWR sessions, in order to identify the emergent strands of learning.

Working with the protocol involved looking at the workshop material without necessarily taking the CHAT conceptual vocabulary as the primary analytical resource, as had been the case when preparing DWR mirror data. In other words, the aim was to provide an analytical evidence base that might substantiate CHAT-based analysis.

We introduced the research team to the general analytic framing of the D-Analysis by describing how it involved a shift from the 'given' to the 'to-be-established'. This analytic shift aimed to move us from framing communication as descriptions corresponding to states in and of the world, and instead to be able to recognise the performative organisation of communicative action. In other words, the team needed to be able to see that what we do with talk and text can be analysed in terms of what it accomplishes (Edwards and Potter 1992; Potter and Wetherell 1987).

For example, how do people use, account for and warrant what it is to do multi-agency work, be a team member and work up their stake and interest in inter-professional collaboration? We emphasised that addressing such issues required a focus on the sequential and contingent organisation of communicative action in each session and across the sessions over time. That is, how people's contributions to the sessions are contingently related to each other in terms of the sequential organisation of their talk.

In drawing analytical attention to the significance of claims to experience we were also able to highlight the temporal organisation of communicative action. As Mercer points out in his presentation of what he terms 'sociocultural discourse analysis', the performative aspects of communicative action extend beyond the immediacies of the situation of production:

> Things that are said may invoke knowledge from the joint past experience of those interacting (e.g. their recall of previous activities they have pursued together), or from the rather different kind of 'common knowledge' which is available to people who have had similar, though separate, past experiences.
>
> (2004: 140)

Just as Mercer develops an analytic framework for the analysis of the development of common understandings in classroom interactions, we also used forms of discursive analysis to trace the emergence of what can be taken as the collective and distributed knowledge of people who are charged with the task of working together. Our aim was to introduce and use discursive analysis for tracking how relevant distinctions concerning multi-agency working were established and made to stick in the emergent learning of what it takes to practise such forms of working.

All the research team participated in the design and execution of the DWR sessions. Running the sessions at each site had involved extended introductions to the methodology and ground rules for participation. Introductions to the sessions in the sites set out both the terms of reference and the selected aims for each session. Focusing on the extent to which these aims were met, evolved, or subverted, provided initial focus of communicative analytical concern, providing an accessible introductory descriptive analysis of what, and how, the sessions were accomplished.

The analysis of the six sessions was informed by notes made at the sessions into narrative accounts of how the sessions evolved at each site, within the overall constraints of the methodology. This descriptive analysis provided a grounding for building the research team's capacities in communicative analysis. It became clear from them that it was possible to take an analytical position on how the participants developed their engagement in the sessions over the period of the interventions.

The DWR sessions provided a forum where practitioners could interrogate how their current working practices and their everyday understandings of these practices either enabled or constrained the development of innovative multi-agency working. On the basis of that interrogation, practitioners could identify how their work could or should be reconfigured in practice. We therefore needed to examine the discussions in the DWR sessions to identify how participants formulated and made visible the consequences for them of session participation. We needed to study what they said as professionals who were required to work across professional boundaries in relation to what they took to be their own professional competence.

A major analytic question was: what forms of communicative action could be identified that demonstrated the participants making visible 'what-it-is-to-learn'? In the first instance we approached the data with what could be termed a minimal operationalisation of what-it-is-to-learn from a participant's perspective. We examined the data for ways participants signalled some forms of awareness that theirs or others' knowledge states were at issue.

If claims to changes in knowledge state are to matter in the context of participation in DWR, we need a way of taking the analysis further in order to pursue visibilities of learning in communicative action. One way to do this is to examine how distinctions concerning the details of practice were worked up to make a difference. In other words, we focused the research team's analytic attention on how participants worked up the significance of details of practice in ways that came to make the difference to how they worked as professionals (cf. Bateson 1972).

The research team's analysis was therefore initially guided by the protocol, which was provided in a summary form in Chapter 8. The first step was to look for how a difference was noticed and worked with by the participants in their discussions in the DWR sessions. The protocol provided three categories that enabled this:

- *Deixis*: identify when there is some nomination or 'pointing' to a particular issue in terms of drawing attention to a distinction that is then worked up to make a difference in subsequent turns.
- *Definition and delineation*: look for how that issue is elaborated in the uptake of others in terms of how the following are warranted and made relevant through: (i) qualifications identifying further distinctions; (ii) orderabilities in the organisation and delivery of past, present and future practice; (iii) expansive elaborations of the problematics of practice.
- *Deliberation*: identify how some working consensus on what is the case emerges in terms of evoking both particularities and generalities of marking distinctive features of past, present or future practice.

The analysis then turned to examining in what ways such sequences mattered. If we identified strands of deixis, definition/delineation and deliberation, what were their contingent consequences for participants? Did they make visible distinctions that made the difference, so that participants could be identified as attending to what it was necessary in order to learn to do multi-agency working. In other words, did the talk lead to, or accomplish, some form of departure or development in claims about the practice of the participants? When this occurred we could assign one or both of the final two categories in the protocol:

- *Departure*: identify shifts towards a qualititatively different position in practices in terms of the formulation of emergent distinctions.
- *Development*: identify when participants specify new ways of working that provide the basis for becoming part of, or have become part of, what they take to be and warrant as a significant reformulation of their practices.

As we demonstrated in Chapter 8, this protocol allowed us to examine the sequential organisation of session talk in terms of identifying distinctions that make the difference for participants in learning to do multi-agency work. It provided a basis for tracking the emergence of what-it-is-to-learn as an analytic focus of concern across sessions at each site. Its cyclical application enabled: reading, reviewing, interrogating, collating and comparing all the audio-visual evidence from the intervention sessions in order to identify the emergent strands of learning.

This allowed the analysis to be taken to the next stage (Daniels *et al.* 2005 and Chapter 8 in this book) where we were able to address the question of how complex and highly contested social dilemmas (Billig 1996) were locally constituted as objects for institutional activity. In other words, how they became part of an institutional order (Smith 2005), which had no ready-made strategy for dealing with such dilemmas.

One challenge of the project was to show how institutionally established categories and ways of arguing could be reformulated and transformed into new strategies and activities as part of learning what it is to become engaged with and in multi-agency work. However, without the comprehensive analysis of the communicative action within the sessions across all the research sites we would not have been able to progress to the final analysis of those transformations (Daniels 2006).

Revealing concepts in use in the analysis of discourse

In his account of the 'New Forms of Learning' study at Helsinki (Engeström 2007b), Engeström begins by outlining the contradictions faced by each of the organisations they studied and then goes on to outline the 'new concept and tools created and adopted by practitioners' as they worked on the contradictions (ibid: 24). He argues that tools and, by extension, how they are used 'open a window into the mentality of the trade' (ibid: 33). This statement is based on Vygotsky's insight that consciousness, that is, how we think about and categorise the world, is revealed in how we engage with it in our actions and talk.

We would, of course, agree with Engeström. In the previous section and in Chapter 8 we have discussed the D-Analysis as a methodological development within CHAT. In this section we suggest that DWR methodology, because it can reveal how we think and categorise, may be a useful addition to the resources of researchers who are interested in revealing the concepts in use in practice.

How practitioners think while they are acting is a problem that has long vexed researchers of professional practice. The most often mentioned research tools for eliciting thinking in practice are thinking aloud protocols; however, these are a methodological minefield (Boren and Ramey 2000). Nielsen *et al.* (2002), for example, point out that thinking aloud in the context of a research study demands the production of explanations, while Boren and Ramey, end their review of the problems associated with these protocols with the proposal that researchers should look at 'speech communication' as a more sound alternative.

We would agree and, inspired by the work of Mäkitalo and Säljö on the hidden categorisations in use in an employment exchange (Mäkitalo and Säljö 2002), we intended to explore the use of everyday situated conversations as an evidence-base for revealing categories in use, as people made decisions about vulnerable children. However, tightened ethical restrictions meant that we could not have access to these conversations and were more reliant than we had anticipated on talk in the DWR sessions. Ultimately this proved a fruitful source, in part because DWR processes pressed participants to develop and reveal the concepts needed to work inter-professionally.

The actual concepts in use that were revealed by the D-Analysis were discussed in Chapter 4 and the analytic processes are discussed in Chapter 8 and the previous section. The concepts outlined in Chapter 4 did not arise in the acts of practice, but in the process of struggling, with other practitioners, to make sense of the acts of practices and the contradictions they gave rise to. If justifications or explanations for action were offered, they were not the end point, as is often the case in thinking aloud techniques. Rather, they were just one element in a process of delineation and deliberation that helped to refine the concepts that emerged in the communicative action of the DWR sessions. The D-Analysis made visible the thinking about practice that wove its way through the sense-making processes demanded by DWR's use of double stimulation (see Chapter 1 and Appendix A).

Attending to the relational and the distributed nature of expertise

The idea that expertise can be seen as distributed across practitioners has been central to our discussions of inter-professional collaboration. We have described it as a collective attribute spread across work systems, which is drawn upon to accomplish tasks and to which practitioners can contribute. It therefore follows that it lies both in the system and in the individual's ability to recognise and negotiate its use. Engeström and Middleton have also given a system level definition of expertise as a collective attribute: the 'collaborative and discursive construction of tasks, solutions, visions, breakdowns and innovations within and across systems' (1996: 4).

While we recognise this definition, we have also focused our gaze at the level between the collective and the individual in order to try to capture the constructing and negotiating that occurs between interacting individuals (Edwards, in press b). This is an important challenge when looking at inter-professional work: although we did find examples of teams in the LIW study, we also worked with systems where practitioners remained in their home organisations and worked at configuring their responses to the needs of children and families with practitioners in other organisations. Recognising that systems, such as children's services, are open knowledge-laden networks with unfolding possibilities for joint action means that notions of systemic expertise, which have developed from studies of the workplace, may not be sufficient. We also need to look at the temporary, shifting configurations of inter-professional activity inside and outside organisations and try to understand better how they are achieved.

This focus takes us immediately to the relational and the idea of relational agency. In Chapter 7 we described relational agency as a capacity for working with others to strengthen purposeful responses to complex problems (Edwards 2005). We described it as a two-stage process within a constant dynamic. It involves:

1   working with others to expand the 'object of activity' or task being working on by recognising the motives and the resources that others bring to bear as they too interpret it;

2   aligning one's own responses to the newly enhanced interpretations, with the responses being made by the other professionals to act on the expanded object.

Relational agency, we suggest, can begin to help us to understand the negotiations and reconfiguring of tasks indicated by Engeström and Middleton by focusing on the capacity for negotiating interpretations of the object of activity and responses to that expanded object. It occupies a conceptual space between a focus on learning as enhancing individual understanding and a focus on learning as systemic change and includes both. It fits squarely within sociocultural readings of mind and world, by seeing mind as outward looking, pattern-seeking and engaged with the world (Greeno: 1997, 2006). Furthermore, by giving emphasis to 'knowing how to know who' as resource for action, it begins to indicate how a more relational form of engaging may be accomplished in both local and more extended configurations of practice.

'Knowing how to know who', as we indicated in Chapter 4, is not simply a matter of gathering information about who knows how to do what so that expertise can be marshalled to respond to a diagnosis made by one professional. It includes a capacity for mutuality and can lead to a form of practice that is enhanced by the interpretations of others and is not simply a matter of co-ordinating the expertise of others to respond to the interpretations made by one practitioner.

The capacity for mutuality is important, as relational practice that is responsive to the needs and strengths of other professionals, and of children and families, involves being able to recognise and take seriously the values and motives shaping the practices of collaborators. In several of the studies of inter-professional work that we have undertaken over the last few years, what has distinguished the collaboration we are discussing here from boundary crossing to access support has been the length of commitment to a constantly renegotiated object of activity that collaboration required. In Chapter 4 we suggested that making values explicit was crucial to inter-professional work as shared values operated as a kind of 'glue', helping trust to develop and creating a shared sense of where they were going. Working on understanding each other's motives and values help them to ascribe to a long-term distant object to which their immediate object-oriented work was ultimately to contribute.

Polanyi's insights (Polanyi 1958/1998) into the relationships between tacit and explicit knowledge as two sides of the same coin, also remind us of just how important it is to understand the motives of others in systems of distributed expert knowledge. Tacitly held knowledge includes motives and beliefs, it therefore links the meanings offered in explicitly shared expert knowledge to the knowledge and value systems in which they emerged. Understanding the knowledge offered by collaborating experts when interpreting the object of activity and when responding to the interpretation with them, therefore also requires that we are sensitive to the tacit aspects of that expertise.

Boundaries as a focus of research

When we started the LIW study, we did not anticipate just how important work on and at boundaries would be. We have provided an extensive analysis of how people worked on organisational boundaries in Chapter 8. Here we simply indicate how the LIW study of what happened at boundaries points to areas for development in CHAT.

In Chapter 5 we discussed Churchman's argument (Ulrich 1988) that boundaries are social constructions that define who is included and excluded from interactions and what knowledge is considered relevant in those interactions. When boundaries become contestable, in the way we outlined in Chapter 8, the threats to exclusive expertise, meaning-making and identity are considerable. Midgley's work on values and boundaries, where he demonstrated how boundaries are places where values can compete and the priorities of the less powerful can be marginalised (Midgley 1992; Midgley *et al.* 1998) similarly point to the importance of analyses of what happens at boundaries.

Kerosuo (Kerosuo 2006; Kerosuo and Engeström 2003), working with activity theory concepts, comes to a similar conclusion and describe boundaries as discursively formed. The discussion in the section that follows this one connects, in part, with Kerosuo's argument as it explains how we can begin to trace links between the mediational potential of institutions and the talk that arises in them. Boundaries as sites of relationships of power and control, for example, may also be amenable to the analyses outlined there. Particularly, the LIW study suggests that an examination of the hybridity of professional language at the boundaries would be worthwhile.

Despite Kerosuo's growing body of work, these contestable spaces have probably received too little attention in CHAT research. Instead, attention has focused on boundary crossing, boundary spanning and the potentially shared objects that mediate links between systems. Konkola's idea of a boundary zone (Konkola 2001), touched on in Chapters 2 and 5, is helpful as it provides an analytic focus. However, the assumption that it is a neutral zone where trust can be generated should not perhaps be taken for granted.

We have already indicated that the DWR sessions in the LIW study operated as boundary zones, which were particularly helpful for the groupings of professionals who were not in the two Multi-Professional Teams in the study. They offered a place where meanings could be explored, values made explicit and where people could re-position themselves in relation to the object of activity that they potentially shared (Edwards in press a). The moves that participants made were outlined in Chapter 5, but we are aware that we are at the start of our work on boundaries and that, for example, we need to know much more about the negotiations that occur at the boundaries that were the focus of attention in Castletown and Seaside. In particular we want to understand better how knowledge that is generated in one place is mobilised and negotiated at boundaries so that messages generated at boundaries work their way into meaning systems of contributing organisations. This is a particularly important question if we are concerned about how knowledge generated in innovative practices can inform the strategic development of policy and institutions. We are quite sure that these analyses will return us to Midgley's categorisations of power in boundary shaping and to Bernstein's work on invisible mediation, to which we now turn.

Analysis of institutional effects

Mäkitalo and Säljö argue that as we talk, we enter the flow of communication in a stream of both history and the future (2002: 63) and that researchers need to have some definition of the situation or activity at hand (ibid: 66).

If activities are to be thought of as socially rooted and historically developed, how do we describe them in relation to their social, cultural and historical contexts of production? If Vygotsky was arguing that formation of mind is a socially mediated process, then what theoretical and operational understandings of the social, cultural, historical production of 'tools' or artefacts do we need to develop in order to empirically investigate the processes of development?

These questions concerning the production of artefacts or tools are a priority for the development of CHAT, as so much of the empirical work that has been undertaken struggles to connect the analysis of the formative effect of mediated activity or tool use with the analysis of tool or artefact production. We need an account of the production of psychological tools or artefacts, such as discourse, that will allow for exploration of formative effects of the social context of production at the psychological level. This will also involve a consideration of the possibilities afforded to different social actors as they take up positions and are positioned in social products such as discourse.

As Bernstein (1993) argued, the development of Vygotskian theory calls for the development of languages of description that will facilitate a multi-level understanding of pedagogic discourse, the varieties of its practice and the contexts of its realisation and production. We therefore need to be able to connect the social cultural historical context to the form of the mediating artefact. When studying processes of social formation, we require a theoretical description of the possibilities for social products in terms of the principles that regulate the social relations in which they are produced. Bernstein's challenge is that we need to understand the principles of communication in terms derived from a study of principles of social regulation.

We have suggested in various parts of this book that different social structures give rise to different modalities of language that have specialised mediational properties. These language modalities have been shaped by the social, cultural and historical circumstances in which interpersonal exchanges arise and they in turn shape the thoughts and feelings, the identities and aspirations for action of those engaged in interpersonal exchange in those contexts. Hence the relations of power and control, which regulate social interchange, give rise to specialised principles of communication.

In Engeström and Middleton's (1996) work on activity theory, the production of the outcome is discussed but not the production and structure of the tool itself. The rules, community and division of labour are analysed in terms of the contradictions and dilemmas that arise within the activity system specifically with respect to the production of the object. The production of the cultural artefact, the discourse, is not analysed in terms of the context of its production that is the rules, community and division of labour that regulate the activity in which subjects are positioned. The language that Bernstein has developed, we think uniquely, allows researchers to capture institutional modalities by describing and positioning the discursive, organisational and interactional practice of the institution. This approach gives some insight into the shaping effect of institutions as well the ways in which they are transformed through the agency of participants.

In LIW, as we outlined in Chapters 3 and 8, we modelled the structural relations of power and control in institutional settings, theorised them as cultural historical artefacts, which invisibly or implicitly mediated the relations of participants in practices in which communicative action takes place. This communicative action was then analysed in terms of the strands of evidence of learning in and for new ways of working. These provided empirical evidence of the mutual shaping of communicative action by organisational structures and relations and the opportunity to recognise the formation of hybrid professional identities.

This approach extends the application of Bernstein's work to the study of the transformation of institutional modalities over time. The analysis of communicative action provides an approach to examining the sequential and contingent development of concepts in specific institutional settings.

Our approach to modelling the structural relations of power and control in institutional settings theorised them as cultural historical artefacts that invisibly or implicitly mediated the relations of participants in practices. Their communicative action was analysed in terms of the strands of evidence of learning in and for new ways of working and gives some insight into the shaping effect of institutions as well the ways in which they are transformed through the agency of participants. It opens up the possibility of developing increasingly delicate descriptions of the rules and division of labour that obtain within and between settings. At the same time it carries with it the possibility of rethinking notions of agency and reconceptualising subject position in terms of the relations between possibilities afforded within the division of labour and the rules that constrain possibility and direct and deflect the attention of participants.

Engaging research participants in the research process

We worked in a period of turbulent policy change, with an inter-ventionist methodology and with practitioners who were being obliged to re-position themselves as professionals. There was a lot to learn for all of us, and the team was usefully strengthened for most of the fieldwork period by local authority-based researchers in the three main English sites. In this section we outline briefly some of issues that arose from our using DWR as a research methodology that engaged closely with the professionals whose learning we were trying to trace. We were driven in our work as educational researchers who want to make a difference, by broader questions about whose knowledge counts and we think that DWR offers one way of revealing the knowledge that is embedded in practices and that is so often overlooked.

DWR provides a rather different model of working with user engagement than, for example, either action research or university-led studies of curriculum or organisational development (Edwards *et al.* 2007). We attempted to work with practitioners to enable them to articulate and refine concepts that we hope help to explain and to take forward understandings of practice. We aimed at enabling profes-sionals to generate fresh ways of explaining what was going on in both existing and emerging practices within relatively long-term research partnerships with them. It was therefore important for us to work with practitioners who were committed to this refining of fresh under-standings of their evolving practices, because the analyses of systems and practices that were necessary to the research process were challenging and time-consuming.

Negotiating entry into the sites therefore required more care than is often the case. Almost every local authority officer we met wanted us to work with their authority, as they rapidly recognised how the methodology could promote practitioners' learning and stimulate the organisational changes they knew were necessary. We learnt from the pilot phase with Brookside and Newhill, however, that we also need to be very clear with the operational staff about what was involved in the study and to negotiate their agreement to engage in a process of individual and organisational change.

If practitioners were not interested in rethinking their practices in relation to their institutional systems, they would dislike the process, the powerful conceptual tools offered by activity theory would be rejected and the contradictions they unearthed resisted. Even where there was an interest among practitioners, participants needed to become gradually aware of how DWR could disrupt assumptions and lead to some quite profound re-positioning. The mini-labs, where people could become accustomed to DWR processes were therefore important.

Once the DWR sessions started, as well as being a site for data collection, they allowed rapid feedback of ongoing analyses to participants: mirror data presented at sessions and the questions asked by the team about the mirror data gave indications of what we were finding in the field within a short time frame. At the same time, the sessions allowed reflexivity, as participants could question our interpretations and offer their own. The facilitator was simply one voice in these multi-voiced settings and he or she focused on capturing the contradictions that arose when the mirror data were discussed, rather than asserting the team's interpretation as the most valid.

Consequently, the team also received regular feedback that could quickly check the validity of its initial interpretations. This feedback, along with interviews with participants who we were seeing regularly in the DWR sessions, meant that we were closely in touch with changes in the field and were able to work with their insights and anticipations to develop aspects of the study in response to these changes.

For example, it became clear that differences in organisational histories and intentions across local authorities were affecting the individual and organisational learning that was occurring. We were able to incorporate this focus within the project, as Chapter 8 indicates. However, we think there is a lesson for funding bodies that desire more practitioner engagement in the research process. Practitioners' concerns, if taken seriously, can fruitfully divert a carefully planned study.

Perhaps, most important of all, the DWR sessions offered a platform where what people knew and needed to know became the focus. Differences were scrutinised and struggled with and practitioners' meaning systems were enriched over time. We were as much part of these emerging meaning systems as were the professionals who were developing new ways of working together. We are therefore certain that the methodology we used has much to offer understandings of how knowledge is constructed in partnerships between universities and the fields in which practices develop.

Conclusion

In this chapter we have pointed, somewhat tentatively, to what we think might be the contribution of the LIW study to growing understandings of CHAT methodologies. In doing so we have also tried to indicate how CHAT approaches connect with and even inform some of the broader methodological concerns of educational research. Above all, in our efforts at following the changing demands of the LIW study we have learnt a lot from each other and the practitioners we met along the way. We therefore end this account of the study with our thanks to them.

Appendix A

Activity theory in the Learning in and for Interagency Working Project

Learning in and for Interagency Working (LIW)

This book is based on the LIW project: one of twelve studies that comprised Phase III of the Economic and Social Research Council's Teaching and Learning Research Programme (TLRP). The project focused on the professional and organisational learning required in order to develop inter-professional collaboration to support the wellbeing of vulnerable children and young people (Daniels *et al.* 2007; Leadbetter 2006, 2007). Directed by Harry Daniels (University of Bath) and Anne Edwards (University of Oxford), the LIW Project ran from January 2004 to December 2007. Two years into the study, a research team led by Tony Gallagher and based in Northern Ireland received TLRP funding to extend the LIW work in a different context.

The LIW Project was driven by activity theory, in particular, the leading-edge work developed at the University of Helsinki by Yrjö Engeström. This appendix outlines the development and key principles of activity theory; Engeström's (1987, 1999a) notion of expansive learning in professional work settings; and the use of developmental work research (DWR), Engeström's method of applying activity theory through interventionist research, in the LIW study.

What is activity theory?

Activity theory is rooted in the work of the Russian psychologist L.S. Vygotsky (1896–1934) and his collaborators and successors in the field, particularly Alexander Luria (1902–77) and A.N. Leont'ev (1904–79). Vygotsky's main concern was to study how relationships between human agents and their environments are mediated by cultural means, tools and signs. His work has therefore allowed us to understand that how we think is revealed in our actions, including our talk. The early development of activity theory, building on Vygotsky's ground-breaking work on mediation, examined human activity in terms of the dynamics between human actors (subjects) and the tools (both material and conceptual) that actors use in order to impact upon aspects the world around them (the object of their activities). For this reason, activity theory is often described as providing object-orientated analyses of human activity, that is, its starting point lies in understanding what it is that individuals (or collectives) are seeking to change, to shift or to act upon. Figure A.1 depicts this triadic conception of how we act in the world and captures Vygotsky's concern with mediation and Leont'ev's emphasis on object and object motive.

Leont'ev's contribution to the development of the theory was twofold. First, he shifted attention from a focus primarily on mediation to a concern with the object of the activity (what was being worked on) and how interpretations of the object give rise to particular ways of acting. In other words, objects contain motives that give shape to how we respond to them. The idea of object motive is very important if we are looking at a value-laden object such as a child's developmental trajectory out of risk of social exclusion, as it may be interpreted differently by different professionals who would then want to work on it in different ways. Second, Leont'ev introduced an emphasis on the division of labour, which he saw as shaping how we think, since, he argued, object-orientated activity is mediated by tools and is also performed in conditions of joint, collective activity.

In the LIW project our analytical approach was object-orientated and concerned with forms of collective activity emerging in multi-agency children's services as they, for example, worked on children's trajectories to remove them from risk of social exclusion. We therefore asked

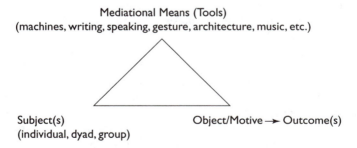

Mediational Means (Tools)
(machines, writing, speaking, gesture, architecture, music, etc.)

Subject(s)   Object/Motive → Outcome(s)
(individual, dyad, group)

Figure A.1 A representation of mediated action and object motive

practitioners to explain what it was that they were working on. When we asked this kind of question we were not so much concerned with the broad outcomes they wanted to achieve, such as improving referral systems, rather we wanted to encourage them to explain the focus of their work and so reveal the object motive and the conceptual and material tools they were using in their work. This question often took them to recognising that they would need to change practices before they could work on the object they identified.

At that point the tools, rules of practice or division of labour would become the object of their work. For example, they might first say that they were working on children's pathways through the local systems of support. However, before being able to work on that with any degree of success they would find that they needed a way of ensuring that a child and family only had to complete one assessment form, rather than a series of forms. In this case, the processing of assessment forms might be the new and temporary object of the activity, various children's services professionals would be the subjects carrying out the activity, and their tool would be the means by which they worked on improving assessment forms, which could be anything from a new electronic entry system to the appointment of a key worker/case co-coordinator to a new diary system.

Engeström and activity theory

Since the 1970s Engeström has pioneered a form of Cultural Historical Activity Theory (CHAT) that builds upon the work of Vygostsky and Le'ontev. In order to develop activity theory, Engeström has expanded the original triangular representation of activity (Figure A.1) to enable an examination of activity at the level of the collective. This 'second generation' of activity theory represents the collective nature of activity through the addition of the analytic elements of community, rules and division of labour and an emphasis on their interactions with each other (Figure A.2).

Engeström (2000) sees object-oriented joint practice as the unit of analysis for activity theory, not individual actions; and sees instability, internal tensions and contradictions as the drivers of change and development in professional and organizational practice. An important aspect of Engeström's version of activity theory is an understanding that object-oriented activity is always characterized by ambiguity, surprise, interpretation, sense making, and potential for change. In short, when we asked participants in the LIW study what they are

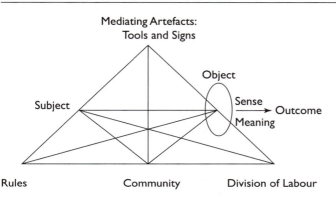

Figure A.2 Second-generation activity theory model (Engeström 1987)

'working on' the answers we received were complex, diverse and often contradictory.

Engeström (1999a) suggests that activity theory may be summarised with the help of five principles:

- The prime unit of analysis is a collective, artefact-mediated, object-oriented activity system, seen in its network relations to other activity systems.
- An activity system is always a nexus of multiple points of view, traditions and interests. The division of labour in an activity creates different positions for the participants; the participants carry their own diverse histories and the activity system itself carries multiple layers and strands of history engraved in its artefacts, rules and conventions. This multi-voicedness increases exponentially in networks of interacting activity systems. It is a source of both tension and innovation, demanding actions of translation and negotiation.
- Activity systems take shape and are transformed over lengthy periods of time. Their problems and potentials can only be understood against their own history. History needs to be considered not only in terms local history of the activity and its objects but also as the history of the theoretical ideas and tools that have shaped professional activity. So, for instance, current developments in children's service provision to counter social exclusion need to be analysed against the history of local organisations and also against the more global history of the social service concepts, procedures and tools employed and accumulated in the local activity.

- Contradictions are historically accumulating structural tensions within and between activity systems, that is, are not the same as problems or conflicts. The definitions of contradictions are outlined in detail in Chapter 6 of the present book. Engeström's activity theory emphasises the importance of contradictions within activity systems as the driving force of change and development and sees them as structural tensions that emerge over time in organisational practices. These contradictions may constrain professional practice at certain points but they may also provide a source of change and development. For instance, in the LIW research we identified numerous instances in which the efforts of different professional groups (such as teachers, educational psychologists, health workers, social care staff) to work on a shared object (such as the trajectories of at-risk young people) revealed contradictions arising from having to work to different professional targets, referral thresholds and assessment procedures (that is, conflicting sets of rules and shifting divisions of labour). These were worked on so that understandings of the object of activity were expanded and, for example, rules were adjusted. This change process takes us to the final principle.
- Activity systems move through relatively long cycles of qualitative transformations. As the contradictions in or between activity systems are aggravated, some individual participants begin to question and to deviate from established norms. In some cases, this escalates into collaborative envisioning of the future and a deliberate collective change effort. An expansive transformation is accomplished when the object and motive of the activity are reconceptualised to embrace a wider horizon of possibilities than in the previous mode of the activity. A full cycle of expansive transformation may be understood as a collective journey through what activity theorists see as the zone of proximal development of the system.

Working across activity systems

Engeström has outlined a 'third generation' of activity theory with which to analyse joint activity or practices that cross traditional professional divisions and categories (Figure A.3).

The third generation of activity theory, as proposed by Engeström, is intended to develop conceptual tools for understanding dialogue, multiple perspectives and networks of interacting activity systems.

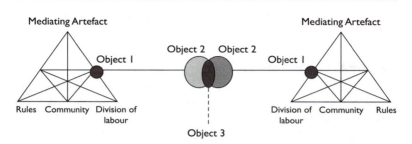

Figure A.3 Third-generation activity theory model (Engeström 1999b)

In arguing that it is important to extend beyond the singular activity system and to examine and work towards transformation of networks of activity, Engeström (2000) sees potential in the exploration of the 'concepts of boundary object, translation, and boundary crossing to analyse the unfolding of object-oriented cooperative activity of several actors, focusing on tools and means of construction of boundary objects in concrete work processes' (Engeström 1999b: 391). He suggests that the transformation of practice grows out of conflict, questioning and dissatisfaction within and between activity systems.

Developmental work research

Much of Engeström's work involves developmental work research (DWR): a mode of research intervention based around series of sessions, which he terms 'change labs', in which researchers and practitioners jointly interrogate the structural tensions in and between the different dimensions of activity, such as the rules, tools and division of labour, that have emerged in collective work practices over time and which constrain the development of future activity. In brief, DWR is a methodology for applying activity theory in order to develop what Engeström (1987, 2001) terms expansive learning in workplace settings

The LIW Project used DWR in its work with children's services professionals in five local authorities to examine and develop emergent multi-agency practices. In the three main case studies we organised our research around a series of six DWR sessions with operational staff in each site. DWR's value to the LIW Project was that it does not assume that practitioners are always learning to master stable, defined bodies of knowledge and skills. Instead, it focuses on the kind of learning that occurs when work practices and organisational configurations are undergoing rapid change and workers are creating new knowledge and new ways of working, as was the case for the practitioners in the LIW study.

Expansive learning

DWR sessions are designed to support cycles of expansive learning (Engeström 1999b, 2007a). Expansive learning cycles are predicated upon a progression from individuals questioning contradictions in current practice through to the modelling and implementation of new forms of practice (Figure A.4). In Chapter 1 we outlined how DWR sessions are based on Vygotsky's idea of dual stimulation, with the tools of activity theory being offered to participants in the sessions so that they might interrogate their practices and reveal the concepts in use as they accomplish their object-oriented activities. In Chapter 6 we explained and illustrated the types of contradiction that can arise as practitioners engage in questioning work practices and their purposes.

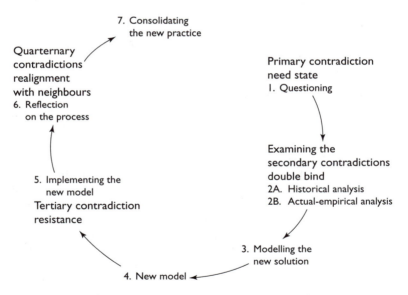

Figure A.4 Cycle of expansive learning (Engeström 1999b)

DWR Sessions in the LIW study

In the three main intervention sites in England our work was organised around a sequence of DWR sessions involving operational staff. Prior to the sessions the research team collected interview and observational data to be jointly scrutinised in them by researchers and professionals. The DWR sessions enabled the team to examine practitioners' 'everyday' interpretations of the practices that were emerging in the shift towards multi-agency working and the organisational conditions that supported these interpretations.

Using activity theory as a shared analytical framework, the sessions were designed to support reflective systemic analysis by confronting these everyday understandings with critical analysis of the ways in which current working practices/activities either enabled or constrained the development of innovative multi-agency working.

In each DWR session, analyses of practices in and for multi-agency working were developed collaboratively between the research team and children's services professionals. These focused upon:

- *past practice* – encouraging professionals to consider the historical development of their working practices;
- *present practice* – identifying structural tensions (or 'contradictions') in current working practices;
- *future practice* – working with professionals to suggest new forms of practice that might effectively support innovations in multi-agency working.

The aim of the DWR sessions was to address the challenges of multi-agency professional learning by:

- encouraging the *recognition* of areas in which there is a need for change in working practices;
- suggesting possibilities for change through *re-conceptualising* the 'objects' that professionals are working on, the 'tools' that professionals use in their multi-agency work and the 'rules' in which professional practices are embedded.

Inside the DWR sessions

In all the three main intervention sites research six DWR sessions were conducted over a period of twelve months at intervals of around two months. Each session ran for two hours and was, on most occasions, conducted by a team of four or five researchers. Sessions were organised around the presentation of 'mirror data', that is, everyday understandings of practices collected from individual interviews with staff and from previous DWR sessions. Professionals and researchers discussed the mirror data, using activity theory as an analytical framework with which to identify structural tensions in the practices of children's services providers and to move towards refining the concepts that were embedded in the practices. This refining led to a set of concepts or understandings that participants could work with and generalise from. These ideas are presented in Chapter 4 of the book.

Research team roles varied slightly at each meeting but usually comprised a session leader who presented mirror data for discussion, a team member summarising and presenting discussion data on flip-charts, a team member constructing a research note on the possible learning outcomes of session, a team member who video recorded the session (video data being used both for subsequent data analysis by the team and to capture data for possible presentation at later session). Numbers of local authority staff attending each session varied: the most viable arrangement, in relation to turn-taking and ease of data capture, was a composition of somewhere between eight and twelve practi-tioners. Figure A.5 indicates the layout of a DWR session (Engeström 2007a).

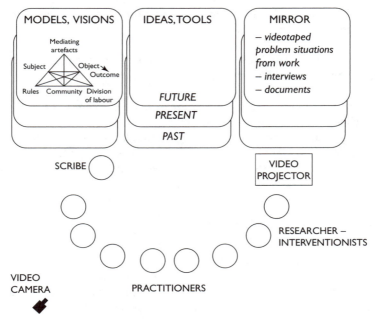

Figure A.5 Plan of a DWR session (Engeström 2007a)

A method used in all three sites to interrogate practice was to invite practitioners to present an anonymised overview of a case around which some form of multi-agency working had taken place. The purpose of these case presentations was for practitioners to discuss the objects (and related elements) of their professional activity. Joint analysis by professionals and researchers was supported though the use of a range of devices and procedures. These included templates or calendars (to summarise important events), maps (to depict the key parties involved) and agreements (summarising the division of labour amongst the parties).

Analysing the data from the DWR sessions

We have explained in Chapters 8 and 9 that analytic protocols were developed in order to analyse the talk in the DWR sessions. These were based on an approach to analysis that focused on the forms of social action that are accomplished in talk and text and the sorts of communicative devices that are used. The particular focus of what became known as the 'D-analysis' grew out of a concern to examine the emergence of what-it-is-to-learn in settings as they developed their inter-professional work, across the three sites. Stages of learning-related talk were identified and used to code the talk in the sessions.

Sequences of communicative action were analysed in the transcripts of the sessions. Related sequences were identified and these were grouped into strands of talk that wove their way through the progress of the each series of sessions. These strands witnessed the progression of learning through and with talk in the sessions. A learning strand was defined as a narrative that focused on one and the same concept and was developmental in its nature, that is, there was a movement from recognising towards proposing an action. These strands revealed the ideas in use as people developed their new ways of working and have been described in Chapter 4. Each sequence prepared the way for the one that followed either in the same session or in subsequent ones. At the end of the project, participants were interviewed about what they gained from the experience and showed that the concepts captured by the D-analysis and outlined in Chapter 4 remained relevant for them.

References

Abreu, G. and Elbers, E. (2005) 'The social mediation of learning in multiethnic schools: Introduction', *European Journal of Psychology of Education*, 20 (1): 3–11.

Alexander, J., Daly, P., Gallagher, A., Gray, C. and Sutherland, A. (1998) *An Evaluation of the Craigavon Two-tier System (Research Report No. 12)*, Bangor: DENI.

Anderson, J.R., Reder, L.M. and Simon H.A. (1997) 'Situative versus cognitive perspectives: form versus substance', *Educational Researcher*, 26 (1): 18–21.

—— (1996) 'Situated learning and education', *Educational Researcher*, 25 (4): 5–11.

Anning, A., Cottrell, D.M., Frost, N., Green, J. and Robinson, M. (2006) *Developing Multi-professional Teamwork for Integrated Children's Services*, Buckingham: Open University Press.

Audit Commission (2004) *The Educational Achievement of Children in Care: A New Improvement Toolkit to Help Local Authorities*, London: Audit Commission.

Baldwin, M. (2004) 'Conclusions: optimism and the art of the possible', in N. Gould and M. Baldwin (eds) *Social Work, Critical Reflection and the Learning Organization*, Aldershot: Ashgate.

Bateson, G. (1972) *Steps to an Ecology of Mind*, Chicago: University of Chicago Press.

Bernstein, B. (2000) *Pedagogy, Symbolic Control and Identity: Theory, Research, Critique* (revised edition), Lanham, Maryland: Rowman and Littlefield Publishers Inc.

—— (1993) 'Foreword', in H. Daniels (ed.) *Charting the Agenda: Educational Activity After Vygotsky*, London: Routledge.

—— (1981) 'Codes, modalities and the process of cultural reproduction: a model', *Language in Society*, 10: 327–63.

Billett, S. (2006) 'Relational interdependence between social and individual agency in work and working life', *Mind, Culture and Activity*, 13 (1): 53–69.

—— (2002) 'Workplace pedagogic practices: co-participation and learning', *British Journal of Educational Studies*, 50 (4): 457–81.

Billig, M. (1996) *Arguing and Thinking: a rhetorical view of social psychology,* Cambridge: Cambridge University Press.

Blackler, F., Crump, N. and McDonald, S. (2000) 'Organizing processes in complex activity networks', *Organization,* 7 (2): 277–300.

Bleakley, A., Brice, J. and Bligh, J. (2008). 'Thinking the post-colonial in medical education', *Medical Education,* 42, 266–70.

Bleakley, A., Hobbs, A., Boyden, J. and Walsh, L. (2004) 'Safety in operating theatres: improving teamwork through team resource management', *Journal of Workplace Learning,* 16: 414–25.

Bleakley, A., Hobbs, A., Boyden, J., Allard, J. and Walsh, L. (2006) 'Improving teamwork climate in operating theatres: the shift from multiprofessionalism to interprofessionalism', *Journal of Interprofessional Care,* 20: 461–70.

Booker, R. (2005) 'Integrated children's services – implications for the profession', *Educational and Child Psychology,* 22 (4): 127–42.

Boreham, N. (2004) 'A theory of collective competence: challenging neo-liberal individualism in performance at work', *British Journal of Educational Studies,* 52 (1): 5–17.

Boren, M.T. and Ramey, J. (2000) 'Thinking aloud: reconciling theory and practice', *IEEE Transactions of Professional Communication,* 43 (3): 261–78.

Brown, J.S. and Duguid, P. (2000) *The Social Life of Information,* Boston: Harvard Business School Press.

Bruner, J.S. (1996) *The Culture of Education,* Cambridge, MA: Harvard University Press.

Burns Report (2001) *Education for the 21st Century: Report of the Post Primary Review Group,* Northern Ireland: Department of Education.

Bynner, J. (2001) 'Childhood risks and protective factors in social exclusion', *Children and Society,* 15 (5): 285–301.

Carlile, P. (2004) 'Transferring, translating and transforming: an integrative framework for managing knowledge across boundaries', *Organization Science,* 15 (5): 555–68.

Chaiklin, S. (1993) 'Understanding the social scientific practice of Understanding Practice', in S. Chaiklin and J. Lave (eds) *Understanding Practice: Perspectives on Activity and Context,* Cambridge: Cambridge University Press.

Chatwin, B. (1987) *The Songlines,* London: Jonathan Cape.

Children's and Young People's Unit (2000) *Tomorrow's Future: Building a Strategy for Children and Young People,* London: Children and Young People's Unit.

Churchman, C.W. (1979) *The Systems Approach and its Enemies,* New York: Basic Books.

Cole, M. (2003) 'Vygotsky and context: where did the connection come from and what difference does it make?', paper presented at the biennial conferences of the International Society for Theoretical Psychology, Istanbul, Turkey, June 22–27, 2003.

—— (1996) *Cultural Psychology: A Once and Future Discipline*, Cambridge, MA: Harvard University Press.

Commission of the European Communities (1993) *European Social Policy Options for the Union* (Green Paper), European Commission.

Costello Report (2004) *Report of the Post Primary Review Body*, Northern Ireland: Department of Education.

Cummings, C., Dyson, A. and Todd, L. (2004) *Evaluation of Extended Schools Pathfinder Projects. Research Report 530*, London: DfES.

Cussins, A. (1992) 'Content, embodiment and objectivity: the theory of cognitive trails', *Mind*, 101: 651–88.

Daniels, H. (2001) *Vygotsky and Pedagogy*, London: Routledge.

—— (2006) 'Analysing institutional effects in Activity Theory: first steps in the development of a language of description', *Outlines: Critical Social Studies*, 2: 43–58.

Daniels, H., Leadbetter, J. and Warmington, P. (2007) 'Learning in and for multi-agency working', *Oxford Review of Education*, 33 (4): 521–38.

Daniels, H., Brown, S., Edwards, A., Leadbetter, J., Martin, D., Middleton, D., Parsons, S., Popova, A. and Warmington, P. (2005) 'Studying professional learning for inclusion', in K. Yamazumi, Y. Engeström and H. Daniels (eds) *New Learning Challenges: Going Beyond the Industrial Age System of School and Work*, Kansai: Kansai University Press.

Dartington Social Research Unit (2004) *Refocusing Children's Services Towards Prevention: Lessons from the Literature DfES (Research Report 510)*, London: DfES.

DfES (2005) *Extended Schools: Access to Opportunities and Services to All* (summary of DfES prospectus), London: DfES.

—— (2004) *The Children Act*, London: HMSO.

—— (2003) *Every Child Matters*, London: DfES.

Douglas, M. (1966) *Purity and Danger: An Analysis of the Concepts of Pollution and Taboo*, London: Ark.

Dyson, A., Millward, A. and Todd, L. (2002) *A Study of the Extended Schools Demonstration Projects (Research Report 381)*, London: DfES.

Edwards, A. (in press a) 'Learning how to know who: professional learning for expansive practice between organisations', in S. Ludvigsen, A. Lund and R. Säljö (eds) *Learning across Sites*, Oxford: Pergamon.

—— (in press b) 'From the systemic to the relational: relational agency and activity theory', in A. Sannino, H. Daniels and K. Gutierrez (eds) *Learning and Expanding with Activity Theory*, Cambridge: Cambridge University Press.

—— (2005) 'Relational agency: learning to be a resourceful practitioner', *International Journal of Educational Research*, 43 (3): 168–82.

—— (2004) 'The new multi-agency working: collaborating to prevent the social exclusion of children and families', *Journal of Integrated Care*, 12 (5): 3–9.

Edwards, A. and Mackenzie, L. (2005) 'Steps towards participation: the social support of learning trajectories', *International Journal of Lifelong Education,* 24 (4): 287–302.

Edwards, A. and Apostolov, A. (2007) 'A cultural-historical interpretation of resilience: the implications for practice', *Outlines: Critical Social Studies,* 9 (1): 70–84.

Edwards, A. and Wiseman, P. (2005) 'Creating conditions for learning across organisations: vertical learning in a complex initiative', paper presented to ISCAR Conference, Seville.

Edwards, A., Sebba, J. and Rickinson, M. (2007) 'Working with users: some implications for educational research', *British Educational Research Journal,* 33 (5): 647–61.

Edwards, A., Barnes, M., Plewis, I. and Morris, K. *et al.* (2006) *Working to prevent the social exclusion of children and young people: final lessons from the national evaluation of the Children's Fund: RR 734,* London: DfES.

Edwards, A., Gilroy, P. and Hartley, D. (2002) *Rethinking Teacher Education: An Interdisciplinary Analysis,* London: Falmer.

Edwards, D. and Potter, J. (1992) *Discursive Psychology,* London: Sage.

Engeström, Y. (2007a) 'Putting activity theory to work: the change laboratory as an application of double stimulation', in H. Daniels, M. Cole and J.V. Wertsch (eds) *The Cambridge Companion to Vygotsky,* Cambridge: Cambridge University Press.

—— (2007b) 'Enriching the theory of expansive learning: lessons from journeys toward co-configuration', *Mind Culture and Activity,* 14 (1and 2): 23–39.

—— (2007c) 'From stabilization knowledge to possibility knowledge in organizational learning', *Management Learning,* 38: 271–75.

—— (2005) 'Knotworking to create collaborative intentionality capital in fluid organizational fields', in M.M. Beyerlein, S.T. Beyerlein and F.A. Kennedy (eds) *Collaborative Capital: Creating Intangible Value,* Amsterdam: Elsevier.

—— (2004) 'Object-oriented interagency: toward understanding collective intentionality in distributed activity fields', paper presented at the Sixth International Conference on Collective Intentionality, October 10–13, 2004, Siena.

—— (2001) 'Expansive learning at work: toward an activity theoretical reconceptualization', *Journal of Education and Work,* 14 (1): 133–56.

—— (2000) 'Making expansive decisions: an activity-theoretical study of practitioners building collaborative medical care for children', in K.M. Allwood and M. Selart (eds) *Creative Decision Making in the Social World,* Amsterdam: Kluwer.

—— (1999a) 'Activity theory and individual and social transformation', in Y. Engeström, R. Miettinen and R.-L. Punamäki (eds) *Perspectives on Activity Theory,* Cambridge: Cambridge University Press.

—— (1999b) 'Innovative learning in work teams: analysing cycles of knowledge creation in practice' in Y. Engeström, R. Miettinen and

R.-L. Punamäki (eds.) *Perspectives on Activity Theory,* Cambridge: Cambridge University Press.

—— (1992) 'Interactive expertise: studies in distributed working intelligence', *Research Bulletin 83,* Helsinki: University of Helsinki Department of Education.

—— (1987) *Learning by Expanding: An Activity-theoretical Approach to Developmental Research,* Helsinki: Orienta-Konsultit.

Engeström, Y. and Middleton, D. (eds) (1996) *Cognition and Communication at Work,* Cambridge: Cambridge University Press.

Engeström, Y., Engeström, R. and Kerosuo, H. (2003a) 'The Discursive Construction of Collaborative Care', *Applied Linguistics,* 24 (3): 286–315.

Engeström, Y., Puonti, A. and Seppänen. L. (2003b) 'Spatial and temporal expansion of the object as a challenge for reorganizing work', in D. Nicolini, S. Gherardi and D. Yanow (eds) *Knowing in Organizations: A Practice-based Approach,* Armonk: Sharpe.

Engeström, Y., Engeström, R. and Vähäaho, T. (1999) 'When the center does not hold: the importance of knotworking', in S. Chaiklin, M. Hedegaard and U.J. Jensen (eds) *Activity Theory and Social Practice,* Aarhus: Aarhus University Press.

Engeström, Y., Brown, K., Christopher, C. and Gregory J. (1997) 'Coordination, cooperation and communication in the courts: expansive transitions in legal work', in M. Cole, Y. Engeström and O. Vasquez (eds) *Mind Culture and Activity: Seminal Papers from the Laboratory of Comparative Human Cognition,* Cambridge: Cambridge University Press.

Engeström, Y., Engeström, R. and Kärkkäinen, M. (1995) 'Polycontextuality and boundary crossing in expert cognition: learning and problem solving in complex work activities', *Learning and Instruction,* 5: 319–36.

Eraut, M. (2007) 'Learning from other people in the workplace', *Oxford Review of Education,* 33 (4): 403–22.

Evans, R., Pinnock, K., Beirens, H. and Edwards, A. (2006) *Developing Preventative Practices: The Experiences of Children, Young People and their Families in the Children's Fund (Research Report 735),* London: DfES.

France, A., Hine, J., Armstrong, D. and Camina, M. (2004) *The OnTrack Early Intervention and Prevention Programme: From Theory to Action. Home Office Online Report 10/04,* London: Home Office.

France, A. and Utting, D. (2005) 'The paradigm of "risk and protection-focused prevention" and its impact on services for children and families', *Children and Society,* 19: 77–90.

Fullan, M. (2001) *Leading in a Culture of Change,* San Francisco: Jossey-Bass.

Fuller, A. and Unwin, L. (2003) 'Learning as apprentices in the contemporary UK workplace: creating and managing expansive and restrictive participation', *Journal of Education and Work,* 16 (4): 407–26.

Fuller, A. and Unwin, L. (1998) 'Reconceptualising apprenticeship: exploring the relationship between the work and learning', *Journal of Vocational Research and Learning,* 50 (2): 153–73.

Furlong, A. and Cartmel, F. (1997) *Young People and Social Change: individualisation and late modernity,* Buckingham: Open University Press.

Gallagher, T. and Smith, A. (2000) *The Effects of the Selective System of Secondary Education in Northern Ireland: Main Report,* Bangor: Department of Education.

Garmezy, N. (1991) 'Resiliency and vulnerability to adverse developmental outcomes associated with poverty', *American Behavioural Scientist,* 34: 416–30.

Gee, J. P. (2003) *What Video Games Have To Teach Us About Learning And Literacy,* New York: Palgrave Macmillan.

Giddens, A. (1991) *The Consequences of Modernity,* Cambridge: Polity Press.

Gilligan, R. (2000) 'Adversity, resilience and young people: the protective value of positive school and spare time experiences', *Children and Society,* 14 (1): 37–47.

Glass, N. (2005) 'Surely some mistake?', *The Guardian,* 5 January.

—— (1999) 'Sure Start: the development of an early intervention programme for young children in the United Kingdom', *Children and Society,* 13 (4): 257–64.

Glisson, C. and Hemmelgarn, A. (1998) 'The effects of organizational climate and interorganizational coordination on the quality and outcomes of children's service systems', *Child Abuse and Neglect,* 22 (5): 401–21.

Greeno, J. (2006) 'Authoritative, accountable positioning and connected general knowing: progressive themes in understanding transfer', *The Journal of the Learning Sciences,* 15 (4): 537–47.

—— (1997) 'On claims that answer the wrong question', *Educational Researcher,* 26 (1): 5–17.

Hager, P. (2004) 'Conceptions of learning and understanding learning at work', *Studies in Continuing Education,* 26 (1): 3–17.

Hakkarainen, K., Palonen, T., Paavola, S. and Lehtinen, E. (2004) *Communities of Networked Expertise,* Amsterdam: Elsevier.

Hardiker, P. (1999) 'Children still in need, indeed: prevention across five decades', in Stevenson, O. (ed.) *Child Welfare in the UK 1948–1998,* Blackwell: Oxford.

Hardy, C., Lawrence, T. and Grant, D. (2005) 'Discourse and collaboration: the role of conversations and collective identity', *Academy of Management Review,* 30 (1): 58–77.

Hargreaves, D.H. (1994) 'The new professionalism: the synthesis of professional and institutional development', *Teaching and Teacher Education,* 10 (4): 423–38.

Hawley, D. and DeHaan, L. (1996)' Towards a definition of family resilience: integrating lifespan and family perspectives', *Family Process,* 35 (3): 283–98.

Heracleous, L. (2004) 'Boundaries in the study of organization', *Human Relations,* 57 (1): 95–103.

Holland, D. and Lachicotte, W. (2007) 'Vygotsky, Mead and the new sociocultural studies of identity', in H. Daniels, M. Cole and J. Wertsch (eds) *The Cambridge Companion to Vygotsky,* Cambridge: Cambridge University Press.

Holland, D. and Lave, J. (eds) (2001) *History in Person,* Oxford: James Currey.

Holland, D., Lachicotte, W., Skinner, D. and Cain, C. (1998) *Identity and Agency in Cultural Worlds,* Cambridge, MA: Harvard University Press.

Home Office (2000) *Report of Policy Action Team 12: Young People,* London: Home Office.

Howard, S., Dryden, J. and Johnson, B. (1999) 'Childhood resilience: review and critique of the literature', *Oxford Review of Education,* 25 (3): 307–23.

Iedema, R. (ed.) (2007) *The Discourse of Hospital Communication: Tracing Complexities in Contemporary Health Care Organizations,* Basingstoke: Palgrave Macmillan.

Il'enkov, E. (1982) *The Dialectics of the Abstract and the Concrete in Marx's 'Capital',* Moscow: Progress.

Jack, G. (2006) 'The area and community components of children's well-being', *Children and Society,* 20 (5): 334–47.

Jensen, K. (2007) 'The desire to learn: an analysis of knowledge-seeking practices among professionals', *Oxford Review of Education,* 33 (4): 489–502.

Jensen, K. and Lahn, L. (2005) 'The binding role of knowledge: an analysis of nursing students' knowledge ties', *Journal of Education and Work,* 18 (3): 305–20.

Kerosuo H. (2006) *An Activity-theoretical Study of Development, Learning and Change in Health Care for Patients with Multiple and Chronic Illnesses,* Helsinki: University of Helsinki Press.

—— (2003) 'Boundaries in health care discussions: an activity theoretical approach to the analysis of boundaries', in N. Paulsen and T. Hernes (eds) *Managing Boundaries in Organizations: Multiple Perspectives,* Basingstoke: Palgrave.

Kerosuo, H. and Engeström, Y. (2003) 'Boundary Crossing and Learning in Creation of New Work Practice', *Journal of Workplace Learning,* 15 (7/8): 345–51.

King's Fund (2001) *Partnerships Under Pressure: A Commentary on Progress in Partnership Working between the NHS and Local Government.* London: King's Fund.

Knorr Cetina, K. (1997) 'Sociality with objects: social relations in post-social knowledge societies', *Theory Culture Society,* 14 (1): 1–29.

Konkola, R. (2001) 'Developmental process of internship at polytechnic and boundary-zone activity as a new model for activity' (in Finnish), cited in T. Tuomi-Gröhn, Y. Engeström and M. Young (eds) (2003) *Between School and Work: New Perspectives on Transfer and Boundary Crossing,* Oxford: Pergamon.

Kozulin, A. (1991) 'Psychology of Experiencing: a Russian View', *Journal of Humanistic Psychology,* 31: 14–19.

Lave, J. (1997) 'Learning apprenticeship and social practice', *Nordisk Pedagogik,* 3: 140–51.

Lave, J. and Wenger, E. (1991) *Situated Learning: Legitimate Peripheral Participation,* Cambridge: Cambridge University Press.

Leadbetter, J. (2006) 'New ways of working and new ways of being: multiagency working and professional identity', *Educational & Child Psychology,* 23, (4): 47–59.

Leadbetter, J., Daniels, H., Edwards, A. *et al.* (2007) 'Professional learning within multiagency children's services: researching into practice', *Educational Research,* 49 (1): 83–98.

Levitas, R. (1998) *The Inclusive Society: Social Exclusion and New Labour,* London: Macmillan

Leont'ev A.N. (1981) *Problems of the Development of the Mind,* Moscow: Progress Publishers.

—— (1978) *Activity, Consciousness and Personality,* Upper Saddle River, NJ: Prentice Hall.

Little, M., Ashford, N. and Morpeth, L. (2004) 'Research review: risk and protection in the context of services for children in need', *Children and Family Social Work,* 9: 105–17.

Lundvall, B.-A. (1996) 'The social dimension of the learning economy', *Druid Working Paper, 96–1,* available: http://papers.ssrn.com/sol3/papers.cfm?abstract_id=66537 (accessed 10 August 2005).

Luthar, S. (1993) 'Annotation: methodological and conceptual issues in research on childhood resilience', *Journal of Child Psychology and Psychiatry,* 34 (4): 441–54.

Luthar, S. and Cicchetti, D. (2000) 'The construct of resilience: implications for interventions and social policies', *Development and Psychopathology,* 12 (4): 857–85.

Mäkitalo, A. and Säljö, R. (2002) 'Invisible people: institutional reasoning and reflexivity in the production of services and "Social Facts" in public employment agencies', *Mind, Culture and Activity,* 9 (3): 160–78.

Masten, A. and Coatsworth, J.D. (1998) 'The development of competence in favorable and unfavorable environments: lessons from research on successful children', *American Psychologist,* 53: 205–20.

Masten, A. and Garmezy, N. (1985) 'Risk, vulnerability and protective factors in developmental psychopathology' in B.B. Lahey and A.E. Kazdin (eds) *Advances in Clinical Child Psychology, Vol. 8,* New York: Plenum.

McLaughlin, R. (2002) 'Branded a problem? A participative research project on the educational experiences of children and young people in care', Belfast: Save the Children, First Key and VOYPIC.

Melhuish, E., Belsky, J. and Leyland, A. (2005) *Early Impact of Sure Start Local programmes on Children and Families. SS Report 13,* London: DfES.

Mercer, N. (2004) 'Sociocultural discourse analysis: analysing classroom talk as a social mode of thinking', *Journal of Applied Linguistics*, 1 (2): 137–68.

Middleton, D., Brown, S., Daniels, H., Edwards, A., Leadbetter, J. and Warmington, P. (in press) 'Making the difference in interagency working: analytic challenges in studying professional learning in communicating what matters', in Candlin, C. and Sarangi, S. (eds) *Handbook of Applied Linguistics Communication in Professions and Organisations,* Berlin: Mouton de Gruyter.

Midgley, G. (1992) 'The sacred and profane in critical systems thinking', *Systems Practice,* 5 (1): 5–16.

Midgley, G., Munlo, I. and Brown, M. (1998) 'The theory and practice of boundary critique: developing housing services for older people', *Journal of the Operational Research Society,* 49 (5): 467–78.

Mills, C. (2004) *Problems at Home, Problems at School: The Effects of Maltreatment in the Home on Children's Functioning at School: An Overview of Recent Research,* London: NSPCC.

Nardi, B. (2005) 'Objects of desire: power and passion in collaborative activity', *Mind Culture and Activity,* 12 (1): 37–51.

Nardi, B., Whittaker, S. and Schwarz, H. (2002) 'NetWORKers and their activity in intensional networks', *Computer Supported Cooperative Work,* 11 (1–2): 205–42.

National Evaluation of the Children's Fund (NECF) (2004) *Collaborating for the Social Inclusion of Children and Young People (Research Report 596),* London: DfES.

Nielsen, J., Clemmensen, T. and Yssing, C. (2002) 'People's heads, people's minds? Theoretical reflections on thinking aloud', in Dai, G. (ed.) *Proceedings of the APCHI2002 – User Interaction Technology in the 21st Century, Vol. 2,* Beijing: Science Press.

Nixon, J., Martin, J., McKeown, P. and Ranson, S. (1997) 'Towards a learning profession: changing codes of occupational practice within the new management of education', *British Journal of Sociology of Education,* 18 (1): 5–28.

Oakley, K. (2003) 'Developing policy as a shared narrative', in T. Bentley and J. Wilsden (eds) *The Adaptive State,* London: DEMOS.

O'Connor, U., Hartop, B. and McCully, A. (2002) *A Review of the Schools Community Relations Programme,* Northern Ireland: Department of Education.

OECD (1998) *Co-ordinating Services for Children and Youth at Risk: A World View,* Paris: OECD.

Office of Public Services Reform (2002) *Reforming out Public Services: Principles into Practice,* London: Office of Public Services Reform.

Orr, J. (1996) *Talking about Machines: An Ethnography of the Modern Job,* Ithaca: Cornell University Press.

Pascal, C., Bertram, T., Gasper, M., Mould, C., Ramsden, F. and Saunders, M. (2001) *Research to Inform the Evaluation of the Early Excellence Centres Pilot Programme (Research Report 259),* London: DfEE.

Peckover, S., White, S. and Hall, C. (in press) 'Making and managing electronic children: e-assessment in child welfare', *Information Communication and Society.*

Pickering, A. (1995) *The Mangle of Practice: Time, Agency and Science,* Chicago, Ill: University of Chicago Press.

—— (1993) 'The mangle of practice: agency and emergence in the sociology of science', *American Journal of Sociology,* 99 (3): 559–89.

Polanyi, M. (1958/1998) *Personal Knowledge: Towards a Post-critical Philosophy,* London: Routledge.

Potter, J. and Wetherell, M. (1987) *Discourse and Social Psychology: Beyond Attitudes and Behaviour,* London: Sage.

Puonti, A. (2004) 'Learning to work together: collaboration between authorities in economic crime investigation', Vantaa, Finland: National Bureau of Investigation.

Rheinberger, H.-J. (1992) 'Experiment difference and writing: I tracing protein synthesis', *Studies in the History and Philosophy of Science,* 23 (2): 305–31.

Roaf, C. (2002) *Co-ordinating Services for Included Children,* Buckingham: Open University Press.

Room, G. (1995) 'Poverty and social exclusion: the new European agenda for policy and research', in G. Room (ed.) *Beyond the Threshold: The Measurement and Analysis of Social Exclusion,* Bristol: Policy Press.

Roth, M., Tobin. K., Elemsky, R., Caeambo, C., McKnight, Y.-M. and Beers, J. (2004) 'Re/making identities in the praxis of urban schooling: a cultural historical perspective', *Mind, Culture, and Activity,* 1 (11): 48–69.

Ryave, A. (1978) 'On the achievement of a series of stories' in J. Schenkein (ed.) *Studies in the Organization of Conversational Interaction,* New York: Academic Press.

Sarangi, S. and Roberts, C. (1999) 'Introduction: discursive hybridity in medical work', in S. Sarangi and C. Roberts (eds) *Talk, Work and Institutional Order: Discourse in Medical, Mediation and Management Settings,* Berlin: Mouton de Gruyter.

Schulz, M. (2001) 'The uncertain relevance of newness', *Academy of Management Journal,* 44 (4): 661–81.

Scribner, S. (1997) 'Mind in action: a functional approach to learning', in M. Cole, Y. Engeström and O. Vasquez (eds) *Mind Culture and Activity: Seminal Papers from the Laboratory of Comparative Human Cognition,* Cambridge: Cambridge University Press.

Sennett, R. (1999) 'Growth and failure: the new political economy and culture', in M. Featherstone and S. Lash (eds) *Spaces of Culture,* London: Sage.

Sfard, A. (1998) 'On two metaphors for learning and the danger of choosing just one', *Educational Researcher,* 27 (2): 4–13.

Sfard, A. and Prusak, A. (2005) 'Telling identities: in search of an analytic tool for investigating learning as culturally shaped activity', *Educational Researcher* 34 (4): 14–22.

Shotter, J. (2005) 'Wittgenstein, Bakhtin and Vygotsky: introducing dialogically-structured reflective practices into our everyday practices', paper from VIKOM Conference, Copenhagen, available at http://pub pages.unh.edu/~jds/ (accessed 15 May 2008).

Sinclair, R. and Franklin, A. (2000) *A Quality Protects Research Briefing: Young People's Participation,* London: Department of Health.

Siraj-Blatchford, I., Clarke, K. and Needham, M. (eds) (2007) *The Team Around the Child: Multi-agency Working in the Early Years,* Stoke on Trent: Trentham Books.

Smith, D. (2005) *Institutional Ethnography: A Sociology for People,* Oxford: AltaMira Press.

Stetsenko, A. (2005) 'Activity as object-related: resolving the dichotomy of individual and collective planes of activity', *Mind Culture and Activity* 12 (1): 70–88.

Toiviainen, H. (2003) *Learning Across Levels: Challenges of Collaboration in a Small-firm Network,* Helsinki: University of Helsinki.

Treasury-DfES (2007) *Policy Review of Children and Young People: A Discussion Paper,* London: HM Treasury.

Ulrich, W. (1988) 'C. West Churchman – 75 years', *Systems Practice and Action Research,* 1 (4): 341–50.

—— (1983) *Critical Heuristics of Social Planning: A New Approach to Practical Philosophy,* Haupt: Berne.

Vasilyuk, F. (1991) *The Psychology of Experiencing: The Resolution of Life's Critical Situations,* Hemel Hempstead: Harvester.

Victor, B. and Boynton, A. (1998) *Invented Here: Maximizing Your Organization's Internal Growth and Profitability.* Boston, MA: Harvard Business School Press.

Vygotsky, L.S. (1999) 'Tool and sign in the development of the child', in R.W. Rieber (ed.) *The Collected Works of L.S. Vygotsky Volume 6: Scientific Legacy,* New York: Plenum Press.

—— (1997a) 'The crisis in psychology' in R.W. Rieber and J. Wollock (eds) *The Collected Work of L.S. Vygostky Volume 3: Problems of the Theory and History of Psychology,* New York: Plenum Press.

—— (1997b) 'Analysis of higher mental functions', in R. Rieber (ed.) *The Collected Works of L.S. Vygotsky Volume 4: The History of the Development of Higher Mental Functions.* New York: Plenum Press.

—— (1994) 'The problem of the environment', in R. Van der Veer and J. Vlasiner (eds) (1994) *The Vygotsky Reader,* Oxford and Cambridge, MA: Blackwell.

—— (1987) 'Thinking and speech', in R.W. Rieber and A.S. Carton (eds) *The Collected Works of L.S. Vygotsky Volume 1: Problems of General Psychology,* New York: Plenum Press.

—— (1986) *Thought and Language,* Cambridge, MA: MIT Press.

—— (1978) *Mind in Society,* M. Cole, V. John-Steiner, S. Scribner and E. Souberman (eds), Cambridge, MA: Harvard University Press.

Walker, R. (1995) 'The dynamics of poverty and social exclusion', in G. Room (ed.) *Beyond the Threshold: The Measurement and Analysis of Social Exclusion,* Bristol: Policy Press.

Walsh, F. (2002) 'A family resilience framework: innovative practice applications', *Family Relations,* 51 (2): 130–37.

Warmington, P., Daniels, H., Edwards, A., Leadbetter, J., Martin, D., Brown, S. and Middleton, D. (2005) *Interagency Collaboration: A Review of the Literature,* Bath: Learning in and for Interagency Working, available at www.bath.ac.uk/research/liw/litreview.html, (accessed 26 May 2008).

Warren, S., Apostolov, A. and Broughton, K. *et al.* (2006) 'Emergent family support practices in a context of policy churn: an example from the Children's Fund', *Journal of Child Care in Practice,* 12 (4): 331–46.

Wertsch, J.V. (2007) 'Mediation', in H. Daniels, M. Cole, and J.V. Wertsch (eds) *The Cambridge Companion to Vygotsky,* New York: Cambridge University Press.

Yanow, D. (2004) 'Translating local knowledge at organisational peripheries', *British Journal of Management,* 15 (S1): 9–25.

Yates, J. and Orliowski, W. (1992) 'Genres of organizational communication: a structurational approach to studying communication and media', *Academy of Management Review,* 17 (2): 299–326.

Index